New York's Historic Armories

New York's Historic Armories

An Illustrated History

NANCY L. TODD

State University of New York Press

Published by
State University of New York

© 2006 State University of New York

For information, address State University of New York Press,
194 Washington Avenue, Suite 305, Albany, NY 12210-2384

Production by Dana Foote
Marketing by Fran Keneston

Library of Congress Cataloging-in-Publication Data

Todd, Nancy L.
    New York's historic armories : an illustrated history / Nancy L. Todd.
        p. cm.
    Includes bibliographical references and index.
    ISBN-13: 978-0-7914-6911-8 (hardcover : alk. paper)
    ISBN-10: 0-7914-6911-5 (hardcover : alk. paper)
    1. Armories—New York (State)—History.   I. Title.

UF544.N48.T64 2006
355.7'5—dc22   2005036300

10 9 8 7 6 5 4 3 2 1

Contents

Foreword

As I travel around New York State, I am always impressed with the vast number and variety of its historic and cultural resources. A great deal can be learned about our history and people by studying institutions that were established to safeguard our population and to ensure the overall growth of civilization. New York's role as a national and global power gave its leaders the impetus to erect many outstanding facilities that testify to America's proud and thriving military tradition.

For many years, I have been especially interested in recognizing and protecting this extraordinary military legacy, not only for our education and enjoyment today, but also for the benefit of future generations. This attractive and engaging book highlights New York's large and distinguished group of historic armories—national treasures associated with a revered history of security and peacekeeping.

Over the past several years, thanks to the commitment and hard work of state and local governments, private individuals and organizations, we have made tremendous progress in preserving New York's military heritage. The New York State Division of Military and Naval Affairs has played a key role in advancing these important efforts. High on the list of accomplishments is the opening of the New York State Military Museum and Veterans Research Center in Saratoga Springs. Housed in a former armory, the museum is dedicated to the preservation and interpretation of our state's extensive collection of military artifacts. With the help of the New York State Office of Parks, Recreation and Historic Preservation, the state's historic military flags are being preserved for safekeeping and exhibition at the museum.

This comprehensive history is the latest initiative to recognize our rich military heritage. I am confident that this book will further our understanding and appreciation of the state's historic armories and their contribution to safeguarding our communities and citizens.

With imposing towers, stately battlements and massive drill halls, the armories remain some of our most prominent civic landmarks and offer new and exciting possibilities for improving the quality and character of our hometowns.

These familiar properties are certainly valuable assets worthy of preservation and renewal. With the cooperation and support of public and private partners, we have the opportunity to rejuvenate our armories so that they can once again play active and productive roles in their communities and the state.

I hope you enjoy this book and thank you for your interest in historic preservation.

—George E. Pataki
Governor, State of New York

Foreword

I am delighted to join Governor Pataki and Major General Taluto in introducing this splendid history of New York State armories. We have one of the oldest, largest and most distinguished collections of historic Army National Guard armories in the country. These monumental buildings played an important role in the development of New York's armed forces and became civic centers in their communities. This publication presents an informative overview of the entire collection.

Begun in the late eighteenth century, New York's extensive armory building program had a significant impact on the development of communities across the state. These major construction projects employed hundreds of workers and involved some of the state's most prominent architects. While most armories shared similar plans, incorporating offices in front and drill halls in the rear, many also included fashionable architectural details. Through the years, the armories were not only important centers of military affairs but also hosted a variety of community activities, such as sporting and social events.

This book draws upon a survey of historic armories by the New York State Office of Parks, Recreation and Historic Preservation and the New York State Division of Military and Naval Affairs. The survey was also used to prepare a National Register Multiple Property Documentation Form, which became the basis for listing numerous armories on the State and National Registers of Historic Places. This recognition has helped to increase our appreciation of the significance of these structures in state history.

As New York's State Historic Preservation Officer for the past eleven years, it has been an honor to oversee the identification and preservation of these historic properties. I am particularly grateful to Nancy Todd of the Historic Preservation Field Services Bureau for her outstanding contribution to the armory project. She played a significant role in documenting this extraordinary legacy, and this book is a reflection of her excellent work.

Today, many of the historic armories are underused or have become obsolete. Safeguarding this remarkable collection presents both challenges and exciting possibilities. Over the past several years, the state has been exploring public and private opportunities to rejuvenate these assets. Thanks to the Governor's encouragement and our agency's partnership with the Division of Military and Naval Affairs, we are confident that these treasures will remain vital resources in their communities.

—Bernadette Castro
Commissioner, New York State Office of Parks,
Recreation and Historic Preservation
State Historic Preservation Officer

Foreword

As the men and women of our New York National Guard continue their great tradition of defending freedom for their fellow citizens, we applaud this exceptional and unique opportunity to remember the past through the beautiful architectural structures that make up the foundation of our force.

Our state militia dates back before the American Revolution. Even the term National Guard was first used in 1824 by a unit of the New York militia. New York went on to establish the first National Guard aviation unit in 1915 when the First Aero Company formed on Long Island.

Today, New York's National Guard has evolved into an effective twenty-first-century force that is ready, responsive and willing to go wherever the call to duty takes them. Our service men and women need and deserve facilities that provide the modern training, and thanks to Governor George E. Pataki's leadership, our soldiers and airmen have or will soon be moving into the armories that will help to keep them ready, proficient and resolute.

But as we replace older armories, we cannot forget those of our communities who came before us. New York State's armories are reminders of the deep personal commitment the New York National Guard's men and women have shown throughout our nation's history. As our armories are replaced with more modern training facilities, many are remaining what they always were—fixtures of their communities.

Recognizing the importance of the New York National Guard throughout our state's history, Governor Pataki has made projects such as this book, the restoration of numerous armories within the Empire State, the preservation of our state's extensive collection of military artifacts and the opening of the New York State Military Museum and Veterans Research Center in Saratoga Springs all possible as means of safeguarding this history.

I wish to thank Governor Pataki, Commissioner Bernadette Castro from the Office of Parks, Recreation and Historic Preservation and the numerous state and local leaders for their steadfast support in ensuring the long-standing tradition of New York's honorable and remarkable military legacy portrayed in this unique book for generations to come to learn and grow from.

—Joseph J. Taluto
Major General, New York Army
National Guard
The Adjutant General

Acknowledgments

There are numerous individuals and organizations whose help and support made this book possible. I am particularly grateful to my colleagues at the New York State Office of Parks, Recreation and Historic Preservation:

Kathleen LaFrank
Raymond W. Smith
Peter D. Shaver
James P. Warren
Mark L. Peckham
David J. Meyersburg
Austin O'Brien
Ruth L. Pierpont

Many officials at the New York State Division of Military and Naval Affairs and the New York State Military Museum and Veterans Research Center also provided invaluable assistance, especially the following:

Colonel (ret.) William W. Knox
Major (ret.) Gayle N. Carpenter
Colonel Michael J. Stenzel
Thomas C. Duclos
Christopher S. Morton

Renee K. Hylton of the National Guard Bureau was instrumental in initiating the project in 1992 and has remained its champion ever since.

In addition, staff at the following organizations were extraordinarily gracious and helpful:

New York State
Brooklyn Public Library, Brooklyn
Broome County Historical Society, Binghamton
Buffalo and Erie County Historical Society, Buffalo
Cayuga County Museum, Auburn
City of New York, Department of Parks and Recreation, New York City
Corning Historical Society, Corning
Fenton Historical Society, Jamestown
Franklin County Historical and Museum Society, Malone
Geneva Historical Society, Geneva
Greater Oneonta Historical Society, Oneonta
Landmark Society of Western New York, Rochester
McKinney Library, Albany Institute of History and Art, Albany
Medina Area Chamber of Commerce, Medina
Museum of the City of New York, New York City
New York City Landmarks Preservation Commission, New York City
New York State Historical Association, Cooperstown
New York State Library, Albany
New York State Military Museum and Veterans Research Center, Saratoga Springs
Office of the City Historian, Dunkirk
Ogdensburg Public Library, Ogdensburg
Oneida County Historical Society, Utica
Onondaga Historical Association, Syracuse

Ontario County Historical Society, Canandaigua
Oswego County Historical Society, Oswego
Rensselaer County Historical Society, Troy
Rensselaer Polytechnic Institute (RPI), Folsom Library, Troy
Seventh Regiment Conservancy, New York City
The Cooper Union, New York City
Whitehall Heritage Area System, Whitehall

Rhode Island
Anne S. K. Brown Military Collection, Brown University, Providence

Washington, D.C.
Company of Military Historians
Historical Services Division, Office of Public Affairs, National Guard Bureau

Lastly, special thanks go to the Legacy Resource Management Program of the U.S. Department of Defense for financially supporting the publication of this book.

Seventh Regiment Armory, 1879. "The Seventh Regiment, N.G.S.N.Y., Taking Formal Possession of the New Armory, April 26th." Frank Leslie's Illustrated Newspaper. *15 May 1880, page 180. Courtesy of the New York State Historical Association.*

Introduction

This book is a pictorial overview of the history of the New York Army National Guard as reflected in approximately 120 arsenals and armories built in the Empire State during the eighteenth, nineteenth and early twentieth centuries. In terms of age and architectural sophistication, the armories built in New York State between 1799 and 1941 compose the oldest, largest and best collection of pre–World War II era armories in the country. The majority of New York's armories are monumental, medieval-inspired, castellated fortresses that were built between the Civil War and World War I. The history of the state's militia paralleled the evolution of citizen soldiery in America, and New York's arsenal and armory building programs reflected, even led, arsenal and armory building programs across the country. Thus, New York's arsenals and armories epitomize the building type and are among the country's most imposing and tangible monuments to the role of the militia in the nation's military history.

A Brief Overview of the History of the New York Army National Guard

For the purpose of understanding the evolution of the New York Army National Guard, American military history can be divided into two major periods. The first, spanning nearly three centuries between the earliest days of the colonial era and the turn of the twentieth century, marks the emergence and eventual preeminence of the militia (officially designated the National Guard during the Civil War), that is, a state-controlled, decentralized army of citizen soldiers. The second, beginning during the first decade of the twentieth century and continuing to the present day, is characterized by the ascent of the regular army, that is, a federally maintained, centralized corps of professional soldiers, and the concurrent transformation of the National Guard into a reserve force of the regular army. The first period can be divided into three phases: the colonial/early republican era (from the early seventeenth century to the early nineteenth century, when compulsory militia service prevailed); the antebellum era (from the 1840s to the outbreak of the Civil War in 1861, when the volunteer militia replaced the compulsory militia); and the Gilded Age (from the 1870s to the late 1890s, when the National Guard flourished as the country's primary domestic peacekeeper during an era of labor-capital conflict). The second period can be divided into two phases: from the turn of the twentieth century to World War II, when the National Guard emerged as the primary reserve force of the U.S. Army; and the post–World War II era, when federal reserves replaced the National Guard as America's primary reserve force.

A Brief Overview of the Arsenal as a Building Type

Prior to the Civil War, most facilities built for New York's militia were called *arsenals*, that is, buildings in which munitions were manufactured, repaired and/or stored. The nearly twenty arsenals built in New York between 1799 and the late 1850s were merely utilitarian warehouses in which to store the often meager supplies of arms, ammunition and war materials issued to the state's militia.[1] This small number of militia-specific facilities erected over a six-decade period does not adequately reflect the size, strength and importance of the militia during the first half of the nineteenth century. Rather, it illustrates the fact that during this period, most of New York's scores of local and regional units were expected not only to supply their own munitions but to locate and pay for their own storage facilities as well. Most units stored their supplies in members' homes or barns; if they could afford to, units occasionally rented locked rooms in a variety of commercial or public buildings in their respective communities. Drill practices were held on village greens or open fields. Meetings, if any, were held in commanders' or members' homes or barns, although financially stable units occasionally leased groups of rooms, even full floors, in a broad range of building types, including churches, inns, taverns, hotels, fraternal halls, commercial blocks and fire stations.

The approximately twenty arsenals built in New York before the Civil War were similar in many features. In terms of function, all were warehouses for the state's munitions. Most were relatively small, vernacular buildings composed of single, rectangular main blocks containing one large room devoted to storage. Few contained separate meeting rooms; even fewer provided spaces for drill purposes. None were designed for sole use by any specific unit, although some came to be associated with or dominated by specific companies or regiments. For safety reasons, given the volatile nature of their contents, all arsenals were of masonry construction with minimal openings. Also for safety reasons, most arsenals were built on the sparsely populated fringes of their respective communities. In terms of design and decoration, the architectural features of these arsenals varied dramatically. Some, especially the earliest arsenals, were unadorned, utilitarian buildings; others displayed relatively sophisticated features derived from the prevailing architectural tastes of their respective dates of construction.

In addition to these twenty arsenals, another handful of facilities are known to have been built for or used by the militia before the Civil War. Several were market armories, which, as the name suggests, housed both the militia and commercial enterprises. One, known as Gothic Hall (1830s), was an older building of unknown origin that was converted for use by one of Brooklyn's local units. Another, the Henry Street Armory (1858), foreshadowed the emergence of the building type after the Civil War as a large, multipurpose headquarters for a specific unit of the state's militia.

A Brief Overview of the Armory as a Building Type

The term *armory* was introduced in the militia's vocabulary in the early 1860s and used almost exclusively after 1870 to describe facilities built or adapted for the sole use of the militia. However, it was not until 1879, when the Seventh Regiment erected its armory in Manhattan's Upper East Side, that the term came to define a new, uniquely American building type.[2] Because of its monumental scale, outstanding architectural design and decoration and prominent location on busy Park Avenue, all of which reflected the wealth and status of the state's premier National Guard unit of the period, the Seventh Regiment Armory was, and still is, the flagship of the building type.

In the broadest sense, armories built after 1879 were multipurpose headquarters built for local units of the state's militia. All were two-part buildings consisting of administration blocks and attached drill sheds. Many were castellated fortresses that reflected construction methods, forms and designs derived from medieval Gothic military architecture. The characteristics of the building type can be divided into four categories: function; form, layout and construction; location and setting; and architectural design and decoration.

Armories had three basic functions: they served as military facilities, clubhouses and public monuments. In their capacity as military facilities, they were headquarters for locally based units of the National Guard. Specifically, they were warehouses where munitions, equipment and uniforms were stored; sheltered places where guardsmen could train and drill; and self-contained centers where the state's domestic security forces could assemble in the event of an emergency. As clubhouses, armories served the social and recreational needs of their respective units' members, many of whom came from the well-to-do middle and upper classes. As public monuments, armories were imposing symbols of military strength and governmental presence within a community, designed to inspire nationalism, patriotism and community pride in law-abiding citizens or fear and awe in those tempted to challenge the status quo. This was particularly true during the post–Civil War era of labor-capital conflict.

In terms of layout and construction, most post-1879 armories followed the formula employed in the Seventh Regiment Armory: they consisted of multistoried administration buildings with massive drill sheds that usually were attached to the rear. Like the Seventh's armory, all later armories were of masonry construction. All late nineteenth-century and some early twentieth-century armories featured load-bearing walls, while most early twentieth-century armories featured structural steel frames sheathed with masonry (usually brick) curtain walls. Visually and aesthetically, the administration buildings of these post-1879 armories dominated their designs; functionally, however, their drill sheds were the buildings' raison d'etre. The need for a safe and unusually large sheltered space motivated the design of the building. Before the Civil War, the militia had drilled outside or in rooms or halls in the upper stories of various types of civic or commercial buildings. Village greens or parade grounds provided ample space, but they were suitable only as weather permitted; indoor facilities provided protection from the elements in all seasons, but they were often cramped and unsafe: too much weight could collapse the upper floors, and emergency egress was virtually impossible. Consequently, the need for safe, extremely large and unobstructed ground-floor space was the primary consideration in creating the new building type.

The construction of drill sheds, often tens of thousands of square feet in size, employed state-of-the-art engineering techniques, including, most notably, massive steel truss work to support soaring roofs. The primary source of inspiration for this massive open floor space was the train shed, a building type recently introduced in large urban railroad depots, such as Grand Central Depot (1871) in New York City. The great exhibition halls built in Europe and the United States for mid-nineteenth-century world's fairs and expositions, such as the Centennial Exhibition (1876) in Philadelphia, also provided models for the engineering and construction of the drill sheds. In the Seventh Regiment's drill shed and in subsequent armories, truss work remained exposed; in fact, exposed trusses are one of the most prominent features in surviving nineteenth- and early twentieth-century drill sheds.

One of the most important functions of armories built after the Civil War was to provide large, sheltered expanses of unobstructed floor space where troops could drill or gather for military actions. In the first photograph, Olean's Forty-third Separate Company poses in its ca. 1889 drill shed. The drill sheds of separate company armories built after the Civil War were generally approximately 10 to 12,000 square feet in extent. The second photograph shows the cavernous drill shed of the Thirteenth Regiment Armory (1892–94) on Brooklyn's Sumner Avenue. It is typical of drill sheds in regimental armories, most of which measure approximately 40 to 60,000 square feet. Both photographs appear courtesy of the New York State Military Museum and Veterans Research Center, in whose archives reside dozens of historic photographs taken of armories built between ca. 1858 and ca. 1920. Individual photographs are not dated, but the series appears to date from the second decade of the twentieth century (ca. 1910s). Many of these photographs depict the interiors of various drill sheds that emphasize the vastness of the unobstructed floor space as well as the variety of truss types employed in the roofing systems. The state-of-the-art museum, opened in 2002, is housed in the Saratoga Armory (1889–91) in Saratoga Springs.

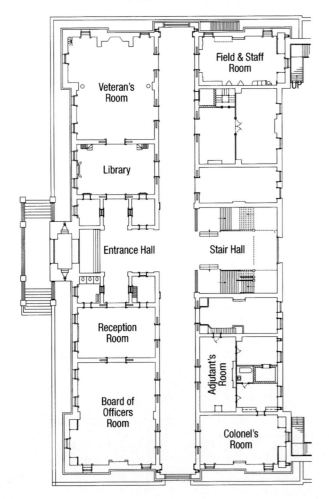

Floor plan of the first story of the Seventh Regiment Armory's administration building. Courtesy of Kirsten Moffett Reoch, Director, Seventh Regiment Armory Conservancy.

In terms of room configuration and space allocation, the Seventh Regiment Armory and later armories followed the same basic pattern. From the street, grand entrances led into large and stylish vestibules; inside, wide corridors were flanked by various types of rooms, including offices, company meeting rooms, officers' quarters, libraries, parlors, studies and/or lounges. Often, large mess halls and recreational facilities, such as swimming pools and bowling alleys, were located in basements under the administration buildings. Rifle ranges were frequently located in basements beneath the drill sheds.

In its location and setting, the Seventh Regiment Armory illustrated the tradition of placing armories in or very near the core of their respective communities, first for the convenience of their members and second to serve as a daily reminder to passersby of governmental and military presence within those communities. Members wanted easy access to their headquarters; they did not want to travel to the fringes of their communities to attend mandatory meetings or enjoy an evening of cards by the fire. Equally important, especially during the Gilded Age, armories served as stalwart fortresses during times of domestic unrest: the militia needed immediate access to their "forts," and these forts needed to be sited at the core of potential conflict.

Finally, in terms of design and decoration, the Seventh Regiment Armory and nearly all subsequent armories reflected the influence of medieval military architecture, primarily castles and fortresses built in Europe between the twelfth and fifteenth centuries. Salient architectural features derived from these sources included raised and battered masonry foundations; tall, narrow windows protected by iron grilles; massive sally ports with portcullises through which troops could march into battle; and machicolated cornices with corbelled brickwork, which, at least during the Middle Ages, allowed a castle's defenders to pour molten lead or boiling oil onto their attackers below. These features were not merely decorative: armories were built to withstand sieges and each of their architectural components fulfilled specific military functions. For example, tall, narrow window openings and battlemented parapets allowed soldiers to shoot at rioters on the streets below; portcullises could be secured to protect the sally ports against intruders. To a greater or lesser degree, virtually every armory built in New York State after the completion of the Seventh Regiment's facility incorporates elements associated with medieval military architecture, ranging from the exuberant and highly picturesque castellated armories of the late nineteenth century to the more subdued Tudor Gothic and classically inspired armories of the early twentieth century.

A Brief Glossary of Architectural Terms

Definitions of the architectural terms used in this book can be found in most general dictionaries and all architectural dictionaries (for example, *Dictionary of Architecture and Construction* by Cyril M. Harris). However, for the convenience of the reader who might be unfamiliar with some of these terms, brief definitions with accompanying illustrations are offered here. The first picture (right), courtesy of the New York State Military Museum, depicts the Saratoga Armory shortly after its completion in 1891. Six of the many architectural terms used throughout this book are illustrated as follows:

1. Sally port: A large, usually round-arched opening around the main entrance, under which a recessed porch or vestibule is sheltered. These extra-wide openings allowed for troops to march out at least four abreast in offensive moves against the enemy.

2. Portcullis: A metal gate that drops or swings into position within the arch of the sally port, providing an additional defense mechanism against would-be intruders.

3. Gable roof: A double-sloped roof whose ends, when viewed head-on, form a triangle.

4. Hipped roof: A roof with four separate slopes and no real "ends."

5. Conical roof: A roof shaped like a cone.

6. Battered foundation: Simple foundations on most building types rise up in a perfectly vertical plane consistent with the walls of the structure. A battered foundation is one that is slightly canted or slanted inward as it moves upward from ground level. In massive masonry structures, battered foundations of tremendous depth and width were needed to support the heavy stone or brickwork above. In medieval military architecture, these foundations were so thick that they provided additional defensive measures—they were virtually impenetrable by even the biggest missiles thrown by the largest catapults. Similarly, many of New York's armories feature battered foundations; certainly, to support load-bearing masonry walls, but also to thwart attackers who might try to break into the facility with pick axes or other such tools or weapons.

Saratoga Armory, 1889–91. Courtesy of the New York State Military Museum.

The second picture (below), courtesy of the Library of Congress (Prints and Photographs Division, Historic American Buildings Survey, #HABS, NY, 31-NEYO, 121-9), portrays a detail of the roofline of the Seventh Regiment Armory (1879; New York City). Illustrated are a crenelated parapet (1) and a machicolated cornice (2). A parapet is a low wall along the top of a building (or any specific part of a building, for example, a tower) that spans or encircles the roofline. A crenelated or battlemented parapet is a fortified wall or platform characterized by alternating solids (also called *merlons*) and voids (also called *crenels*). Crenelated parapets were highly functional in medieval Gothic military buildings: the protectors of castles and fortresses would stand or crouch behind the merlons for safety but could fire with ease through the crenels. The cross-shaped openings in the merlons of the Seventh's parapet evoke the idea of balistrariae, tall, narrow slits through which a man with a crossbow could shoot arrows. Also depicted in this picture is a machicolated cornice.

Thirteenth Regiment Armory, 1892–94. Historic postcard from the collection of the author.

Seventh Regiment Armory, 1879. Detail of the crenelated parapet and machicolated cornice. Courtesy of the Library of Congress.

A cornice is the trim on the exterior of a building where the roofline meets the wall. It can also form the trim on a specific element of the building; for example, a lintel above a door or window opening can have a decorative cornice. (On the interior of a building, cornices often decorate the junctions of walls and ceilings.) In medieval military architecture, a machicolation was a slightly overhanging structure or projection at the top of a castle or fortress that featured an opening in its floor through which boiling oil could be poured upon anyone attacking the fortification. Thus, in this picture, the tall, narrow openings between the striated or slightly stepped brickwork of the cornice are the channels through which the oil (or any type of missile) could be poured (or dropped) upon the heads of the enemy.

The third illustration (above) is a historic postcard of the Thirteenth Regiment Armory (1892–1894) in Brooklyn. It shows several previously defined components, including a sally port, crenelated or battlemented parapets and machicolated cornices. Also depicted are medieval-inspired bastions, turrets and bartizans. A bastion is essentially a tower, but often is associated with the corners of a building. To clarify, the entrance of the Thirteenth Regiment Armory is flanked by large, round towers (1), while the front and rear corners of the administration building are articulated by octagonal bastions (2). Turrets and bartizans are essentially tiny towers, or projecting structures, attached to the upper stories of a building or above a building's entrance or sally port, designed to hold sentries (or actual warriors in times of battle). In this picture, the tower-like accretion on the large, round tower to the left of the entrance is called a *bartizan* (3), but it could just as accurately be called a large *turret*. The smaller structures on the large, round, right-hand tower and above the sally port are called *turrets* (4), but could just as easily be called *bartizans*. Fortified turrets and bartizans often feature crenelated parapets (5) and/or machicolated cornices (6).

A Brief Overview of the Arrangement of the Book

Chapter 1 provides a brief history of the Army National Guard in New York State during the four major phases of its evolution.[3] Chapters 2, 3, and 5 through 9 begin with summaries of the various arsenal and armory building programs in New York between 1799 and World War II. (Chapter 4 is devoted to the Seventh Regiment and its 1879 armory on Park Avenue.) Each overview is followed by detailed discussions of each arsenal/armory within its respective theme. The level of information included in these individual catalog entries varies dramatically. Some entries include only the name of the facility, its approximate date of construction and a single drawing or photograph. Others contain lengthy discussions about the armory itself, the history of the unit for which it was built, the architect who designed the building and the contractor who built the building and are augmented by extensive illustrations in the form of drawings, paintings and/or photographs.[4] Where applicable, notations of previous and/or subsequent armories built either in the same city or for the specific unit under discussion are provided under the heading "Others." The unequal coverage of the individual facilities in no way reflects either the superiority or

inferiority of any specific armory or group of armories; rather, the disparity is the product of programmatic priorities and financial constraints inherent in the project, as well as the accessibility of primary and secondary sources.

Whenever possible, efforts were made to note the changing names and/or affiliations of the various units housed in each facility. An accurate catalog of the official designations and/or compositions of the almost constantly evolving units, particularly after the Spanish American War in 1898, is beyond the scope of this book. Discerning the ancestral origins of the various units is equally difficult. For example, guardsman and military historian DeWitt Clinton Falls wrote a series of articles entitled "Regimental Historical Sketches" for publication in the *New York National Guardsman* over a seven-year period, between 1925 and 1932. By 1929, seemingly chagrined by readers' criticisms, he quips that virtually every unit can easily trace its descent to the "Garden of Eden Defense Force originally organized by Adam."[5]

The following tables (grouped chronologically according to the chapters in which the individual arsenals and armories are discussed) list the facilities built for New York's militia between 1799 and 1941.[6] The entries that are shaded denote the facilities that no longer survive. When known, the current ownership and/or functions of those facilities no longer owned by DMNA are discussed in the descriptions of the specific facilities throughout the text of the book.[7] Of the extant facilities, the twenty-eight listed below are still owned by DMNA for use by the New York Army National Guard:

Binghamton, Broome County, Binghamton Armory (1932–34), 85 West End Avenue

Brooklyn, Kings County, Forty-seventh Regiment Armory (1883–84), 355 Marcy Avenue

Brooklyn, Kings County, Troop C Armory (1903–07), 1579 Bedford Avenue

Buffalo, Erie County, Connecticut Street Armory (1896–99), 184 Connecticut Street

Buffalo, Erie County, Masten Avenue Armory (1932–33), 27 Masten Avenue

Geneva, Ontario County, Geneva Armory (1892; 1906), 300 Main Street

Glens Falls, Warren County, Glens Falls Armory (1895), 147 Warren Street

Gloversville, Fulton County, Gloversville Armory (1904–05), 87 Washington Street

Hoosick Falls, Rensselaer County, Hoosick Falls Armory (1888–89), Church Street

Hornell, Steuben County, Hornell Armory (1894–96), 100 Seneca Street

Jamaica, Queens County, Jamaica Armory (1936), 168th Street

Jamestown, Chautauqua County, Jamestown Armory (1932), Porter Avenue

Kingston, Ulster County, Kingston Armory (1932), North Manor Road

New York City, New York County, Seventh Regiment Armory (1879), 643 Park Avenue

New York City, New York County, Sixty-ninth Regiment Armory (1904–06), 68 Lexington Avenue

New York City, New York County, 369th Regiment Armory (early 1920s; 1930–33), 2366 Fifth Avenue

Newburgh, Orange County, Newburgh Armory (1931–32), South William Street

Niagara Falls, Niagara County, Niagara Falls Armory (1895), 901 Main Street

Ogdensburg, St. Lawrence County, Ogdensburg Armory (1898), 225 Elizabeth Street

Olean, Cattaraugus County, Olean Armory (1919), 119 Times Square

Peekskill, Westchester County, Peekskill Armory (1932–33), 955 Washington Street

Poughkeepsie, Dutchess County, Poughkeepsie Armory (1891–92), 61 Market Street

Rochester, Monroe County, Culver Road Armory (1917), 145 Culver Road

Saratoga Springs, Saratoga County, Saratoga Armory/New York State Military Museum (1889–91), 61 Lake Avenue

Schenectady, Schenectady County, Schenectady Armory (1936), 125 Washington Avenue

Staten Island, Richmond County, Staten Island Armory (1922), 321 Manor Road

Utica, Oneida County, Utica Armory (1929–30), 1700 Parkway East

Whitehall, Washington County, Whitehall Armory (1899), 62 Poultney Street

Chapter 2: Arsenals and Armories Built in New York State during the Republican, Antebellum and Civil War Eras

Date	Name	Location	Unit (if applicable)
1799	Albany Arsenal	Albany	
1808	Canandaigua Arsenal	Canandaigua	
ca. 1809	Russell Arsenal	Russell	
1830s	Centre Market Armory	Manhattan	Seventh Regiment
1836–37	Center Market Armory	Rochester	
1830s	Fulton Market Armory	Troy	
1835	Old Market House	Oswego	
1830s	Gothic Hall	Brooklyn	
1844	Downtown Arsenal	Manhattan	First Division
1848	Central Park Arsenal	Manhattan	Seventh Regiment
1857–60	Tompkins Market Armory	Manhattan	Seventh Regiment
1858	Henry Street Armory	Brooklyn	Thirteenth Regiment
1863	Twenty-second Regiment Armory	Manhattan	Twenty-second Regiment
1858	State Arsenal, First Division	Manhattan	First Division
1858	State Arsenal, Second Division	Brooklyn	Second Division
1858	Albany Arsenal	Albany	Tenth Regiment Third Division (South)
1858	Broadway Arsenal	Buffalo	Sixty-fifth and Seventy-fourth regiments, Eighth Division (North)
1858–59	Syracuse Arsenal	Syracuse	Fifty-first Regiment Sixth Division
1858	Ogdensburg Arsenal	Ogdensburg	Fourth Division
1858	Ballston Spa Arsenal	Ballston Spa	Third Division (North)
1858	Dunkirk Arsenal	Dunkirk	Eighth Division (South)
1858	Corning Arsenal	Corning	Seventh Division (South)
1862	Utica Arsenal	Utica	Twenty-eighth Separate Company
1868	Schenectady Arsenal	Schenectady	Fifth Division
1868–70	Rochester Arsenal	Rochester	Fifty-fourth Regiment Seventh Division (North)
1868	Virginia Street Armory	Buffalo	Seventy-fourth Regiment

Entries that are shaded denote facilities that no longer survive.

Chapter 3: Armories Built in New York City during the 1870s and in Upstate New York during the 1870s and 1880s

DATE	NAME	LOCATION	UNIT (IF APPLICABLE)
1872–73	Clermont Avenue Armory	Brooklyn	Twenty-third Regiment
1874–75	Flatbush Avenue Armory	Brooklyn	Thirteenth Regiment
1877–78	North Portland Avenue Armory	Brooklyn	Fourteenth Regiment
1873	East Side Armory	Oswego	Forty-eighth Regiment
1873	Syracuse Armory	Syracuse	Fifty-first Regiment
1873	Auburn Armory	Auburn	Forty-ninth Regiment
1879	Kingston Armory	Kingston	Fourteenth Separate Company
1879	Newburgh Armory	Newburgh	Fifth and Tenth separate companies
1879	Watertown Armory	Watertown	Thirty-ninth Separate Company
1882	Virginia Street Armory	Buffalo	Seventy-fourth Regiment
1884	Sixty-fifth Regiment Armory	Buffalo	Sixty-fifth Regiment
1884–86	Virginia Street Armory	Buffalo	Seventy-fourth Regiment
1880s	Binghamton Armory	Binghamton	Sixth Battery and Twentieth Separate Company
1884–86	Troy Armory	Troy	Fourth Battery and Sixth, Twelfth, and Twenty-first separate companies
1885	Oneonta Armory	Oneonta	Third Separate Company
1886	Walton Armory	Walton	Thirty-third Separate Company
1886–88	Elmira Armory	Elmira	Thirtieth Separate Company

Entries that are shaded denote facilities that no longer survive.

Chapter 5: Armories Built in Brooklyn and Manhattan during the 1880s and 1890s

DATE	NAME	LOCATION	UNIT (IF APPLICABLE)
1883–84	Forty-seventh Regiment Armory	Brooklyn	Forty-seventh Regiment
1892–94	Thirteenth Regiment Armory	Brooklyn	Thirteenth Regiment
1891–95	Twenty-third Regiment Armory	Brooklyn	Twenty-third Regiment
1891–95	Fourteenth Regiment Armory	Brooklyn	Fourteenth Regiment
1886–87	Twelfth Regiment Armory	Manhattan	Twelfth Regiment
1888–89	Eighth Regiment Armory	Manhattan	Eighth Regiment
1889–92	Twenty-second Regiment Armory	Manhattan	Twenty-second Regiment
1892–94	Seventy-first Regiment Armory	Manhattan	Seventy-first Regiment
1894–96	Ninth Regiment Armory	Manhattan	Ninth Regiment
1894–95	Squadron A Armory	Manhattan	Squadron A

Entries that are shaded denote facilities that no longer survive.

Chapter 6: Upstate Armories Designed by Isaac G. Perry between 1888 and 1899

Date	Name	Location	Unit (if applicable)
1889–93	Washington Avenue Armory	Albany	Tenth Battalion
1895	Amsterdam Armory	Amsterdam	Forty-sixth Separate Company
1896–99	Connecticut Street Armory	Buffalo	Seventy-fourth Regiment
1888–89	Catskill Armory	Catskill	Sixteenth Separate Company
1892–93	Cohoes Armory	Cohoes	Seventh Separate Company
1892	Geneva Armory	Geneva	Thirty-fourth Separate Company
1895	Glens Falls Armory	Glens Falls	Eighteenth Separate Company
1888–89	Hoosick Falls Armory	Hoosick Falls	Thirty-second Separate Company
1894–96	Hornell Armory	Hornell	Forty-seventh Separate Company
1898	Hudson Armory	Hudson	Twenty-third Separate Company
1890–92	Jamestown Armory	Jamestown	Thirteenth Separate Company
1891–92	Malone Armory	Malone	Twenty-seventh Separate Company
1891–92	Middletown Armory	Middletown	Twenty-fourth Separate Company
1891–92	Mohawk Armory	Mohawk	Thirty-first Separate Company
1888–89	Mount Vernon Armory	Mount Vernon	Eleventh Separate Company
1895	Niagara Falls Armory	Niagara Falls	Forty-second Separate Company
1898	Ogdensburg Armory	Ogdensburg	Thirty-fifth Separate Company
1889–91	Olean Armory (drill shed only)	Olean	Forty-third Separate Company
1891–92	Poughkeepsie Armory	Poughkeepsie	Fifteenth Separate Company
1889–91	Saratoga Armory	Saratoga	Twenty-second Separate Company
1898–99	Schenectady Armory	Schenectady	Thirty-sixth and Thirty-seventh separate companies
1896–97	Tonawanda Armory	Tonawanda	Twenty-fifth Separate Company
1893–94	Utica Armory	Utica	Fourty-fourth Separate Company
1895–96	Walton Armory	Walton	Thirty-third Separate Company
1899	Whitehall Armory	Whitehall	Ninth Separate Company
1890s	Yonkers Armory	Yonkers	Fourth Separate Company

Entries that are shaded denote facilities that no longer survive.

Chapter 7: Armories Built in New York City between 1900 and World War I

DATE	NAME	LOCATION	UNIT (IF APPLICABLE)
1904–06	Sixty-ninth Regiment Armory	Manhattan	
1903–07	Troop C Armory	Brooklyn	
1908–11	Franklin Avenue Armory	Bronx	Second Battery
1911	Fort Washington Avenue Armory	Manhattan	Twenty-second Regiment Corps of Engineers
1901–03	First Battery Armory	Manhattan	
1904–06	Seventy-first Regiment Armory	Manhattan	
1912–17	Kingsbridge Armory	Bronx	Eighth Coastal Artillery District
1909–11	Dean Street Armory	Brooklyn	Second Signal Corps
1911	Clermont Avenue Armory	Brooklyn	First Battalion of Field Artillery

Entries that are shaded denote facilities that no longer survive.

Chapter 8: Armories Built in Upstate New York between 1900 and World War I

Date	Name	Location	Unit (if applicable)
Armories designed by George L. Heins			
1904–06	Binghamton Armory	Binghamton	Sixth Battery and Twentieth Separate Company
1902–07	Masten Avenue Armory	Buffalo	Sixty-fifth Regiment
1904–05	Flushing Armory	Flushing	Seventeenth Separate Company
1906	Geneva Armory	Geneva	Thirty-fourth Separate Company
1904–05	Gloversville Armory	Gloversville	Nineteenth Separate Company
1901	Medina Armory	Medina	Twenty-ninth Separate Company
1904–05	Oneonta Armory	Oneonta	Third Separate Company
1906–08	Oswego Armory	Oswego	Forty-eighth Separate Company
1904–07	East Main Street Armory	Rochester	Third Regiment
1906–07	West Jefferson Street Armory	Syracuse	Forty-first Separate Company
1902	Troy Armory	Troy	Sixth and Twelfth separate companies
Armories designed by Franklin B. Ware			
1909–10	White Plains Armory	White Plains	Forty-ninth Separate Company
Armories designed by Lewis F. Pilcher			
1914	New Scotland Avenue Armory	Albany	Troop B
1917	West Delavan Avenue Armory	Buffalo	Troop I
1914–18	Ithaca Armory	Ithaca	
1919	Olean Armory	Olean	Forty-third Separate Company
1917	Culver Road Armory	Rochester	Troop H (later F)
1918–19	Troy Armory	Troy	
1918	Yonkers Armory	Yonkers	

Entries that are shaded denote facilities that no longer survive.

Chapter 9: Armories Built in New York State between World War I and World War II

Date	Name	Location	Unit (if applicable)
Armories built in the 1920s, arranged chronologically			
1922	Staten Island Armory	Staten Island	
1924–26	Brooklyn Arsenal	Second Avenue, Brooklyn	
1927–29	Hempstead Armory	Hempstead	
Upstate Armories designed by William E. Haugaard in the 1930s, arranged alphabetically			
1932–34	Binghamton Armory	Binghamton	
1932–33	Masten Avenue Armory	Buffalo	Sixty-fifth Regiment
1935–36	Corning Armory	Corning	
1932	Jamestown Armory	Jamestown	
1932	Kingston Armory	Kingston	
1931–32	Newburgh Armory	Newburgh	
1929–30	Oneida Armory	Oneida	
1932–33	Peekskill Armory	Peekskill	
1936	Schenectady Armory	Schenectady	
1941–43	East Genesee Street Armory	Syracuse	
1935	Ticonderoga Armory	Ticonderoga	
1929–30	Utica Armory	Utica	
Armories built in New York City during the 1930s, arranged chronologically			
1930–33	369th Regiment Armory	Manhattan	
1936	Jamaica Armory	Jamaica	Fourth Regiment

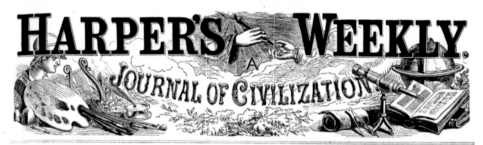

HARPER'S WEEKLY.
A JOURNAL OF CIVILIZATION.

Vol. XXI.—No. 1076.]   NEW YORK, SATURDAY, AUGUST 11, 1877.   [WITH A SUPPLEMENT. PRICE TEN CENTS.

Entered according to Act of Congress, in the Year 1877, by Harper & Brothers, in the Office of the Librarian of Congress, at Washington.

Throughout the seventeenth, eighteenth and nineteenth centuries, the militia—that is, conscripted or volunteer citizen soldiers—formed the backbone of the American military system. However, it wasn't until the late nineteenth century, when the United States was embroiled in a tumultuous era of labor-capital conflict, that the National Guard achieved widespread acclaim as the nation's primary keeper of domestic peace. Pictured here, on the front cover of the 11 August 1877 issue of Harper's Weekly, is the National Guard suppressing rioters during the height of the Great Railroad Strike of 1877. This was the first of many late nineteenth-century revolts by laborers against the middle and upper classes in which the Guard was called in to restore order.

Chapter 1
History of the Army National Guard

The history of the militia can be divided into two major periods. From the colonial era to ca. 1900, America's military system was dominated by the militia, that is, a state-controlled, decentralized army of citizen soldiers commanded by the various colonial (later state) governments. After ca. 1900, the militia was replaced by the regular army, that is, a centralized corps of professional soldiers under federal control. Dating back to the arrival of the first settlers in the New World, the actions and rhetoric of various groups and individuals expressed America's preference for a decentralized militia rather than a centralized army. For example, on the eve of the War of Independence, the Provincial Convention of Maryland proclaimed that "a well-regulated militia, composed of gentlemen freeholders and other freemen, is the natural strength and only stable security of a free government."[1] Nearly a century later, the adjutant general of New York State echoed that sentiment when he remarked in his annual report for 1867 that "a large permanent army [is] correctly considered [to be] the most formidable menace to the liberties of the people."[2] Three and one-half decades after that, the author of an article in a 1901 issue of the *Forum* remarked that "we are a peaceably disposed people, and only take up the sword when no other alternative is left us. . . . A military system should be an evolution of the war spirit of the people. The American people in the rare periods in which their war spirit has been aroused have shown clearly that they prefer a volunteer soldiery."[3]

The era of the citizen soldier can be divided into three distinct phases. The first phase, encompassing the colonial and early republican eras, represents the establishment and dominance of a compulsory militia in the New World. The second, beginning during the second quarter of the nineteenth century and ending with the Civil War, signals the demise of mandated militia service and the rise of the volunteer militia.[4] The last phase, spanning nearly four decades between the end of the Civil War and the beginning of the twentieth century,

marks the heyday of the National Guard as the primary force of the American military system. It was during this era of labor-capital conflict that New York's militia achieved its greatest acclaim as a domestic peacekeeper.

Colonial Era to the War of 1812

Upon their arrival in the New World, the first European settlers, most of whom were English, immediately adopted a militia system (based on British precedent) in which all able-bodied men were required by law to bear arms in times of need. Virginia codified the first laws for a militia in 1611; Massachusetts followed suit in 1636. Most other colonies also adopted policies that established short-term, compulsory military service.

In the Dutch settlement of New Amsterdam (later New York City), the first militia law was passed at the 9 May 1640 meeting of the New Amsterdam Council.[5] However, it was not until 1653 that the Dutch militia, dubbed the Burgher Guard, was mustered into service to ward off English encroachment into New Netherland (later New York State) territory. Militia units in rural areas of New Netherland appear to have been established as early as 1654, but New Amsterdam's Burgher Guard appears to have been the most organized and best trained. A primary mandate of many of these units was firefighting duty. In 1663 the three companies of the Burgher Guard were summoned to the village of Esopus (later Kingston) to defend the settlement against the Esopus Indians. When the British finally took over New Amsterdam in 1664, the Burgher Guard, consisting of only 180 militiamen, simply surrendered. In 1686 the former Burgher companies were reorganized as a Regiment of Foot, under Colonel Nicholas Bayard.[6]

This drawing, which accompanied an article by Daniel Morgan Taylor in the March 1890 issue of the Cosmopolitan, *provides a late nineteenth-century journalist's interpretation of what members of the militia might have looked like during the colonial era. The caption for the drawing on page 569 of the magazine identifies the militiamen as follows, from left to right: a member of the Philadelphia City Troops; a New England Minuteman; a New York Rifleman; a member of the Connecticut Foot-guards; and a Virginia Rifleman.*

Each colony was responsible for funding and operating its own militia. In virtually every case, related costs devolved upon the individual militiamen themselves. As a result, militias in different colonies varied widely in terms of levels of training, leadership and equipment. Nonetheless, the colonial militia generally managed to fulfill both the defensive and offensive needs of the settlers; in fact, such troops even proved worthy of assisting the British in defending the Empire's interests in North America during the French and Indian War (1754–1763).

The militia also served during the Revolutionary War as an auxiliary force of the Continental Army, that is, the provisional force of soldiers furnished by the individual colonies and directly accountable to the Continental Congress. Many historians agree that the war was won in spite of, rather than because of, the involvement of the militia; records abound documenting the inadequacies of citizen

This 1987 rendering of a Virginia Militiaman during the Revolutionary War, painted by the renowned military artist Don Troiani, illustrates a rather ill-equipped farmer called into service to augment the Continentals during the rebellion against Britain. In agreement with many military historians, Troiani states that the militia's performance was "less than stellar" during several specific battles, but, in concert with the regulars, the militia ultimately redeemed its reputation. Thus, the way was paved for the solidification of the role of the citizen soldier during the early republican era. Painting by Don Troiani, www.historicalartprints.com.

soldiers. Nonetheless, during the conflict as well as after the victory, the militia was sanctioned on numerous occasions. On 18 July 1775, three months after the "shot heard 'round the world" was fired in Concord, Massachusetts, the Continental Congress passed the first militia act. On 22 August 1775 New York passed its own Provincial Militia Act. Both the U.S. Constitution, signed in 1789, and the U.S. Militia Act of 1792, which fleshed out the Militia Act of 18 July 1775, reaffirmed the fledgling nation's commitment to the concept of citizen soldiery, despite violent protests expressed by postwar Federalists who argued for replacing the militia with a centralized, regular army composed of full-time, professional soldiers. In 1786 New York's militia was formally organized into two divisions. The First Division encompassed all units in Manhattan (then known as New York City)[7] and the Second Division comprised all other units in the state.

The first real test of the new republic's military organization occurred in the middle of the first decade of the nineteenth century, when America's commercial interests and seafaring rights were suffering the effects of the ongoing feud between the British and French empires. In an effort to protect itself, the United States enacted the Embargo Act of 1807, and on 12 February 1808, New York State passed the Act for the Defense of the Northern and Western Frontiers. Tensions continued to increase until finally, in June 1812, the United States declared war on Britain and a three-year conflict ensued.

Technically, America won the War of 1812, but the victory had little to do with the young republic's military prowess. First of all, despite the rhetoric about the superiority of the militia system, America's volunteer soldiers were, in reality, woefully ill-equipped and poorly led, primarily because, until 1806, Congress had never provided a single penny for the proper outfitting and training of militiamen. Secondly, Britain only half-heartedly applied herself to the War of 1812; her primary resources were directed toward the conflict with France on the European continent. Moreover, upon finally defeating Napoleon in 1814, Britain turned her attention away from North America and toward colonizing the Near East. While not acknowledging defeat, Britain offered peace to the United States on 11 February 1815; a treaty was ratified eight days later.

Despite the fact that the federal government had mandated the militia to be the primary force and the Regular Army to be the secondary force in the newly formed United States, few states were willing or able to adequately train or equip their citizen soldiers. Thus, on the eve of the War of 1812, the militia was ill-prepared for battle, as portrayed in this late twentieth-century painting of a farmer called to serve his country in defense against British forces. Nonetheless, the militia managed to redeem its reputation and was ratified as the primary force of the American military system during the antebellum era. Image, entitled "52nd Regiment, NY Militia, 1810–1816" (Plate 537), courtesy of David M. Sullivan, Company of Military Historians.

Some used America's "victory" in the War of 1812 as evidence of the credibility of the militia system. Proponents of a regular army, on the other hand, were quick to cite the incompetence of the non-professional soldiers. A number of follies committed by citizen soldiers made it easy to ridicule them. For example, there is the tale of several Rockland County companies stationed in New York City during the autumn of 1814. Repeatedly denied permission to return home to harvest their crops, the militiamen abandoned their posts and marched off one night for home en masse. However, it must be noted that once they harvested their crops, they marched back to camp and resumed their military responsibilities.[8]

Despite the frequent and often accurate criticism of the militia, the anti-Federalists prevailed and a decentralized, state-controlled system of citizen soldiery persisted, at least in theory, after the War of 1812. However, neither the federal nor the state government made available sufficient funds to carry out the mandates outlined in the militia acts. Coupled with the war-weariness that pervaded the nation in the late 1810s, the militia, at least in its compulsory form, died out during the first quarter of the nineteenth century.

The Antebellum Era

The volunteer militia emerged during the 1820s to replace the defunct compulsory militia. Several factors contributed to the popularity of the "new" militia. First, relatively stable economic, social and political conditions resulted in a class of wealthy young men of leisure who had both the time and the money to invest in social or fraternal activities. Second, as memories of the horrors of war faded with each passing year, subsequent generations succumbed to romanticized memories of the glorious battles of the American Revolution and the War of 1812. Consequently, hundreds of young men fascinated by the pomp and circumstance of the military joined the volunteer militia.

In New York State, notable units that were either established or greatly expanded during this antebellum period include the Second Battalion (later the National Guards), the Pulaski Cadets (later the New York City Guard) and the Washington Greys in Manhattan; the Light Guard and the Chasseurs in Brooklyn; the Washington

This tinted stipple engraving by Louis François Charon, dating from ca. 1815, shows a romanticized version of an early nineteenth-century militia officer from an unidentified New York unit. Courtesy of the Anne S. K. Brown Military Collection.

Continentals in Albany; the Twenty-eighth Artillery in Buffalo; the Willard Guards in Auburn; the DeWitt Guards in Ithaca; the Oswego Guards in Oswego; and the Penfield Pioneers near Rochester.[9]

During these years three roles for the volunteer militia crystallized: first and foremost, it was a military body charged with ensuring both domestic and international peace; second, it was a civic entity whose responsibilities included appearing at both somber and festive

Members of the Pulaski Cadets (later renamed the New York City Guard) were pictured on the front cover of the 10 May 1856 issue of Leslie's. The caption describes the costumes, from left to right, as follows: Lieutenant's full uniform; Captain, full dress overcoat; Captain, full dress; First Lieutenant, regimental uniform; full dress, Private; regimental uniform, Private, undress.

21

public events; finally, it was an elite fraternal organization for members of New York's middle and upper classes. These roles would become clearly defined during the late nineteenth century, and all three would exert a profound impact on the evolution of the armory as a specific building type.

As a military organization, the volunteer militia gained widespread prestige during the antebellum era for its success in quelling domestic disturbances in both urban and rural settings. The earliest signs of unrest appeared in New York City, one of the first cities in the country to experience the social and economic turmoil that accompanied America's transition from a rural agrarian and light manufacturing nation into a fledgling urban, industrial giant. Accompanying this transition were harbingers of the ill-effects of rampant industrialization, urbanization and immigration (for example, overcrowded and unsanitary living conditions, long hours spent toiling in unsafe work environments and gross inequities in pay scales) that later sparked a series of strikes and riots that nearly paralyzed the nation.

Although domestic uprisings during the antebellum period were sporadic and generally unorganized, local police forces were quickly proven unequal to the task of controlling the violence; in desperation, authorities called upon the militia to assist. Disturbances in the New York City area in which the militia served included the Flour Riots of 1826, the Election Riot of 1834, the Abolition Riot of July 1834, the Stonecutters' Riot of 1835, the Stevedore Riots of 1836, the Croton Water Riots of 1840, the Astor Place Riot of 1849, the Dead Rabbits Riots of 1857 and the Staten Island Quarantine Riots of 1858.[10] These pre–Civil War conflicts were quite varied in their causes and the natures of their protagonists. For example, the Stonecutters' Riot erupted in opposition to the use of convict labor in the building industry. The Astor Place Riot, one of New York City's bloodiest disputes during the antebellum era, began as a shouting match between rival groups of theater patrons but soon snowballed into a full-scale street brawl. William Swinton, in his 1869 history of New York's Seventh Regiment, recalls the role of the unit during the mayhem on Astor Place:

Fully twenty thousand men and boys, the dregs of the city, gathered around the theater, armed with stones, sticks and pistols. . . . Three hundred police were driven back, after a gallant struggle to disperse them; and at length . . . the Seventh Regiment . . . was ordered up. At 9 p.m. the regiment arrived at Astor Place, preceded by the National Guard Troop and a company of cavalry. The mounted men, ten abreast, charged through the place from Broadway; but their horses, galled by the fire of the mob, became unmanageable, and they reached Third Avenue, having accomplished nothing. The Seventh Regiment then followed . . . clearing a way to Third Avenue; thence in columns of companies, clearing Eighth Street, and finally, again moving through Broadway into Astor Place, and forming a line in front of the theater. The volleys of stones from the mob there became very severe;

The Astor Place Riot in New York City in 1849 was one of dozens of localized strikes, riots or disturbances during the antebellum era that were quelled by the militia. This rendering of the Astor Place Riot appears in Colonel Emmons Clark's History of the Seventh Regiment (1890), *the two-volume history of the unit that is still widely considered to be the definitive chronicle of the regiment.*

but the regiment preserved its magnificent discipline under the trying ordeal. . . . The first volley was purposely aimed high; the second was point-blank, and was delivered with terrible effect; and pressing hard on the flying mob, the troops soon cleared Astor Place of rioters.[11]

According to Swinton, "from that eventful night dates, perhaps, the civic popularity and national prestige of the Seventh Regiment. Its courage, promptness, discipline and steadiness were long the theme of conversation, and no honors of the city or citizens were thought too high to be paid to these trustworthy guardians of law and order."[12]

Eight years later, the Dead Rabbits and the Bowery Boys, two particularly contentious gangs of young men, clashed in the Dead

Rabbits Riots during the Fourth of July holiday in 1857.[13] In 1858, the Quarantine (Sepoy) Riots broke out when angry residents of Tompkinsville, Castleton and Southfield on Staten Island, ostensibly fearful for their health, set fire to a nearby hospital full of patients afflicted with yellow fever.[14] Because most of the patients were recent immigrants, the Quarantine Riots foreshadowed one of the root causes of many post–Civil War disputes: the middle and upper classes' fear of and anger toward newcomers.

Several upstate militia units were also called upon to maintain law and order during the antebellum period. During the anti-rent riots of the 1830s and 1840s on the Hardenburgh Patent (Delaware County) and Rensselaerwyck (Albany County), the militia was ordered to suppress tenant farmers who were rebelling against the

The Sepoy Riots, often referred to as the Quarantine War, paralyzed much of Staten Island when a hospital treating patients afflicted with yellow fever was destroyed by angry mobs. During the initial mayhem and the weeks-long aftermath, virtually every militia unit in the First Division was called upon to assist authorities in restoring and maintaining order. This drawing, one of many illustrations accompanying an article in the 25 September 1858 issue of Leslie's, *depicts the changing of the guards at the encampment of the Eighth Regiment. Subsequent issues of the newspaper, particularly the 6 November 1858 issue, provide full coverage of the entire range of services provided by the various New York City regiments during the crisis. Courtesy of James Spring, DMNA.*

During the antebellum era, the militia was expected to perform a broad range of ceremonial duties at a variety of local, state and national events. In 1825 the Second Battalion (later the famous Seventh Regiment) participated in the closing ceremonies at the end of the Marquis de Lafayette's year-long visit to America. This image, part of the National Guard Heritage Series, is one of more than sixty oil paintings commissioned from various artists by the National Guard Bureau (NGB; Washington, D.C.) since 1962. The original paintings are owned by NGB; copies are available to the public.

feudal-like system of land control that persisted in New York well after the Revolutionary War. In western New York, the militia was called up to suppress insurrections against the Holland Land Company's offices in Mayville (Chautauqua County) and Batavia (Genesee County). In Auburn (Cayuga County), members of the Willard Guards were expected to provide assistance in the event of an uprising at the state prison and to protect local citizens from would-be escapees. In Oswego (Oswego County), the militia turned out to quell a riot that took place on West Seneca Street "between a party of Canadian excursionists and citizens of Oswego."[15] In Buffalo (Erie County), the Sixty-fifth Regiment was called upon to subdue rioting laborers on the Erie Canal. In Rensselaer County, the Troy Citizens' Corps dispersed a mob that had sacked and burned a house of ill-repute.[16]

As a civic entity, like a police force or fire company, the militia was expected to participate in all sorts of public events, from the grandest, most exalted national celebrations to the smallest, most pedestrian local gatherings. For example, Manhattan's Washington Greys, who later became the Eighth Regiment, and the Second Battalion, Eleventh New York Infantry, who later became the Seventh Regiment, paraded in New York City in 1824 in honor of the arrival of the Marquis de Lafayette. The following year, the Second Battalion, by then known as the National Guards, paraded again at the end of Lafayette's year-long visit to the United States.

Throughout the antebellum era, many of New York's individual units participated in numerous high-profile, national events of either somber or festive nature. For example, the Eighth Regiment paraded in 1850 at the funeral of President Zachary Taylor. In 1858, when the remains of former President James Monroe were disinterred and returned to Virginia, the Eighth Regiment served as Guard of Honor at New York City Hall and the Seventh Regiment served as special escort on the long trip to Richmond, Virginia.

Two years later, the Seventh Regiment participated in the celebratory unveiling of Clark Mills's statue of George Washington in

Featured on the front page of the 24 July 1858 issue of Leslie's, *this rendering portrays the officers of the Eighth Regiment who participated in the funeral obsequies of President James Monroe. The Eighth Regiment served as Guard of Honor as the remains of President Monroe lay in state at New York City Hall. Courtesy of the New York State Military Museum.*

The 24 July 1858 issue of Leslie's *contained an extensively illustrated article about the ongoing role of the militia in the interment of President Monroe. In this drawing, members of the Seventh Regiment serve as Guard of Honor as the president's coffin is delivered to Richmond, Virginia. Courtesy of the New York State Military Museum.*

Washington, D.C., in 1860 as recounted in a contemporary issue of *Harper's Weekly:*

> The principal feature of the whole procession was the presence of the Seventh Regiment. On the route of the march they proceeded in columns by companies. . . . [There were] eight full companies, each extending nearly from curb to curb. . . . The carriage of the men was erect, their band discoursed most excellent music, and they moved with the precision of a grand piece of machinery.[17]

Later that year, many of New York City's units turned out in honor of the visiting Prince of Wales:

> Then passed before [the Prince] in marching order our splendid corps of volunteer soldiers, and most nobly did they sustain the honor and reputation of the city. Firm and elastic in step, manly and well disciplined in bearing, they seemed the very beau-ideal of the citizen soldier.[18]

In addition to being called upon by local, state or national authorities to participate in specific events, the militia often performed for the public in a variety of monthly or annual parades, drills and mock battles. This image, published by the National Guard Association on page 16 of The Nation's National Guard *(1954), recalls a mid-1852 review of the Seventh Regiment in New York City. Courtesy of the New York State Military Museum.*

On a local level, most communities expected their respective units to turn out for a variety of public events, such as Independence Day parades, county fairs and local political ceremonies. No civic activity was considered complete without the participation of the local militia in full dress.

As for the more private social and recreational aspects of the militia, local units often functioned as elite fraternal organizations. Some units, such as Rochester's Irish Volunteers, Rochester's German Grenadiers, two German units from the Williamsburgh neighborhood of Brooklyn and Manhattan's Sixty-ninth Regiment (composed of first- and second-generation Irishmen), were established by like-minded members of various ethnic groups. Leisure activities ranged from musical soirees to extravagant military balls staged for the community's elite; from smoking cigars and playing cards by the fire to boisterous excursions to destinations both near and far. Writing in his

During the antebellum era, militiamen engaged in a variety of social and recreational activities that illustrated the fraternal camaraderie within and between their respective units. For example, many units commissioned musical pieces for either their own personal enjoyment or for public appearances, as seen in this 1842 song sheet for "Bayeaux's Quick Step." Commissioned by the Albany Burgesses Corps, the tribute was arranged for the piano forte, performed by the Burgesses Band, and dedicated to the officers and members of the corps. Courtesy of the New York State Military Museum.

Although dating from 1878, this ticket to the Company G, Eighth Regiment's annual reception is a perfect example of the types of social and fraternal activities enjoyed by the militia during the antebellum era. Courtesy of the New York State Military Museum.

memoirs in 1866, a member of Ithaca's DeWitt Guards provided a vivid account of the lively camaraderie and good-natured rivalry between his unit and the Willard Guards of nearby Auburn. Apparently any excuse was used by the Ithaca militiamen to justify an excursion down Cayuga Lake to meet their fellow guardsmen in Auburn. The memoirs recall one summer weekend in 1859, when "the Smiles of Heaven seemed to be upon us, and everything seemed given to conduce our happiness [as we] floated down the beautiful Cayuga."[19] Upon their arrival in Auburn on a Saturday in mid-July, the DeWitt Guards were received by three companies out of Auburn and the Tompkins Blues of Trumansburg. They were treated to dinner, lively entertainment and a trip to the Auburn Cemetery to visit the grave of a former member of the DeWitt Guards. Festivities on Sunday included a visit to the state prison and state insane asylum, along with parades and drills in the afternoon with the battalion, during which "each company displayed a thorough discipline in military tactics, the movements being of almost mathematical precision."[20]

Mid-nineteenth-century Changes in the New York Militia

Since 1786, the state's militia comprised two divisions: the First Division included all of Manhattan and the Second Division encompassed the remainder of the state. In an effort to organize more efficiently the large number of local and regional units that had emerged during the second quarter of the nineteenth century, particularly in Manhattan, legislation entitled "An Act for the Organization of the First Division of the New York State Militia" was passed in 1847. This led to the official establishment or redesignation of many regiments in Manhattan, including the Seventh, Eighth and Twelfth. The Second Division followed suit and restructured or redesignated many of its units in 1847 and 1848. In Brooklyn, for example, the Thirteenth and Fourteenth regiments were formalized; in Upstate New York, the Sixty-fifth Regiment in Buffalo was one of several new regiments.

(Most of these regiments retained their 1847–1848 designations until 1917, when sweeping changes in the structure of the National Guard and the U.S. Army necessitated numerous redesignations.) In 1854 the First and Second divisions were reorganized into eight divisions, an official structure that lasted until 1882.

Divisions	Counties Included in Divisions Between 1854 and 1882
First	New York and Richmond
Second	Kings, Orange, Putnam, Queens, Rockland, Suffolk and Westchester
Third	Albany, Columbia, Dutchess, Greene, Rensselaer, Saratoga, Sullivan, Ulster and Washington
Fourth	Clinton, Essex, Franklin, Jefferson, Lewis, St. Lawrence and Warren
Fifth	Broome, Chenango, Cortland, Delaware, Fulton, Hamilton, Herkimer, Madison, Montgomery, Otsego, Schenectady and Schoharie
Sixth	Cayuga, Oneida, Onondaga, Oswego, Schuyler, Seneca, Tioga and Tompkins
Seventh	Chemung, Livingston, Monroe, Ontario, Steuben, Wayne and Yates
Eighth	Allegany, Cattaraugus, Chautauqua, Erie, Genesee, Niagara, Orleans and Wyoming

Within each division, there were usually three brigades; within each brigade, usually three regiments; within each regiment, two to four companies. By the late 1850s, the various regiments included approximately 220 companies of infantrymen, 41 of cavalrymen and 37 of riflemen, for a total of approximately 18,000 troops.[21] This figure represents only those who officially belonged to active units. New York's enrolled militia, that is, those able-bodied men subject to conscription if needed, numbered, as of 1859, approximately 350,000.

The Civil War and the Draft Riots of July 1863

When the Civil War broke out in 1861 and President Abraham Lincoln called for troops, New York State was ready, willing and able to supply its quota. In fact, during the course of the war, New York supplied nearly 20 percent of the entire northern forces; many soldiers on the front were well-trained, highly experienced militiamen. Furthermore, the commanding officers of many of the North's wartime regiments were recruited directly from New York's existing militia units. New York's militia was so strong and well organized that not only did the state send regiments to the front but it was also able to maintain many fully staffed home guard units.

During the war, some of New York's existing units, such as Manhattan's Sixty-ninth and Seventh regiments, served intact under their antebellum designations; other units served intact under new designations. For example, Brooklyn's Fourteenth Regiment was redesignated the Eighty-fourth New York Volunteer Infantry, even though it was commonly known as the Fourteenth Brooklyn. Other preexisting regiments, as well as most of the smaller separate companies, were split up again and again to complete various newly created, wartime regiments. Still others, such as the Twenty-second, Twenty-third and Forty-seventh regiments, were organized at the outbreak of the conflict and continued to thrive long after the end of the war.

Despite conflicting opinions about the performance of citizen soldiers at the front, there is one specific, Civil War–related episode that attracted widespread praise for the militia: the New York City Draft Riots of July 1863. The Thirteenth, Twenty-third, Forty-seventh and Seventy-first regiments were all called into state service. Some units even returned from the front to battle angry mobs rioting against the implementation of conscription.[22] The militia is credited with assisting, and even leading, local authorities in regaining control of the situation and restoring law and order. Its success in dispersing

Mustered into federal service in August 1861, the Seventh Regiment was one of the best-trained, well-equipped militia units to fight in the Civil War. This image of a representative member of the Seventh, painted by Don Troiani in 1993, depicts the epitome of a physically fit, finely attired citizen soldier during the Civil War era. Painting by Don Troiani, www.historicalartprints.com.

The militia was called in to suppress the 1863 Draft Riots when local police forces proved insufficient to contain the mayhem. In an extensively illustrated article in the 1 August 1863 issue of Harper's Weekly, *police are depicted charging rioters who were sacking the printing house of the* Tribune.

the draft rioters, in addition to the respect it had gained during the antebellum period, was a major factor in establishing the National Guard's primary role as the keeper of domestic peace during the late nineteenth-century era of labor-capital conflict.

Post–Civil War Era: Labor-Capital Conflict

The antebellum disturbances and the Civil War Draft Riots paled in comparison with the labor-capital conflicts that plagued much of the nation during the Gilded Age, which spanned the last third of the nineteenth century. Urbanization, industrialization and immigration increased astronomically after the Civil War, especially after America rebounded from the devastating economic Panic of 1873. Clever, ambitious and sometimes unscrupulous entrepreneurs and leaders of burgeoning new industries ascended to previously unimaginable heights of wealth and power; concurrently, many others descended into the depths of poverty and despair. America, previously a classless society, at least compared to her counterparts in Europe, was suddenly stratified, with an ever-widening gap between rich and poor. The destitute, many of whom were immigrants, were crowded into unheated and unventilated tenements without adequate utilities or running water. Those who were lucky enough to find employment often toiled endlessly in dangerous and unsanitary factories; eight-hour days, medical insurance and disability compensation were unheard of. Not surprisingly, unrest among the unemployed and working poor began to ferment. America's first labor unions were established during this period: the National Labor Union (NLU), the Knights of Labor and the American Federation of Labor (AFL) were created in 1866, 1869 and 1886, respectively.[23]

The tension between "labor" (the workers and their sympathizers) and "capital" (the owners/managers and their allies) was exacerbated by the arrival of a relatively small but volatile and vociferous contingent of Eastern European anarchists, socialists and communists. Labeled rebels by the increasingly uneasy members of America's middle and upper classes, these political radicals joined forces with the already restless lower-class laborers and unemployed, causing widespread panic among many Americans who began to fear that the country was on the brink of all-out class warfare. During the last quarter of the nineteenth century, the National Guard emerged as the defender and ultimate savior of the status quo.

The late nineteenth-century era of labor-capital conflict was ushered in with the Great Railroad Strike of 1877. The conflict began in mid-July in West Virginia, Maryland and Pennsylvania when firemen and brakemen on the freight lines of the Baltimore and Ohio (B&O) Railroad Company revolted against their employer for cutting wages. Rapidly spreading throughout the Northeast, the strike crippled and ultimately paralyzed much of the country for several weeks. Many states called out their volunteer militia units to restore order along the affected rail lines, while President Rutherford B. Hayes ordered the regular army into service in the worst-hit areas of West Virginia. In New York, the center of unrest occurred in Hornellsville (Steuben County), when firemen and brakemen on the western division of the Erie Railroad stopped all trains and tore up the tracks. The Twenty-third Regiment of Brooklyn was ordered to Hornellsville, the Eighth Regiment of Manhattan to Buffalo and the Ninth Regiment, also of Manhattan, to Albany. While Pennsylvania and West Virginia sustained great disruption and extensive property damage, the presence of the New York militia is credited with keeping the level of mayhem and destruction along the Empire State's rail corridors to a minimum.

Numerous ever-bloodier conflicts followed in the wake of the Great Railroad Strike of 1877, as workers in a broad range of industries rebelled against low wages, long hours and dangerous working conditions. At the national level, these included the Haymarket (Anarchist) Affair of 1886 in Chicago, the Carnegie Steel Strike of 1892 in Homestead, Pennsylvania, and the Pullman Strike of 1894 in Chicago.[24] In New York, notable instances of unrest were the Buffalo Switchmen's Strike of 1892 and the Brooklyn Trolley Strike of 1895.

The Buffalo strike began in August, when switchmen employed by the Philadelphia & Reading, the Erie, the New York Central and the Buffalo, Rochester & Pittsburgh railroad companies rebelled against low wages and poor working conditions. National Guard units from all across the state were called out to restore order along 800 miles of track. It took more than 7,000 troops nearly two weeks to end the mayhem.

The Brooklyn Trolley Strike broke out on 14 January 1895, when labor organizations controlling the motormen, conductors and other employees of the trolley system rebelled against low wages and long hours. Tracks were blocked, trolley cars were overturned or burned, trolley wires were cut and "the hoodlum element, ever present in great cities, and ready to welcome disorders in which they may gain something, if only amusement . . . made haste to join the disturbances."[25] The local police force proved unable to contain the rioters, particularly because many policemen were in sympathy with the strikers. It was not until 28 January that 4,000 troops from the First Brigade (Manhattan) and 3,000 troops from the Second Brigade (Brooklyn) were able to restore order along the trolley system.

Smaller but equally disturbing riots in communities throughout the state included a strike by laborers on the Erie Canal near Rochester in 1871, an insurrection at the cement works in Rosendale (Ulster County) in 1875, a switchmen's strike in Waverly (Tioga County) in 1892 and an uprising against a cholera quarantine camp on Fire Island (Long Island Sound, Suffolk County) in 1892.[26] The National Guard was called out on each of these occasions and largely succeeded in suppressing the rioters. Although the militiamen incurred the wrath of pro-labor factions and were condemned as brutal policemen of industry, for the most part they drew the praise and respect of the general public as valiant keepers of domestic peace.

Press Coverage: The National Guard and Labor Disputes

Naturally, the press covered labor-capital conflicts, especially those that affected large regions of America or the entire nation. Since most newspapers, journals and magazines were owned and operated by and written for the educated upper classes, their reports supported the interests of capital and condemned the actions of labor. For example, E. L. Godkin, one of the most famous publishers and spokesmen of the

The Twenty-third Regiment played a pivotal role in suppressing the Brooklyn Trolley Strike of 1895. Photograph (1895) courtesy of the New York State Military Museum.

conservative, antilabor wing during the late nineteenth century, wrote a scathing account of the Great Railroad Strike in an 1877 issue of the *Nation*. He advocated dealing harshly with the "riotous poor," the "day-laborers of the lowest class" and the immigrants "who carry in their very blood traditions which give universal suffrage an air of menace to many of the things which civilized men hold most dear."[27] Other popular, conservative journals, such as the religiously oriented *Independent* and the secular, widely circulated *North American Review*, expressed similar views.

Many popular weekly newspapers and magazines also published alarmist accounts of the Great Railroad Strike. For example, the 11 August 1877 issue of *Harper's Weekly* was peppered with phrases such as "the reign of terror," "lawless and howling mobs" and "deeds of violence written in fire and blood."[28] The following week, another article in the same magazine praised the state's militia for its role in suppressing the strike: "The New York National Guard, the flower of American citizen soldiery, have by their attitude and conduct earned the grateful respect of all good citizens everywhere in the country."[29]

Nationally circulated publications also covered the Buffalo Switchmen's Strike of 1892 and the Brooklyn Trolley Strike of 1895. An article in the March 1895 issue of *Outing* by Daniel S. Mercein reported that in Brooklyn "the presence of the State troops seemed to arouse the baser passions of what was now a lawless mob, the strikers' ranks having been augmented by many gangs of the tougher element of Brooklyn's lower classes."[30] The trolley strike was broken after Governor Levi P. Morton called up the entire First Brigade, bringing the number of troops to nearly 7,000. The members of the various units of the National Guard returned home as heroes, as recounted by Mercein,

> This masterly demonstration of force by civic and military authorities proves that to successfully enforce respect for and obedience to the law, and to secure every man his individual liberty and rights, a State must have a large, disciplined, well-equipped and enthusiastic National Guard. New York can well be proud of its citizen soldiery, who have on many occasions forsaken business and home comforts, sacrificed pleasure for duty, to stand shoulder to shoulder and protect the lives and property of its citizens.[31]

In more general terms, the author of a series of articles in the March, April and May 1895 issues of the *Bostonian* despaired that America's cities were

> teeming with immigration of all kinds, from every nation under the sun, and staggering under the loathsome burden of such ignorance, prejudice and corruption as go far to threaten with dire failure the huge experiment of our republican regime. . . . [The rioters are] as ignorant and untutored as horses or donkeys. . . . They must be taught—by moral suasion, if possible; by force, if there should be need.[32]

A few late nineteenth-century publications attempted to counter the mainstream press. For example, the *Arena*, a monthly journal of social reform published in Boston, featured a lengthy article by B. O. Flower in October 1894 that condemned the increase of militarism in America:

> [The country] is becoming a mighty armed camp, with enormous armories, not infrequently erected and furnished by individuals, for companies and regiments of troops who can be relied upon as being absolutely loyal to capital in any struggle between plutocracy or corporate greed and slaving industry. . . . Monopoly in land, class legislation, special privileges and gambling have enabled a handful of men to acquire wealth earned by millions, and with that wealth to corrupt government and crush industry into practical serfdom. . . . It is always to the military arm that an oppressive government, of whatever character, looks for a continuation of power. And for this reason every true patriot and lover of the republic should discourage the war spirit and seek to check the spread of the military tendency which plutocracy is so energetically fostering at the present time. . . . [Armories are] bastiles of death which speak in such an unmistakable manner of the real materialism of the age and the absence of soul kinship with the Prince of Peace.[33]

However, Flower did not speak for the majority of Americans who perceived the National Guard as ensuring, rather than threatening, their way of life. Thus, by the end of the nineteenth century, thanks to its effectiveness in suppressing working-class uprisings, the militia was at its peak in terms of public support. Whether citizen soldiers acted as brutal policemen of industry or trustworthy guardians of law and order is a question best left to military and labor historians; suffice it to say that the National Guard paved the way for orderly and productive industrial activity in capitalist America. And furthermore, despite continued debate about a centralized versus a decentralized armed force, the volunteer militia remained the backbone of the American military system throughout the remainder of the nineteenth century. The sudden increase in armory construction during the 1880s and the 1890s in New York State was a direct reflection of this meteoric rise in prestige and popularity of the National Guard during the Gilded Age.

Early 1880s to Late 1890s: Camp Smith, the Consolidation Act of 1882 and the Armory Law of 1884

Several noteworthy developments occurred during the 1880s and 1890s that affected the evolution of the state's militia during the latter years of the Gilded Age. In 1882 a state training camp, Camp Smith, was established near Peekskill (Westchester County) for the annual training of troops. While not directly impacting the state's armory construction program, the creation of the centralized training camp served to unite the state's geographically scattered units into a more cohesive entity. Mandatory biannual, one-week (later

Camp Smith, established in 1882 near Peekskill, New York, was an open-air training ground for the state's militia units, all of which were mandated to one week (later two weeks) of annual training. Hundreds, even thousands, of photographs were taken of various units at the camp during the late nineteenth and early twentieth centuries; many are stored in the archives of the New York State Military Museum.

two-week) training sessions allowed militiamen to bond with their comrades, thereby fostering loyalty and commitment to the system. The centralized gatherings also allowed the state's high-ranking officers regularly to review, evaluate and more systematically control the individual units.

The Consolidation Act of 1882 reduced the state's eight National Guard divisions, which had been created in 1854, to four divisions. By 1886 these four divisions were renamed *brigades*.[34] More important, at least in terms of impact upon armory building programs of the period, was the passage of the Armory Law of 1884, a critical component of which provided for the creation of the New York City Armory Board. This quasi-public board, composed of local and state politicians, military representatives and private consultants, immediately had a profound impact on the construction of new armories in Manhattan and, after 1898, in all boroughs of New York City.

Several changes at the federal level paralleled these legislative initiatives in New York. During the mid-1880s, several amendments were made to the Militia Law of 1792, which, for nearly a century, had been the supreme military law of the land. The most important amendment doubled the federal government's annual appropriation of $200,000, a sum that had remained unchanged since 1806. The $400,000 appropriation was to subsidize all financial needs of the various state militias. However, it was a ridiculously low figure considering, for example, that the average cost of constructing a single regimental armory in New York City during the 1880s and 1890s was at least $500,000. As in the past, the federal government imposed mandates on the state militias and foisted the burden of implementation on the states and localities. While many states would not, or could not, fulfill these mandates, New York willingly and eagerly assumed its responsibilities: between ca. 1880 and ca. 1900, millions of state tax dollars were spent building nearly fifty armories across the state.

1900 to World War II

During the first half of the twentieth century, the National Guard underwent a radical transformation. Once the backbone of the American military system, the guard began to assume an auxiliary role as a reserve force of the U.S. Army. In terms of federal legislation, the change was marked by the passage of the Dick Act in 1903 and the National Defense Acts of 1916 and 1920, all three of which sanctioned the regular, centralized armed forces as the official mainstay of the American military system.[35] These legislative acts were the culmination of trends dating back to the late 1890s that foreshadowed the downsizing of the militia. The two most important events at the national level were the election of President William McKinley in 1896 and America's surprisingly decisive victory in the Spanish American War of 1898.[36] The prowess of the U.S. armed forces, particularly the U.S. Navy, displayed against Spain in the interest of liberating Cuba and the Philippines, catapulted America into a position of international leadership. Federalists, who for centuries had argued for the preeminence of a centralized army, renewed their efforts to persuade government and military officials as well as the general public that a decentralized militia was incapable of meeting the country's military needs.

These arguments were reinforced by social and economic changes that were undermining the role of the militia. By 1900 the fear of class warfare that had nearly paralyzed the country between the mid-1870s and the mid-1890s began to subside, primarily because the middle and upper classes had essentially succeeded in silencing the lower classes: first, via military might, and second, via employers' and society's concessions to some of the workers' more serious complaints. In particular, an eight-hour workday replaced the twelve-hour shifts that previously dominated industry; a minimum-wage law was enacted; and new tenement laws required improvements in heat, water, light and ventilation systems in housing for the poor and working classes. Furthermore, although sporadic strikes and riots continued into the twentieth century, the public's perception of the conflict changed dramatically. Strikes were viewed simply as annoying disturbances to productivity rather than harbingers of the breakdown of the capitalist economy or the republican form of government. Equally important, fledgling state police forces began to replace the militia as the preferred tool for labor suppression. Finally, taxpayers, many still paying off debts incurred by the late nineteenth century armory construction projects, were simply tired of subsidizing their increasingly expensive militia units.

Thus the way was paved for the passage of the three pivotal congressional acts that redefined, but did not abolish, the National Guard during the early twentieth century. Local units of state-controlled citizen soldiers remained stable and even served in active duty during the Mexican border dispute (1916), World War I (1918–1919) and World War II (1941–1945). In terms of noncombat duty, National Guard units began to evolve into proactive community organizations in their hometowns and cities, and their armories began

In the midst of its changing role in terms of military structure and responsibility, the National Guard remained a popular civic, social and fraternal organization. In the public realm, the militia continued to impress and entertain crowds in all sorts of parades, reviews and drills, as seen in this historic photograph of the Seventh Regiment marching in full dress in New York City. Photograph (undated, but believed to have been taken during the second decade of the twentieth century) courtesy of the New York State Military Museum.

35

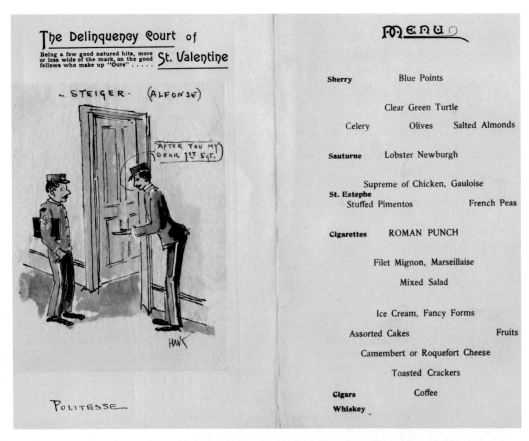

The Delinquency Court of

Being a few good natured hits, more or less wide of the mark, on the good fellows who make up "Ours" . . . . . **St. Valentine**

STEIGER - (ALFONSE)

"AFTER YOU MY DEAR 1ST SGT."

HWT

POLITESSE

MENU

Sherry	Blue Points
	Clear Green Turtle
Celery	Olives Salted Almonds
Sauturne	Lobster Newburgh
St. Estephe	Supreme of Chicken, Gauloise
	Stuffed Pimentos French Peas
Cigarettes	ROMAN PUNCH
	Filet Mignon, Marseillaise
	Mixed Salad
	Ice Cream, Fancy Forms
Assorted Cakes	Fruits
	Camembert or Roquefort Cheese
	Toasted Crackers
Cigars	Coffee
Whiskey	

On the more private side, members of the various units continued to amuse themselves with social outings, attendance at cultural events or private dinners. The menu depicted is from a dinner held by the Eighth Regiment in 1904. The menus, each of which was illustrated with a hand-painted cartoon designed for a specific member of the unit (in this case, Sergeant Alfonse Steiger), also served as place cards. About two dozen of these place cards are in the Eighth Regiment archives at the New York State Military Museum.

to function as civic centers, particularly after World War I. The congressional acts had preserved the integrity of locally based militia units, thereby ensuring the survival of National Guard traditions that fostered camaraderie among young men, loyalty to country and local civic responsibility. Many National Guard units quickly became pivotal public entities whose interests in community stability and well-being were equal to those of local politicians, businessmen and private citizens.

Post–World War II History of the National Guard

After World War II, the federal reserve forces replaced the state-controlled militias as the country's primary reserve force. The National Guard became the U.S. Army's secondary reserve force. During the cold war era, the National Guard's primary mission was military readiness, although in reality, citizen soldiers were seldom called out for combat duty. Instead, the National Guard flourished as a provider of domestic security during times of natural disasters or localized incidents of civil unrest. At the national level, the National Guard is remembered for subduing war protesters at Ohio's Kent State University in 1970 and assisting local police during the Los Angeles Race Riots of 1992. In New York, the National Guard was called out to restore order during a riot at Attica State Prison in 1971. The fall of the Berlin Wall in 1989 signaled the end of the Cold War; subsequently, virtually all levels of the military were downsized accordingly. The National Guard was among the hardest hit: it suffered severe cutbacks in both funding and enrollment.

During the 1990s, the New York Army National Guard began to experience a period of rejuvenation. New York's citizen soldiers responded when the Blizzard of 1996 hit New York City and the Ice Storm of 1998 paralyzed New York's North Country. Beginning in 1996, special units of the New York National Guard were sent to augment NATO peacekeeping forces in Bosnia. In terms of community service, the National Guard won acclaim for airlifting abandoned cars out of the ecologically sensitive Pine Barrens in Southampton

(Suffolk County) and the similarly fragile Pine Bush Preserve in Colonie (Albany County). In order to retain existing enrollment and attract new enlistees, Governor Pataki signed a tuition reimbursement bill in 1997 that provided funds to cover new enlistees' college expenses. The following year, guardHELP, a program charged with spearheading community service projects, was launched.

In the wake of the 11 September 2001 terrorist attacks on the World Trade Center in Manhattan and the Pentagon in Arlington, Virginia, the National Guard has once again ascended to a paramount position in the American military system. Numerous units were immediately activated by their respective states to perform security and relief duties in the metropolitan areas of New York City and Washington, D.C. Subsequently, National Guardsmen and women from all across the country have been systematically called to full-time, active duty in the Global War on Terror. To date, members of the New York Army National Guard are among the most distinguished, most highly decorated citizen soldiers in Operation Iraqi Freedom and Operation Enduring Freedom in Afghanistan.

Throughout the cold war era, the National Guard remained an important, state-based reserve force within the American military system. Although Guardsmen participated in nearly every post–World War II military engagement, their most widely recognized function was as disaster-relief workers and as aids to local, state or federal forces during times of civil unrest. In New York, for example, National Guardsmen were mobilized in September 2005 to assist a variety of local, state and federal authorities responding to Hurricane Katrina, which devastated parts of Louisiana, Mississippi and Alabama.

After the 11 September 2001 terrorist attacks on America, the National Guard reasserted its pivotal role in the American military system. According to a late 2005 quote from Lieutenant General Steven H. Blum, Chief of the National Guard Bureau in Washington, D.C., "We have moved from simply being the nation's strategic reserve to serving as a full operational force, where Homeland Defense is Job One and overseas deployments are Homeland Defense in depth." Pictured here is a New York National Guardsman stationed on the front in Iraq (2005; courtesy of DMNA).

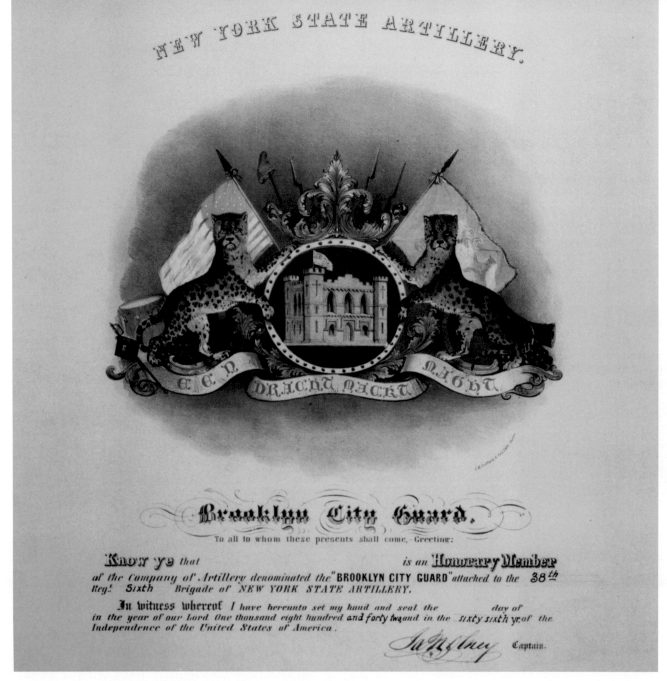

Brooklyn City Guard.

To all to whom these presents shall come, Greeting:

Know ye that   is an Honorary Member of the Company of Artillery denominated the "BROOKLYN CITY GUARD" attached to the 38th Reg.t Sixth Brigade of NEW YORK STATE ARTILLERY.

In witness whereof I have hereunto set my hand and seal the   day of   in the year of our Lord One thousand eight hundred and forty two and in the sixty sixth yr. of the Independence of the United States of America.

Captain.

This template for an 1842 Certificate of Honorary Membership in the Brooklyn City Guard conveys the feeling of pride and patriotism enjoyed by members of the volunteer militia during the antebellum era. The City Guard was one of several units in New York's Second Division that formed the nucleus of the Thirteenth Regiment, officially organized in 1847. The building in the center of the certificate is Gothic Hall, an older building converted for use as an armory during the 1830s by Brooklyn's citizen soldiery.

Chapter 2

Arsenals and Armories Built in New York State during the Republican, Antebellum and Civil War Eras

The heritage of the New York militia between the War of Independence and the end of the Civil War is reflected in more than two dozen arsenals, armories and market armories built between 1799 and the mid-1860s. All of these facilities served as storage facilities for the militia, all were of masonry construction and all were located in or near the centers of their respective communities. The earliest of this group was a state arsenal constructed in Albany in 1799; other facilities include several small-scale arsenals built around 1808, several prominent market armories, seven relatively large-scale arsenals or armories built between the 1840s and early 1860s in New York City and about a dozen mid-scale arsenals built in Upstate New York between the late 1850s and the late 1860s. Together these buildings chronicle the emergence of the volunteer militia during the second quarter of the nineteenth century as a replacement for the compulsory militia that had dominated the colonial and early republican eras.

Earliest Armories and Arsenals to the 1830s

One of the earliest documented arsenals in New York State was built in 1799 in Albany to the design of the regionally renowned architect Philip Hooker. Like Hooker's other civic and residential buildings in Albany, the arsenal was a monumental, Federal-style building finely crafted in brick with stone trim.

The first statewide arsenal construction program began in 1808, when New York passed an "Act for the Defense of the Northern and Western Frontiers" in response to the federal Embargo Act of 1807. Among other things, the act authorized the construction of arsenals at Batavia, Canandaigua, Elizabethtown, Malone, Plattsburgh, Syracuse (then known as Onondaga Hollow), Rome, Russell and Watertown.[1] Fortuitously, Congress simultaneously amended the 1792 Militia Law

to provide an annual appropriation of $200,000 to the states for supporting and developing their citizen soldiery. New York was one of the few states to avail itself of this financial assistance, and construction on several of the proposed arsenals was begun immediately.

Few details about the actual construction or fate of most of these buildings are known; however, by the outbreak of the War of 1812, there were arsenals in seven of the eight authorized upstate locations.[2] It is not clear whether any or all of these arsenals were completely new structures built to serve solely as military facilities or whether existing buildings were simply adapted to serve as arsenals. In Malone, a two-story stone arsenal was built in 1812 in the east part of what was formerly known as Arsenal Park.[3] Plattsburgh's arsenal, built in 1809 at St. John's Academy on Broad Street, burned in 1813 or 1814.[4] The Canandaigua Arsenal, built in 1808, was destroyed by fire in 1879. The Rome Arsenal, located on a three-acre compound now bounded by West Dominick Street, Arsenal Street and West Erie Boulevard (the former Erie Canal), was destroyed by fire at an unknown date. The Russell Arsenal was later used as a village school.

Slightly more is known about the two ca. 1808 arsenals erected in New York City. The first of these, located on Fifth Avenue at East 64th Street, was a city arsenal; the second, bounded by White, Elm, Center and Franklin streets in lower Manhattan, was a state arsenal. Oriented toward Franklin Street, the arsenal included a "handsome three-story brick dwelling, the residence, at that time, of the Commissary General, who had charge of the establishment."[5] In a complicated land exchange between state and city officials, the state arsenal was razed in 1844 to make way for a new city arsenal, while the city arsenal was razed in 1848 to build a new state arsenal.

In addition to these early nineteenth-century arsenals, there were several market armories that served as quarters for specific militia units. For example, New York City's Seventh Regiment occupied the upper floors of Centre Market, a large commercial building on the corner of Centre and Grand streets in Manhattan's Lower East Side. In western New York, Monroe County's early nineteenth-century militia was housed in a commercial facility known as Center Market. Located in the heart of downtown Rochester, it was built around 1836. In Rensselaer County, Troy's militia occupied a portion of the fashionable Fulton Market on River Street. In Oswego County, the nucleus of the Forty-eighth Regiment was housed in the Old Market House on Water Street in downtown Oswego.

Most units, however, did not have specific quarters to call their own, although some of the wealthier units were able to arrange long-term leases for various types of spaces in buildings in their respective communities. For example, Auburn's Willard Guards (along with the old Auburn Guard and the Continentals) were quartered above the John H. Beach Block, built in 1837 on State Street. The Utica Citizens' Corps, founded in 1837, was housed in the old Chubbuck Hall on Hotel Street. Antecedents of Brooklyn's Thirteenth and Fourteenth regiments occupied Gothic Hall, an older building that had been converted for use by the militia.

Arsenals and Armories in New York City from the 1840s to the Early 1860s

Two large, new arsenals, the Downtown Arsenal and the Central Park Arsenal, were built in New York City during the 1840s. Both were designed in a Gothic mode that anticipated the fortress-like, castellated armories of the late nineteenth century. The Downtown Arsenal was built by the city in 1844 for the First Division. Constructed on the site of the old ca. 1808 state arsenal at White, Elm, Center and Franklin streets, the new city arsenal was a two-story stone building surmounted by a crenelated parapet. The Central Park Arsenal was erected by the state in 1848 at the intersection of Fifth Avenue and East 64th Street on the site of a former city arsenal (ca. 1808).[6] It was designed by Martin E. Thompson and featured stalwart corner bastions and crenelated parapets. An interesting footnote to the construction of

this arsenal was the allegation that the Commissary General in charge of the project had "expended moneys most unwarrantably."[7] It is not clear whether this referred to graft or abuse of state funds or simply to an excess of money spent; the critics may have meant that the building was far too lavish for its intended purpose.

In addition to these 1840s arsenals, there were three armories built in New York City for specific regiments during the late 1850s/early 1860s. The Tompkins Market Armory in Manhattan, a large and fashionable, Italianate-style, cast-iron commercial building funded and shared by the Seventh Regiment and a group of butchers, was built in 1857–1860 on Third Avenue at the Bowery. The Henry Street Armory in Brooklyn was built in 1858 by the city for all of its local units, although the Thirteenth Regiment dominated the large brick and stone building for the next two decades. The Twenty-second Regiment Armory, built in Manhattan in 1863, was a fashionable Renaissance/Second Empire–style building.

The State's 1858 Arsenal Building Program

In conjunction with the 1854 reorganization of the New York militia into eight divisions, the state embarked on an aggressive arsenal construction program. Funds for the building campaign, which came to fruition in 1858, were derived from the state's sale of its 1848 Central Park Arsenal to New York City on 15 April 1857 for $275,000. The earliest facilities were erected in 1858 for the First Division in Manhattan and for the Second Division in Brooklyn. The First's new arsenal, located on Seventh Avenue at West 35th Street, was a three-story, fortress-like brick building on a raised, rough-hewn stone foundation. The Second's, similar in appearance to the First's, was erected on North Portland Avenue in Brooklyn.

Twelve new arsenals were also authorized in 1858 for construction in Upstate New York to serve various components of the Third through Eighth divisions. The communities chosen to receive new facilities were Albany, Auburn, Ballston Spa, Buffalo, Corning, Dunkirk, Ogdensburg, Oswego, Rochester, Syracuse, Troy and Utica.

During the next two years, arsenals were erected in seven of the twelve designated communities.[8] The outbreak of the Civil War interrupted the building campaign in Upstate New York. Only one, the Utica Arsenal (1862), was completed during the war years. Rochester did not receive its arsenal until 1868–1870. For unknown reasons, Oswego, Auburn and Troy were dropped from the 1858 plan and Schenectady was added. The Schenectady Arsenal was built in 1868. Despite their post-1861 dates of construction, the Utica, Schenectady and Rochester arsenals are included in this group of antebellum arsenals because in terms of purpose, planning, funding and overall appearance they belong to the 1858 set.

Few of these ten arsenals in Upstate New York displayed any consistent or recognizable features that united, or even identified them as military buildings. Stylistically, some were designed in picturesque Victorian modes, while others reflected the equally popular, but opposing, classical tastes of the period. Of particular note is that five of these arsenals were designed by a single architect, Horatio Nelson White. A Syracuse architect who had recently achieved recognition for his design of the Onondaga County Courthouse (1856–1857), White happened to be a member of Syracuse's Fifty-first Regiment. The first arsenal designed by White was for his hometown unit in Syracuse; almost immediately, White received commissions for arsenals in Ballston Spa, Dunkirk and Ogdensburg. His designs for these three may have been inspired by the 1844 and 1848 arsenals in Manhattan: all featured crenelated parapets, central towers, corner bastions and tall, narrow window openings. The fifth arsenal attributed to White was built in Utica in 1862.[9]

Among the four other arsenals included in the 1858 plan, the ones in Albany and Buffalo were nearly identical, despite having been designed by different architects: both were castellated-style buildings similar to New York City's Downtown and Central Park arsenals. The Schenectady Arsenal was similar to White's 1862 Utica Arsenal in its asymmetrical massing and multistoried corner tower. The Corning Arsenal, distinguished by a multistoried central tower, and the Rochester Arsenal, anchored by stout corner bastions, were symmetrical.

Five arsenals built in Upstate New York during the state's 1858 arsenal building campaign were designed by Horatio Nelson White, pictured in this historic photograph of one of the earliest and most prolific architects in the Syracuse area. Courtesy of the Onondaga Historical Association, this picture shows White, a member of Syracuse's Fifty-first Regiment, posing in his dress uniform.

1799 ALBANY ARSENAL
ALBANY, ALBANY COUNTY

Broadway at North Lawrence Street
Architect: Hooker

Other arsenals/armories in Albany:
1858   Albany Arsenal, Hudson and Eagle streets
1889–93   Washington Avenue Armory
1914   New Scotland Avenue Armory

The Albany Arsenal was built in 1799 to the design of Philip Hooker, an architect renowned for designing numerous Federal-style buildings in the state's capital during the late eighteenth and early nineteenth centuries. Typical of the Federal era, the arsenal was a rectangular, gable-roofed building with regular fenestration. The tripartite façade was articulated by a subtly projecting three-bay pavilion surmounted by a gabled pediment. The arsenal served as a regional storage facility for militia units located in the Hudson and Mohawk valleys.

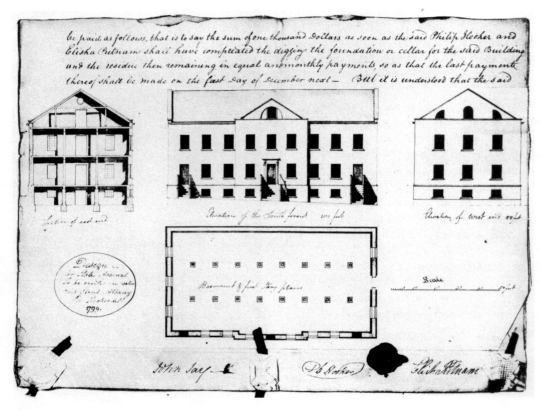

Albany Arsenal, 1799. The design for Albany's first arsenal is presented in a 1799 contract between the regionally renowned, Federal-period architect, Philip Hooker, and New York's Governor John Jay. The original contract is on file in the Freedom Train Collection of the New York State Archives at the New York State Library.

One of Albany's earliest militia units was the Eighty-ninth New York Infantry, established in 1819. The Eighty-ninth was eclipsed during the second quarter of the nineteenth century by several volunteer units, including the Albany Burgesses Corps, the Albany Republican Artillery, the City Cavalry, the Albany Scotch Light Infantry (later part of the Caledonian Guards) and the Washington Continentals.[10] Several of these units served during the anti-rent wars, particularly in the Helderberg area of western Albany County in the late 1830s and 1840s. It is not clear whether or not the area's militia units had access to the arsenal for unit-specific activities.

The state sold the 1799 arsenal to the city in 1858, when the Third Division, created in 1854, received a new state arsenal at the intersection of Hudson and Eagle streets in Albany. In 1859 the city remodeled the old arsenal for use as an eight-room public school (Public School 13). The school was demolished in the 1960s during Albany's urban renewal campaign.

This ca. 1840 lithograph of the Albany Burgesses Corps, one of the city's most prominent volunteer militia units during the antebellum era, is provided courtesy of the Anne S. K. Brown Military Collection.

Hooker's 1799 arsenal was remodeled in 1859 for use as a school, a purpose it served until the 1960s when it was demolished. Photograph courtesy of the McKinney Library, Albany Institute of History and Art.

1808 CANANDAIGUA ARSENAL
      CANANDAIGUA, ONTARIO COUNTY

Arsenal Hill
Architect: unknown

Canandaigua, one of the earliest, most prosperous settlements in the Finger Lakes Region during the first quarter of the nineteenth century, received a new state arsenal in 1808. In September 1812, "a regiment of militia composed of 400 or 500 of the best blood of the country marched through the village with four wagons which stopped at the arsenal to pick up arms and ammunition to be taken to the front" during the War of 1812.[11] The arsenal was a two-story, gable-roofed masonry building sited atop what had been dubbed Arsenal Hill. The arsenal was destroyed by fire in 1879.

This 1874 painting of the Canandaigua Arsenal was executed by Lydia J. Atwater, a locally renowned artist whose uncle had donated the land on which the arsenal was built. The original painting is in the collections of the Ontario County Historical Society in Canandaigua and this reproduction is courtesy of that organization.

CA. 1809   RUSSELL ARSENAL
           RUSSELL, ST. LAWRENCE COUNTY

Russell-Pyrites Road
Architect: unknown

Built around 1809, the arsenal was a three-story, gable-roofed, 30' x 50' building constructed of locally quarried stone. Like the Canandaigua Arsenal (1808), the Russell Arsenal was an unadorned, utilitarian structure that resembled vernacular industrial, civic or commercial buildings of the period. According to an 1853 history, "it stands on a commanding elevation, a little north of the village, on a lot given to the state by Mr. [Russell] Attwater [the founding father of the town and the builder of the village's first saw mill]. . . . [It] is a massive stone building three stories high, thirty by fifty feet on the ground, and originally surrounded by a high stone wall, bristling with iron spikes. The lower story was destined [designed, *sic*] for artillery, the second for small arms, and the third for ammunition."[12] Overlooking the Grasse River and prominently located on the St. Lawrence Turnpike from Sackets Harbor, the Russell Arsenal was expected to be a stronghold for St. Lawrence County if the British invaded the northwestern frontier of New York via Canada. Instead, the British focused their attention to points along the St. Lawrence River, leaving much of inland St. Lawrence County untouched.

   Used infrequently after the War of 1812, the arsenal was finally sold at auction around 1850 and subsequently converted for use as a schoolhouse. In 1913 it became a storage facility behind the newly built Knox Memorial High School; in 1942 it was put back into use as auxiliary classroom space. It was destroyed by fire in 1945.

The Russell Arsenal (ca. 1809) served as a storage facility for Northern New York's militia for about four decades. In 1850 it was converted for use as a school, as seen in an early twentieth-century postcard. Courtesy of Marie Rocca, Russell Town Historian.

1830s CENTRE MARKET ARMORY (SEVENTH REGIMENT)
MANHATTAN, NEW YORK COUNTY

Grand and Centre streets
Architect: unknown

Other arsenals/armories for the unit:

1848	Central Park Arsenal, Fifth Avenue
1857–60	Tompkins Market Armory, Third Avenue at the Bowery
1879	Seventh Regiment Armory, Park Avenue

The Centre Market Armory was the first home of the Seventh Regiment, the nucleus of which was formed around 1806. Beginning in 1839, the Seventh Regiment occupied the upper stories of this two-and-one-half-story, Greek Revival–style commercial building on the

This late nineteenth-century photograph, found in the archives of the Eighth Regiment at the New York State Military Museum and hand labeled "Centre Market Armory," appears to be taken from Grand Street, looking northward up Centre Street. The rear or south pediment of the 1830s market is visible in the far background of the row. An 1891 map of the city labels the entire block bounded by Grand, Centre, Broome and Lafayette streets on the south, west, north and east, respectively, as "Central Market."

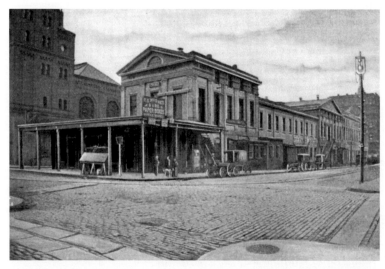

A rare rendering of the Centre Market Armory (1830s) appeared in the Seventy-first Regiment's Souvenir *booklet that commemorated the grand opening of its new armory in 1884. A study of early and late nineteenth-century maps suggests that the narrow, pedimented north end of the building overlooked Broome Street while the long, west side of the building fronted Centre Street. Courtesy of the New York State Military Museum.*

Lower East Side; the attic story contained a large drill hall. According to currently available information, the north (front) façade overlooked a large, open-air marketplace on Broome Street and the west (side) elevation overlooked Centre Street. A late nineteenth-century photograph of the building depicts a veneer of late Victorian ornamentation in the form of a crenelated parapet, corner turrets and a machicolated cornice.

The regiment occupied the market armory until around 1848, when it relocated to the newly completed Central Park Arsenal on Fifth Avenue. After being vacated by the Seventh, Centre Market housed a succession of militia units, including the Eighth and Seventy-first regiments. The date of the building's demise is unknown.

1836–37	CENTER MARKET ARMORY
	ROCHESTER, MONROE COUNTY

Front and Market streets
Architect: unknown
Other arsenals/armories in Rochester:

1868–70	Rochester Arsenal, Woodbury Boulevard
1904–07	East Main Street Armory
1917	Culver Road Armory

Monroe County's militia was housed in the basement of the Center Market Armory, an elegant Greek Revival–style building overlooking the Genesee River. In 1838 a writer described it as a credit to the city:

There is but one market-house in the Union, and that is in Boston, which can be compared with this market in its general composition. It is about two hundred feet long, extending along the west bank of the Genesee River. . . . The edifice is substantially as well as tastefully constructed, the basement story being of cut stone and the superstructure of brick. The parts of the main building fronting on the square are supported by stone columns, with large doors and windows with green blinds, presenting an appearance unsurpassed by the lower part of any range of stores in the city.[13]

The area's oldest unit, Penfield's Pioneer Riflemen, was formed in 1818. Under the command of Captain Ashbel W. Riley, the Pioneer Riflemen had achieved regional renown as they escorted the Marquis de Lafayette from Rochester to Canandaigua in 1824. Other early units housed in Center Market included the following, with their dates of organization noted in parentheses: the Irish Volunteers (November 1828; under the command of Captain P. J. McNamara); Van Rensselaer's Cavalry (1834; under the command of the proprietor of the locally renowned Eagle Hotel); Williams's Light Infantry (1838; under Major John Williams, who later became mayor of Rochester); Rochester Union Grays (1838; first as an infantry unit and later as an artillery company); the Rochester City Cadets (1839; later reorganized as the Rochester Light Guards); the German Grenadiers (1840); the Rochester Artillery (1840); the Rochester City Guards (1844); the German Union Guards (1847); and the Rochester City Dragoons (1850).

In 1849 the various separate companies in the western half of the county were officially combined to form the Fifty-fourth Regiment. By 1855, the Fifty-fourth embraced all units throughout the entire county, many of which continued to have access to the Center Market in Rochester for meeting, drilling and storing ordnance. The Fifty-fourth occupied the building until around 1870, when the regiment relocated to a new state arsenal on Woodbury Boulevard.

The Center Market Armory, a sophisticated, classically inspired commercial building in downtown Rochester, was the first home of Monroe County's militia. The illustration, courtesy of the Landmark Society of Western New York, appeared in the 1984 reprint of Henry O'Reilly's 1838 Sketches of Rochester with Incidental Notices of Western New York.

1830s	FULTON MARKET ARMORY (TROY CITIZENS' CORPS) TROY, RENSSELAER COUNTY

River Street at Fulton Street
Architect: unknown

Other armories in Troy:

1884–86	Troy Armory, Ferry Street
1902	Troy Armory, Ferry Street
1918–19	Troy Armory, Fifteenth Street

The Troy Citizens' Corps, the nucleus of the much later Sixth Separate Company, was organized in September 1835 and took up residence in the newly built, Greek Revival–style Fulton Market on River Street. The unit assisted authorities in suppressing anti-rent rioters in the Helderbergs in 1839; in 1849 it was called out to disperse a mob that had attacked and pillaged a local house of ill-repute.[14] Troy's militia vacated the Fulton Market in 1884 and moved to its new quarters at the corner of River and Ferry streets.

One of the more architecturally sophisticated market armories of the antebellum era, the Fulton Market Armory in Troy was an imposing civic building that featured a two-story, projecting pediment with a full entablature supported by massive square columns with Doric order capitals. Photograph (date unknown) courtesy of the Rensselaer County Historical Society.

Water Street
Architect: unknown

Other armories in Oswego:
1873   East First Street Armory
1906–08   Oswego Armory, West Jefferson Street

The Oswego Guards, the core of what later became the Forty-eighth Regiment (and, still later, the Forty-eighth Separate Company), was organized on 19 July 1838. The unit achieved regional recognition for its service during the Rensselaerwyck anti-rent wars in the 1840s; it also helped contain a riot that took place on West Seneca Street "between a party of excursionists and citizens of Oswego."[15]

The market house is a sophisticated example of Greek Revival–style commercial architecture. The third story of the building contains a ballroom that was used by the regiment as a drill hall during the winter. The ballroom was also the village's primary social and political hall. The unit vacated the market in 1873 and moved to its new armory on East First Street.

The Old Market House—home to Oswego's militia—was a grand, classically inspired civic building adjacent to the city's bustling shipping port. Taken in 1876, this picture shows the newly built, Mansard-roofed tower that replaced the original, Federal-style belvedere. Courtesy of the Oswego County Historic Society.

Adams Street
Architect: unknown

Other armories for the Thirteenth:
1858   Henry Street Armory
1874–75   Flatbush Avenue Armory
1892–94   Thirteenth Regiment Armory, Sumner Avenue

Other armories for the Fourteenth:
1858   North Portland Avenue Arsenal
1877–78   North Portland Avenue Armory
1891–95   Fourteenth Regiment Armory, Eighth Avenue

Gothic Hall, Brooklyn's first permanent facility for its militia, was an older building that had been "fitted up as an armory, and there balls and other gatherings of a social character were held."[16] Between the early 1830s and late 1840s, Gothic Hall housed antecedents of the Thirteenth and Fourteenth regiments, both of which were officially created in 1847. An artist's rendering of Gothic Hall is the centerpiece of the illustration reproduced on page 38 of this volume.

The Thirteenth was formed by consolidating the following independent units: Brooklyn City Guard (formerly Right-flank Company, light artillery; descended from the Sixty-fourth Regiment of Foot during the Revolutionary War); Company A (Pearson Light Guard); Company B (Washington Horse Guard); Company C (Brooklyn Light Guard); Company D (Williamsburgh Light Artillery); Company E (Williamsburgh Light Artillery)[17]; Company F (Oregon Guard); Company G (Washington Guard Rifles); and Company H (Jefferson Guard).

The individual companies within the Thirteenth frequently changed compositions and designations over the next few years; some left the regiment altogether. For example, the two German units from Brooklyn's Williamsburgh neighborhood left in 1849 to create the short-lived Twenty-eighth Regiment. The Williamsburgh units were replaced by the City Cadets and the Greenwood Rifles, companies D and E, respectively. Several other companies seceded in 1858 when they refused to trade in their colorful uniforms for the Thirteenth's newly adopted, regimental gray attire. In 1860, companies B and C were joined under the name of Company C, and the Fourteenth Regiment's Company B transferred into the Thirteenth and became Company B, Thirteenth Regiment.[18] To further confuse the regiment's history and geneology, several of the Thirteenth's companies quit the unit during the early years of the Civil War to form the Twenty-third Regiment; ten years later, the City Guard, one of the Thirteenth's oldest, most esteemed founding units, defected from (or may have been transferred to) the Twenty-third Regiment.[19]

The nucleus of the Fourteenth Regiment was the Brooklyn Chasseurs, formed during the second quarter of the nineteenth century. Little else is known about the antebellum configuration of the regiment. The Thirteenth and Fourteenth regiments shared Gothic Hall until 1849, when both units moved to the recently vacated, old city hall on Henry Street at Cranberry Street.[20] Gothic Hall was subsequently occupied by a series of Brooklyn units, including the Twenty-third Regiment and the Third (Gatling) Battery. The battery occupied the facility from early 1882 until 19 December 1882, when the building was destroyed by fire.

1844   Downtown Arsenal (First Division)
Manhattan, New York County

White, Elm, Center and Franklin streets
Architect: unknown

Other arsenals for the division:
1848   Central Park Arsenal, Fifth Avenue
1858   State Arsenal, Seventh Avenue

The Downtown Arsenal was built in 1844 on the site of the old state arsenal (ca. 1808). Funded and controlled by the city on behalf of the First Division, the Downtown Arsenal was "131 x 84 feet and two stories high. It [was] built of bluestone and [was] supplied with narrow windows for easy defense against mobs."[21] According to an unlabeled clipping in the files of the New York State Military Museum, the thirteen-foot-high first story was used as a gun room and a meeting room, and the thirty-foot-high second story was a drill room and rendezvous point in case of a riot. As of 1871, the building was occupied by three batteries of the First Artillery; as of 1888, the building had been acquired by a private owner and converted for use as a center of commercial/light industrial activity.[22] Its later fate is unknown.

Downtown Arsenal, 1844. This drawing, on a loose page, hand labeled "1854," is on file at the New York State Archives (New York State Library).

Fifth Avenue at East 64th Street
Architect: Thompson

Other arsenals for the division:
1844   Downtown Arsenal, White, Elm, Center and
                  Franklin streets
1858   State Arsenal, Seventh Avenue

The Central Park Arsenal was built in 1848 on the site of the ca. 1808 city arsenal, which the state had acquired in 1844 and promptly demolished. With funds derived from the state's recent sale of its "military works upon Staten Island" to the federal government,[23] state officials constructed a new arsenal on Fifth Avenue to store the First Division's equipment and munitions. Although designed as a centralized storage facility for the entire division, the facility was usurped by the Seventh Regiment for its sole use during the 1850s. No records survive to explain the unusually long period of time expended on the building's construction: it appears not to have been completely finished until 1854, although most secondary sources continue to use 1848 as the official date of construction.

According to a contemporary account, "the facade extends two hundred feet, and the depth is fifty feet, not including the eight towers. The basement story . . . is of brown stone, and extends the entire length of the building. The upper part is of thick walls of brick. The first story, twelve feet six inches in height, is used as a place of deposit for small arms, the second story is nine feet six inches in height, and the upper story sixteen feet. This latter contains munition and guncarriages. . . . The arsenal was erected in 1848, at a cost of forty thousand dollars, and contains all the arms and munition belonging to the state, which are not in use. . . . Every arrangement indicates much taste and neatness."[24]

Central Park Arsenal, 1848. This image, hand labeled "1857, Gleason's [Pictorial Drawing-Room Companion]," is courtesy of the New York State Military Museum.

In 1857 the state sold the nine-year-old arsenal and the adjacent 152 parcels to the city for incorporation into Manhattan's Central Park. (Shortly thereafter, the Seventh Regiment relocated to its new facility, the Tompkins Market Armory [1857–1860].) For a short time the building housed a menagerie, but the city allowed the militia to use the building during the Civil War era. In 1869 the arsenal was converted to house the collections of the newly created Museum of Natural History, a weather observatory and a neighborhood division of the city police. When the museum moved to new quarters on Central Park West in 1874, the arsenal was used by a variety of municipal offices. The building now contains the New York City Department of Parks and Recreation.

This ca. 1870 photograph of the rear (west) elevation of the Central Park Arsenal, courtesy of OPRHP (SHPO, NR files), shows the building a year after its conversion for use as storage and exhibition space for the newly organized Museum of Natural History. A new managerie, which appears in the foreground of the photograph, was built to house the animals that had, during the mid- to late 1860s, been housed on a temporary basis in the arsenal. During the late 1860s, the crenelated parapets of the central towers and corner bastions were replaced with low-pitched hipped roofs.

1857–60   TOMPKINS MARKET ARMORY (SEVENTH REGIMENT)
          MANHATTAN, NEW YORK COUNTY

Third Avenue at the Bowery between East 6th and East 7th streets
Architect: Bogardus, Lefferts and Clinton

Other arsenals/armories for the unit:

1830s	Centre Market Armory, Grand Street
1848	Central Park Arsenal, Fifth Avenue
1879	Seventh Regiment Armory, Park Avenue

The Tompkins Market Armory, a facility paid for and occupied by the Seventh Regiment and a consortium of butchers, was begun in 1857, when the unit was evicted from its comfortable quarters in the Central Park Arsenal. The market armory was a large-scale, Italianate-style, cast-iron commercial building with meat market stalls on the first floor and meeting rooms and a drill hall on the upper floors. Its design is attributed to James Bogardus and Colonel Marshall Lefferts. Interior features are believed to have been designed by Charles W. Clinton (a member of the Seventh's Company K), who later designed the Seventh Regiment Armory (1879) on Park Avenue.

The building was officially opened on 5 September 1860, and a gala opening, covered in the 12 January 1861 issue of *Frank Leslie's Illustrated Newspaper*, occurred on 28 December 1860.[25] The Seventh Regiment remained in the Tompkins Market Armory until 1879, when it moved to its new armory on Park Avenue. The same year, the Sixty-ninth Regiment moved into Tompkins Market, where it stayed until 1906. Shortly after the Sixty-ninth left, the market armory was demolished.

The Tompkins Market Armory, 1857–60, as it appeared in The Manual of the Seventh Regiment, National Guard, S.N.Y., *a 236-page government publication printed in 1868 on file at the New York State Archives (New York State Library). The Tompkins Market Armory was the third of four armories occupied by the Seventh Regiment.*

Henry Street Armory, 1858. The 11 May 1861 issue of Harper's Weekly depicts the Thirteenth Regiment marching off to war in front of its four-story, Italianate-style armory on Henry Street. Although it served with distinction in battle, the Thirteenth's most important contribution during the Civil War era was its participation in subduing angry mobs during the New York City Draft Riots of 1863. When the Thirteenth Regiment moved out of the Henry Street Armory in 1875, the Third (Gatling) Battery moved in.

Henry Street at Cranberry Street
Architect: unknown

Other arsenals/armories for the Thirteenth:
1830s   Gothic Hall, Adams Street
1874–75   Flatbush Avenue Armory
1892–94   Thirteenth Regiment Armory, Sumner Avenue

Other arsenals/armories for the Fourteenth:
1830s   Gothic Hall, Adams Street
1858   North Portland Avenue Arsenal
1877–78   North Portland Avenue Armory
1891–95   Fourteenth Regiment Armory, Eighth Avenue

The Henry Street Armory was built for the Thirteenth and Fourteenth regiments, both of which were formed in 1847 by combining numerous older, independent units that had shared quarters in Gothic Hall since the 1830s. In 1849 both regiments moved to new quarters in the recently vacated old city hall on Henry Street. The militiamen quickly outgrew the former city hall and, in 1858, Brooklyn officials razed the old building and erected a new armory on the site. Both regiments fought at the front during the Civil War. However, the Thirteenth is best remembered for its service back home during the New York City Draft Riots of 1863.

In 1875 the Thirteenth vacated the building for a new armory on Flatbush Avenue. At that time, the Third (Gatling) Battery, initially formed in 1864, moved into the Henry Street facility. Most sources agree that in 1878 the Fourteenth left the Henry Street Armory and moved into new quarters on North Portland Avenue.[26] The battery appears to have been the sole occupant of the Henry Street facility until March 1882, when the city sold the building to a private concern. When the building was demolished in 1930, the contents of the cornerstone were removed to the Brooklyn Historical Society for safekeeping.

West 14th Street near Sixth Avenue
Architect: unknown

Other armories for the unit:
1889–92   Twenty-second Regiment Armory, Western Boulevard
1911   Fort Washington Avenue Armory

The Twenty-second Regiment was organized as an infantry unit in 1861 by consolidating three formerly independent companies, the Lindsey Blues, the Federal Chasseurs and the Union Greys.[27] While most of the members of the Twenty-second Regiment were serving at the front during the early years of the Civil War, several influential members were waging battle back home in Manhattan to obtain permanent quarters for their unit.[28] The regiment proposed to finance the construction of a new facility itself but sought assistance from county officials to lease the land and pay the annual taxes. In April 1863 the county agreed to lease a large lot on West 14th Street, just west of Sixth Avenue, on behalf of the regiment. Then known as the Palace Garden, the grounds extended all the way back to West 15th Street and consisted of an older building (later used by the regiment for drilling) and several vacant lots. The regiment then raised $20,000 by issuing bonds and began to build its new facility. According to George Wingate in his 1896 *History of the Twenty-second Regiment*:

> The rooms in the new armory were fitted up by the different companies and the board of officers at their own expense, at a cost of from $3,000 to $5,000 each, Colonel Aspinwall loaning to the officers a magnificent set of massive ebony furniture of Chinese manufacture, which the board of officers used for many years. . . . The first meeting of the Board of Officers in this new armory took place on May 5, 1863, the administration building being then unfinished.[29]

According to an article in the 20 November 1858 issue of Leslie's, the Lindsey Blues (later incorporated into the Twenty-second Regiment) was formed on 25 October 1851 under the command of Captain William A. Day. Information in the accompanying article states that "May last the Lindsey Blues established their armory at No. 481 Broadway, where they have rooms splendidly fitted up for meetings, drill, &c."

On 20 January 1872 part of the armory was destroyed by fire. Piecemeal repairs, expansions and improvements were made during the next decade to keep the building functional, but by 1882 it became clear that a new facility was needed. Eight years later, the Twenty-second vacated the 1863 armory and moved into new quarters on Western Boulevard. The West 14th Street building was razed in 1894 to make way for a new armory for the Ninth Regiment.

The Twenty-second Regiment Armory (1862–63) is shown here in a drawing by Mark L. Peckham (OPRHP) in 2005. Inspiration for the drawing was provided by an illustration in the 14 October 1865 issue of Leslie's *that reported on the annual Agricultural and Mechanics' Fair, which was held at the Twenty-second's recently completed armory. (*Leslie's *courtesy of the New York State Historical Association.)*

1858 STATE ARSENAL (FIRST DIVISION)
      MANHATTAN, NEW YORK COUNTY

Seventh Avenue at West 35th Street
Architect: Cleveland and Backue

Other arsenals for the division:
1844   Downtown Arsenal, White, Elm, Center and
              Franklin streets
1848   Central Park Arsenal, Fifth Avenue

When the state sold the Central Park Arsenal (1848) to New York
City in 1857, $100,000 of the $275,000 profit was allocated for the

This rendering of the collapse of the roof during the construction of the new state arsenal (1858) for the First Division, New York City, accompanied an article in the 4 December 1858 issue of Leslie's. The article goes on to explain the inability of traditional wooden rafters to withstand the weight of a roof that was designed to span—without intervening support columns—the 82-foot-wide drill shed. The collapsed roof was replaced by a new roof whose traditional rafters were strengthened with iron ties. It was not until after the Civil War that the use of structural steel trusses allowed for large areas of unobstructed space within the later armories' drill sheds.

construction of a new arsenal for the First Division. Located on Seventh Avenue at West 35th Street in Manhattan, the building was ready for occupancy in 1859, despite the collapse of the slate-clad roof in mid-November 1858 during construction. An account of the roof collapse in a December 1858 issue of *Leslie's* included the following information about the new arsenal:

> The plan of Mssrs. Cleveland & Backue was accepted, and to that firm was awarded the superintendence of the building. The contract for construction was awarded to Richard Calrow, junior, for sixty-three thousand seven hundred dollars. The building was eighty-two feet in the clear on Seventh Avenue by one hundred eighty-four in the clear on [West 35th Street]. A turret was erected on each corner of the building—the highest of which was one hundred and twenty feet in height. The walls to the second story were constructed of Hastings stone; above they were of brick . . . each being eight inches in thickness, with a space of four inches between the two.[30]

According to currently available information, this is one of the first facilities for the militia that included a drill shed, a feature that would later characterize all armories. The unobstructed floor space of the drill shed measured 183 feet by 83 feet.[31] The National Guard used the facility until 1923, when it was sold to a private concern; the building was subsequently demolished.

State Arsenal, First Division, New York City, 1858. Photograph (ca. 1910s) courtesy of the New York State Military Museum.

The 16 March 1867 issue of Leslie's offered a rare glimpse of the interior of the First Division's State Arsenal. Pictured here is group of men conducting a trial of breech-loading firearms in the drill shed. Note the simple beams that support the roof, the method of construction favored before the introduction of metal trusses in the late nineteenth century.

State Arsenal, Second Division, Brooklyn, 1858. Few primary records—graphic or otherwise—regarding the early history of the militia in Brooklyn survive. Although further research eventually may have turned up an image of the Second Division's arsenal as built in 1858, the only readily available rendering is the facility after its expansion and renovation for use by the Fourteenth Regiment in 1878 as portrayed on page 823 of The Eagle and Brooklyn: History of the City of Brooklyn *(1893) by Henry W. B. Howard. Stylistically, it is very similar to the First Division's arsenal in Manhattan, but one can only guess as to its original size. Perhaps, like the First's, it was about 82 feet wide and 184 feet deep with one 120-foot-tall corner tower. If that were true, it appears that the 1858 building was nearly tripled in size (at least along the width of the administration building) in 1878 and embellished with two more monumental towers.*

1858   STATE ARSENAL (SECOND DIVISION)
        BROOKLYN, KINGS COUNTY

North Portland Avenue
Architect: unknown

Other arsenals for the division:
1924–26   Brooklyn Arsenal, Second Avenue

Far less is known about the Second Division's arsenal than the First's, primarily due to the lack of records pertaining to the division, the city of Brooklyn or Kings County. However, based on a late nineteenth-century photograph of the facility on North Portland Avenue, taken after the arsenal was expanded in 1878 for use by the Fourteenth Regiment, it appears that the original arsenal may have been similar to the First Division's 1858 facility in Manhattan, that is, a five-bay-wide, ten-bay-deep, hip-roofed building with a single corner tower. Primary occupants of the arsenal between the mid-1860s and 1878 were the Fourteenth Regiment and the Third (Gatling) Battery. The date of and reason for the building's demise are unknown. In 1926 a new state arsenal, located on Second Avenue between 63rd and 64th streets, was erected to serve Brooklyn's militia.

1858   ALBANY ARSENAL (THIRD DIVISION SOUTH AND TENTH
            REGIMENT)
        ALBANY, ALBANY COUNTY

Hudson Street (later Avenue) and Eagle Street
Architect: von Steinwehr

Other arsenals/armories in Albany:
1799   Albany Arsenal, Broadway
1889–93   Washington Avenue Armory
1914   New Scotland Avenue Armory

The Albany Arsenal was one of twelve new arsenals authorized in 1857 for construction in Upstate New York with profits derived from the state's sale of its 1848 Central Park Arsenal. Completed in 1858, it was designed by Adolf von Steinwehr with a $25,000 appropriation

Albany Arsenal, 1858. Rendering from the 16 August 1862 issue of an unidentified newspaper, courtesy of the McKinney Library, Albany Institute of History and Art.

from the state.[32] Similar to the 1848 Central Park Arsenal, the Albany Arsenal was a three-story, rectangular brick building distinguished by a bold, crenelated parapet, a central pavilion articulated by paired four-story towers and three-story, octagonal corner bastions. It was nearly identical to the Broadway Arsenal (1858) in Buffalo that was designed by Calvin N. Otis.

    Prior to 1858, the numerous Albany area militia units were housed in the old 1799 Albany Arsenal on Broadway. Two years after the opening of the new arsenal on Hudson Street, the area's units were joined to form the Tenth Regiment, Third Division. The regiment comprised Company A (the Albany Zouave Cadets), Company B (the Washington Continentals), Company C (initially formed as Company K), Company D (the Caledonian Guards) and Company R (the Albany City Cavalry; later Troop B). Many members of the Tenth, especially those attached to companies A and B, served during the Civil War. The Tenth expanded to ten companies in 1862 for wartime duty and served as the 177th New York Volunteer Infantry.

In 1866 the Tenth assisted local authorities in quelling anti-rent riots in southern Albany County, where tenant farmers continued to rebel against the not quite dethroned lords of Rensselaerwyck. In 1877 the Tenth, augmented by the Ninth Regiment of New York City, was called upon to suppress rioters at the railroad shops in West Albany

during the Great Railroad Strike. In 1881 the regiment was reduced to a battalion. Despite the decrease in size, the unit continued to thrive and attract members of Albany's social and economic elite. By the mid-1880s, the Tenth Battalion had outgrown the Hudson Street facility and plans were underway for a new armory on Washington Avenue.

The 1858 arsenal, vacated by the Tenth in 1891, was subsequently remodeled for use as the Catholic Union Building by the Roman Catholic Diocese of Albany and, still later, became the Eagle Street Theater. The theater, along with approximately 1,500 nearby buildings in a fifty-block area of downtown Albany, was demolished in the 1960s to make way for the Governor Nelson A. Rockefeller Empire State Plaza.

The 1 June 1861 issue of Harper's Weekly *provided an illustrated article about troops in Upstate New York mobilizing for the Civil War. The drawing, entitled "The Armory at Albany, New York," provides a completely fictitious interpretation of Albany's 1858 arsenal.*

1858   BROADWAY ARSENAL (SIXTY-FIFTH AND SEVENTY-FOURTH
        REGIMENTS)
        BUFFALO, ERIE COUNTY

Broadway (formerly Batavia Road)
Architect: Otis

Other armories for the Sixty-fifth:
1884   Sixty-fifth Regiment Armory, Broadway
1902–07   Masten Avenue Armory
1932–33   Masten Avenue Armory

Other armories for Seventy-fourth:
1868   Virginia Street Armory, Virginia Street at North
              William Street
1882   Virginia Street Armory, Virginia Street at Fremont
              Place
1884–86   Virginia Street Armory, Virginia Street at Elmwood
              Avenue
1896–99   Connecticut Street Armory

The Broadway Arsenal was built in 1858 for the Sixty-fifth and Seventy-fourth regiments and as headquarters for the northern components of the Eighth Division.[33] According to *Souvenir, 74th Regiment, N.G., S.N.Y.*, a booklet published in 1899, the Broadway Arsenal was designed by Calvin N. Otis of Buffalo. The cornerstone for the new building was laid on 5 May 1858 by the Grand Lodge of Masons of the State of New York. Dozens of state and local politicians and military officials were on hand, and the local press estimated that nearly 10,000 celebrants from all across Western New York attended the festivities. It was paid for with a $45,000 state appropriation and was ready for occupancy in January 1859. It was nearly identical to the Albany Arsenal (1858), which was designed by Adolf von Steinwehr for the Third Division.

The Sixty-fifth Regiment, Buffalo's oldest militia unit, dates to 24 April 1818. The unit expanded to regimental size in 1827 and was designated the Twenty-eighth Artillery. In 1847, when the state reorganized most of the units within the First and Second divisions, the Twenty-eighth was redesignated the Sixty-fifth Regiment. Two years later, the regiment assisted local authorities in dispersing a group of

rioting laborers along the Buffalo section of the Erie Canal. By 1855 the regiment was headquartered in rented space in a building at Court and Pearl streets, where it remained until the Broadway Arsenal opened in 1858.

The roots of the Seventy-fourth Regiment date to 30 December 1837, when a ten-company regiment, the Buffalo City Guard (a.k.a. the Thirty-seventh Regiment), was mustered for state service during the Patriot War (Canadian Rebellion) of 1837. The regiment appears to have broken up after the hostilities, but Company D of the short-lived regiment persisted; "it made journeys to Detroit, Rochester, Meadville and other places, and helped to celebrate the anniversary of the battle of Tippecanoe at Toledo in 1840. . . . Its balls in the old Eagle Street Theatre in the [1840s] were famous for their brilliancy."[34] In 1847 Company D was attached to the Sixty-fifth Regiment.

Four years later, however, Company D withdrew from the Sixty-fifth Regiment and embarked on a campaign to form a separate regiment. The company's wishes were granted in June 1854, when it became the founding unit of the Seventy-fourth Regiment. For a while, the Seventy-fourth was a regiment in name only; Company D was its only component. (Regiments needed at least eight companies to form an official regiment.) The first addition to the Seventy-fourth was in November 1854, when the Spaulding Guards were attached to Company D. The regiment continued to expand during the late 1850s and early 1860s. Many members of the Seventy-fourth served during the Civil War as components of various wartime regiments. Portions of the Seventy-fourth also assisted authorities in New York City during the Draft Riots of July 1863.

In 1868 the Seventy-fourth vacated the Broadway Arsenal and moved to a new armory on Virginia Street. The Sixty-fifth, now sole occupants of the old arsenal, flourished during the 1870s and early 1880s and quickly outgrew the 1858 building. However, instead of erecting a separate facility like they had for the Seventy-fourth Regiment, county officials simply expanded the existing arsenal. In 1884 a huge new drill shed and administration building were added to the front of the old arsenal, which became a minor rear wing of the Sixty-fifth's "new" armory. The 1884 armory, which became the Broadway Auditorium during the first decade of the twentieth century, survives in a much altered state. The 1858 arsenal was destroyed by fire in 1948.

Broadway Arsenal, Buffalo, 1858. Photograph (ca. 1900) courtesy of the Buffalo and Erie County Historical Society.

1858–59 Syracuse Arsenal (Sixth Division and Fifty-first
            Regiment)
         Syracuse, Onondaga County

West Jefferson Street
Architect: White

Other armories in Syracuse:
1873   Syracuse Armory, West Jefferson Street
1906–07   West Jefferson Street Armory
1941–43   East Genesee Street Armory

In 1857 Syracuse received $4,000 toward the erection of an arsenal to store state ordnance for the Sixth Division and to house Onondaga's Fifty-first Regiment. The regiment (formed in 1851 and expanded in 1858) was, according to local accounts, the second largest regiment in the country. Horatio Nelson White, a talented young architect who had recently achieved acclaim for his design of the Onondaga County Courthouse in 1856–1857, was selected to prepare plans for the arsenal. White's membership in the Fifty-first Regiment undoubtedly helped him secure the commission. In February 1858 the contract was awarded to local contractor David Wilcox, the lowest bidder at $3,450.

When White's final plans were revealed to the public, most local folks (militiamen, politicians and citizens alike) were a bit disappointed with what they considered the plainness of the two-story brick building, the restraint of which was attributed to the relatively small budget. After all, they argued, the arsenal would be not only a facility for one of New York's largest, most prestigious militia units but also the centerpiece of the newly created Jefferson Park.[35] A nonpartisan committee was formed almost immediately, and an additional $4,825 was raised, allowing White to enlarge and expand his original design substantially. Wilcox stayed on as general contractor and, on 15 July 1859, the imposing three-story, brick and stone building with tall, round-arched windows and multistoried towers and turrets was completed.

Syracuse Arsenal, 1858. Undated photograph courtesy of the Onondaga Historical Association.

The facility was formally dedicated in September 1859 with two days of parades, speeches and ceremonies, concluding with an elegant ball. According to the Syracuse Standard, "the Ball in the evening was a grand and extensive affair. The Large Drill Room or Hall of the Armory was filled with youth and beauty and the glittering trappings of the military gentlemen, and the bright eyes and elegant attire of the ladies formed a brilliant and attractive scene."[36] The 1859 building was razed to make way for a new armory in 1873.

Ogdensburg Arsenal, 1858. Historic photograph courtesy of OPRHP (SHPO, NR files).

1858 OGDENSBURG ARSENAL (FOURTH DIVISION)
OGDENSBURG, ST. LAWRENCE COUNTY

100 Lafayette Street
Architect: White

Other armories in Ogdensburg:
1898   Ogdensburg Armory, Elizabeth Street

Major General Schuyler F. Judd, commander of the militia in Northern New York, was instrumental in obtaining the services of Horatio Nelson White to design a headquarters for the Fourth Division in Ogdensburg. On 23 February 1858 White's drawings were displayed to the public in the office of General Judd, and sealed bids were opened by the general on 13 March. The contract was awarded to Urias Pearson, a renowned, local general contractor, who had built many of Ogdensburg's finest buildings during the 1840s and 1850s. The weekly *St. Lawrence Republican* reported on 27 April 1858 that "Pearson . . . has broken ground upon [the new armory]. The trenches are already dug and the stones and material are rapidly accumulating upon the ground wherewith to raise the structure. The site is a commanding one, being on the slight eminence just above the mill dam on the east side of the Oswegatchie River."[37] The cornerstone was laid on 18 May 1858. Built of square blocks of hewn bluestone from a local quarry, the arsenal was officially completed on 29 November 1858. Finishing touches were added the following year, as reported in the *St. Lawrence Republican*:

> The additional appropriation of $1,000 to complete the armory at this place has been secured, as was the original appropriation, mainly through the efforts of General S. F. Judd. The $1,000 appropriation will be expended to provide the building with iron shutters, grading the grounds and constructing walks. Very few of our citizens know what a substantial and tasty building the armory is, and when we consider the small appropriation consumed in its construction, we must acknowledge the superior judgment of the

General in the expenditure of public funds. With the completion of the anticipated improvements, the armory will be a point of attraction as well as an ornament to the place.[38]

The arsenal was acquired by the city in 1873 for $1,400 and was used to store waterworks equipment. (It is not clear where the divisional headquarters and Ogdensburg's Fortieth Separate Company went; the city's second armory was not built until 1898.) On 8 January 1895 the former arsenal was extensively damaged by fire and subsequently abandoned for sixteen years. The Board of Water Commissioners resurrected the burned-out shell and adapted it for use by the Water Authority. The building, still extant although underutilized, was purchased from the city by a private corporation in 1960.

Ballston Spa Arsenal, 1858. Photograph (2003) by the author.

1858   BALLSTON SPA ARSENAL (THIRD DIVISION, NORTH)
        BALLSTON SPA, SARATOGA COUNTY

Ballston Avenue
Architect: White

Ballston Spa, the county seat of Saratoga County, was a focal point of regional militia activity during the eighteenth and early nineteenth centuries. Active militia units in the area during this period included the Black Plumed Riflemen under Captain Vandenburgh and the Saratoga Springs Light Infantry under Captain Partelo.[39] Thus, the village was a logical location for one of the twelve state arsenals authorized in 1857 for construction in Upstate New York. The cornerstone for the building was laid on 26 August 1858; construction was completed later that year. For the next several decades, the arsenal served as headquarters for the northern components of the Third Division, the bulk of which was concentrated further south in Albany and served by the Albany Arsenal (1858). In design and decoration, the Ballston Spa Arsenal was nearly identical to the 1858 arsenals in Ogdensburg and Dunkirk, both of which were also designed by H. N. White.

Shortly after the building's completion, however, the village was virtually eclipsed by the nearby resort community of Saratoga Springs. By the early 1870s, Saratoga County's militia had stagnated and the Ballston Spa Arsenal was obsolete; it was sold to the adjacent Christ Episcopal Church in 1873 and was converted to a parish hall. At some point during the late nineteenth/early twentieth century, the central tower's battlemented parapet with a large, central finial was replaced by a small, multigabled roof and the tall, narrow front windows on the first story were replaced by single-paned picture windows.

There appear to have been no active militia units in Ballston Spa in particular or Saratoga County in general during the mid-1870s; but, by 1878, the county's citizen soldiers were revitalized under the name of the Citizens' Corps (later the Twenty-second Separate Company) in Saratoga Springs. A new armory was built in 1889–1891 on Lake Avenue for the Twenty-second.

Dunkirk Arsenal, 1858. This photograph, taken in 1890, portrays the newly built Dunkirk City Hall on the left and the 1858 arsenal on the right. Although essentially serving as a side wing to the new city hall, the old arsenal retained its monumental presence in the community. Photograph courtesy of Robert Harris, Dunkirk City Historian.

1858 DUNKIRK ARSENAL (EIGHTH DIVISION, SOUTH)
DUNKIRK, CHAUTAUQUA COUNTY

Central Avenue and East Fourth Street
Architect: White

The Dunkirk Arsenal, designed by H. N. White, was built for the southern components of the Eighth Division. (The Eighth's most prominent units, the Sixty-fifth and Seventy-fourth regiments, were housed in Buffalo's Broadway Arsenal, also built in 1858.) Nearly identical to White's 1858 arsenals in Ogdensburg and Ballston Spa, the Dunkirk Arsenal featured a central tower, a crenelated parapet, machicolated cornices and chamfered corner bastions. Several decades after its construction, the arsenal was turned over to Dunkirk city officials, who promptly erected an imposing new city hall on the site, incorporating the former arsenal as a secondary wing. Neither component of that municipal facility survives.

1858 CORNING ARSENAL (SEVENTH DIVISION, SOUTH)
CORNING, STEUBEN COUNTY

First Street between Washington and Hamilton streets
Architect: unknown

Other armories in Corning:
1935–36   Corning Armory, Centerway

The Corning Arsenal was built in 1858 for companies C and D of New York's Seventh Division.[40] In 1857, when the state legislature authorized the construction of twelve new arsenals in Upstate New York, Corning's representative to the state assembly was R. B. VanValkenburgh, who happened to be a colonel in the militia. As a member of the legislature's Military Committee, VanValkenburgh may have been instrumental in securing a $14,000 appropriation from the state to build an arsenal in his hometown. This figure was almost five times the amount received by similarly sized communities, such as Ballston Spa, Dunkirk and Ogdensburg, and more than three times the amount received by several larger communities (e.g., Syracuse).

Corning Arsenal, 1858. Photograph (late nineteenth century) courtesy of the Corning Historical Society and the Market Street Restoration Agency.

Interestingly, Corning boasted only two militia units (companies C and D) of the eight-company Sixtieth Regiment, which was headquartered in nearby Elmira. Perhaps due to the influence of Colonel VanValkenburgh, Corning, instead of the more logical Elmira, was chosen to receive the coveted new arsenal.

Built of locally quarried stone on land donated by the city's founding family, the Corning Arsenal was built by James M. Hawley, a local contractor, for $12,900. In terms of design and decoration, it was a symmetrical, rectangular building with a multistoried front tower, octagonal corner bastions and crenelated parapets. Like many units in New York, Company C and Company D (dubbed the Irish Brigade) languished after the Civil War; little use was made of the new arsenal. Around 1872–1873, the Corning Arsenal was sold to St. Mary's Parish and became a convent for the Sisters of Mercy as well as headquarters for the St. Joseph's Orphan Asylum. By 1902, however, the nuns had outgrown the former arsenal and plans were made to erect a new convent. The outer edges of the four-acre parcel were subdivided into small residential lots; proceeds from their sale were applied to the construction of a new convent elsewhere in the city. The great masonry wall around the perimeter of the original parcel was dismantled; the stones were distributed among the purchasers of the individual lots to construct foundations for their new houses. The nuns moved out of the arsenal in 1906 and the building was converted for use as a kindergarten. By mid-century, the former arsenal was vacant and deteriorating; it was razed in 1965 to make way for a modern apartment complex, aptly named Castle Garden Apartments.

1862   UTICA ARSENAL (TWENTY-EIGHTH SEPARATE COMPANY)
        UTICA, ONEIDA COUNTY

Bleecker Street
Architect: attributed to White

Other armories in Utica:
1893–94   Utica Armory, Rutger and Steuben streets
1929–30   Utica Armory, Parkway East

The earliest militia unit in Utica was known as the Utica Independent Company, which, in 1837, became the Utica Citizens' Corps under the command of Captain E. K. Barnum.[41] The unit was initially housed in the old Chubbuck Hall on Hotel Street. At some point before the Civil War, the Citizens' Corps was reorganized as the

Utica Citizens' Corps. Image derived from the front cover of the unit's semicentennial anniversary publication, 1887; courtesy of the New York State Military Museum.

Twenty-eighth Separate Company. In 1858 Utica was chosen to receive a new facility for its militia as part of the state's late 1850s arsenal building program. However, the Utica Arsenal was not completed until 1862. Its design is attributed H. N. White, who had designed four of the five arsenals within the 1858 plan. Like White's other arsenals, the Utica Arsenal was built of masonry construction and featured a bold, multistoried tower; however, unlike the others, the Utica Arsenal was asymmetrical. In overall appearance it was similar to the Schenectady Arsenal (1868), which also featured a four-story corner tower.

In March 1887, the Twenty-eighth was joined by the newly formed Forty-fourth Separate Company. (Conflicting sources indicate that the Citizens' Corps became the Forty-fourth in 1887; the discrepancy is attributed to the fact that both the Twenty-eighth and Forty-fourth claim the Corps as their antecedents.) The two units shared the Bleecker Street arsenal until 1894, when they moved to a newly built armory on Steuben Park. The old arsenal was razed shortly thereafter to make way for the Schubert (later Colonial) Theater.

Utica Arsenal, 1862. Photograph (ca. 1900) courtesy of the Oneida County Historical Society.

1868   SCHENECTADY ARSENAL (FIFTH DIVISION)
SCHENECTADY, SCHENECTADY COUNTY

State Street at Crescent (now Veterans') Park near Nott Terrace
Architect: unknown

Other armories in Schenectady:
1898–99   Schenectady Armory, State Street
1936   Schenectady Armory, Washington Avenue

The origin of Schenectady's militia dates to 1839, when a unit called the Washington Continentals was organized. During the Civil War, it was mustered into federal service as a component of the Eighty-third Regiment. After the war and under the command of Robert Furman, a prominent Schenectadian and state assemblyman, the Washington Continentals succeeded in persuading the state to fund a new arsenal. Furman obtained a $30,000 legislative appropriation on 19 January 1866.[42] John W. Veeder and Judson S. Landon of Schenectady were appointed commissioners of construction for the project. The site chosen was the summit of a hill overlooking Crescent (now Veterans') Park. Like most of the arsenals in the ca. 1858 set, the design of the Schenectady Arsenal resembled a civic or religious building. With its asymmetrical massing and four-story corner tower, the Schenectady Arsenal closely resembled the Utica Arsenal (1862).

 The Continentals were joined in 1873 by a newly formed unit called the Citizens' Corps; on 12 June 1880, the two units were officially mustered into the National Guard as the Thirty-seventh and Thirty-sixth separate companies, respectively. Both companies shared the 1868 arsenal until 1898, when it was demolished to make way for a new armory.

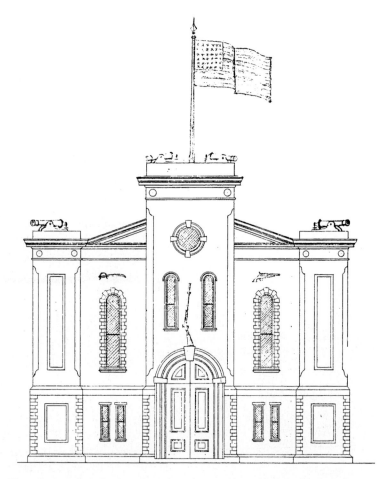

The architectural rendering of the front elevation of the proposed Schenectady Arsenal is, along with a series of undated elevations and floor plans, in the archives of the Schenectady County Historical Society. Special thanks to the late Wayne Harvey, Schenectady, New York.

Schenectady Arsenal, 1868. This undated historic photograph of the arsenal shows that the final design of the building deviated from the earlier drawings. Courtesy of the Schenectady County Historical Society.

1868–70   ROCHESTER ARSENAL (SEVENTH DIVISION, NORTH, AND
              FIFTY-FOURTH REGIMENT)
          ROCHESTER, MONROE COUNTY

Woodbury Boulevard at Washington Park
Architect: Warner

Other arsenals/armories in Rochester:
1836–37   Center Market Armory, Front and Market streets
1904–07   East Main Street Armory
1917   Culver Road Armory

In 1858 Rochester was selected to receive a new arsenal to house the Fifty-fourth Regiment and to serve as headquarters for the northern components of the Seventh Division.[43] For unknown reasons, construction was delayed for several years. The outbreak of the Civil War further delayed the project; it was not reactivated until 1865. Several more years were wasted as local officials (particularly city councilmen) argued over the location for the proposed facility. Finally, a site on Woodbury Avenue was agreed upon. The project, however, continued to be plagued with difficulties. For example, in 1868 the construction firm of Gorsline and Aldrich consumed the entire $23,000 allocation in putting up just the outer walls, "necessitating further delays until the state could be persuaded to vote an additional $44,000 to finish and equip the building."[44]

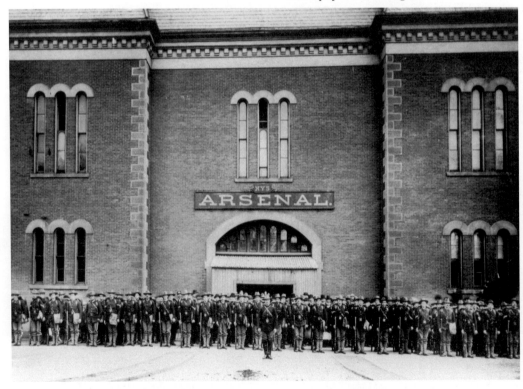

Rochester Arsenal, 1868–70. Photograph courtesy of the Landmark Society of Western New York.

Two years and $70,000 later, the arsenal was complete. Built to the design of regionally renowned architect Andrew Jackson Warner, it was a two-story, mansard-roofed brick building with Italianate- and Romanesque Revival–style features. Excerpts from Rochester's *Union Advertiser* in 1869 and 1870 reflected a popular dissatisfaction with the facility: one editorial complained that the arsenal was being used for balls and parties rather than for military purposes, while another editorial lamented that "it is so far a failure at every point. Its architecture is horrible. The men who designed and carried out their work into execution probably had no idea of anything but getting state money with the least outlay of labor possible." The following year, however, the reputation of the Fifty-fourth was redeemed when it suppressed an oarsmen's riot on the Erie Canal at Oxbow Bend just west of Fairport. In both 1871 and 1872, the regiment helped maintain order at two public executions, where crowds of spectators verged on rioting.[45]

The Fifty-fourth Regiment was officially disbanded in December 1880, but the Eighth Separate Company persisted. Over the next few years, the Eighth was joined by the First Separate Company, the Second Separate Division and a subunit of the New York naval militia. All four units vacated the arsenal in 1907 for a new armory on East Main Street. The city subsequently acquired the old arsenal and expanded it for use as a convention hall. Neoclassical-style wings were added to the east and west sides of the old drill shed and, on the interior, a proscenium arch and stage and a balcony were added. The building was again altered in 1949 when the U.S. Naval Reserve renovated the building for use as its headquarters. The building now houses the GEVA Theater Company and thrives as one of Rochester's most popular performing arts venues.

After the National Guard vacated the Rochester Arsenal in 1907, the facility was converted for use as a civic center, a capacity in which it served until it became an armory for Rochester's naval militia in 1949. Historic postcard courtesy of the author.

1868 VIRGINIA STREET ARMORY (SEVENTY-FOURTH REGIMENT)
BUFFALO, ERIE COUNTY

Virginia Street at North William Street (later Fremont Place, later
Elmwood Avenue)
Architect: unknown

Other arsenals/armories for the Seventy-fourth:
1858   Broadway Arsenal
1882   Virginia Street Armory, Virginia Street at
            Fremont Place
1884–86   Virginia Street Armory, Virginia Street at Elmwood
            Avenue
1896–99   Connecticut Street Armory

The origin of the Seventy-fourth Regiment dates to 1837, when the
Buffalo City Guard was formed. The Guard, a ten-company regiment,
was short-lived: only Company D seems to have persisted between the
late 1830s and late 1840s. In 1847 Company D was officially attached
to the Sixty-fifth Regiment. In 1851, however, Company D withdrew
from the regiment in hopes of reestablishing its own independent
regiment. In June 1854, the Seventy-fourth Regiment was officially
recognized with Company D as its founding unit, but the regimental
status existed on paper only until enough individual companies could
be created (or annexed) to constitute a full regiment. In the mean-
time, a group of students from a "Mr. Ernst's School" joined to form a
cadet company called the Spaulding Greys (August 1854). Shortly
thereafter the unit's name was changed to the Spaulding Guards. In
November 1854, the unit was officially designated as Company B and
attached to Company D, thus forming the two-part nucleus of the
Seventy-fourth Regiment. The fledgling unit shared quarters with the
older Sixty-fifth Regiment in the Broadway Arsenal when it opened
in 1858.

Both regiments flourished between the late 1850s and mid-
1860s. After the Civil War, the county decided to build a new facility
for the Seventy-fourth. A large site on Virginia Street at the corner of
North William Street (later Fremont Place and, still later, Elmwood

*This ticket (1884), from the archives of the Seventy-fourth Regiment on file at the
New York State Military Museum, illustrates the fact that many units continued to use
their original, informal names regardless of subsequent, more "official" designations
assigned to them later in the nineteenth century. For example, the Spaulding Guards,
an independent militia unit, was organized in August 1854 in Buffalo. Three months
later, it was officially linked with Company D (originally called the Buffalo City
Guards) and assigned the formal designation of Company B in November 1854 to
form the nucleus of the newly created Seventy-fourth Regiment, which was housed in
the Broadway Arsenal. Nonetheless, thirty years later, members of the unit continued
to call themselves the Spaulding Guards. This tradition, expressed countless times
across the state, illustrates the militia's deep respect for its specific local heritage and,
consequently, its long-standing community spirit; similar pride persists to this day in
many National Guard units. The original ticket, along with a variety of similar
ephemera, is on file in the archives of the New York State Military Museum.*

Avenue) was acquired. The new armory, ready for occupancy in 1868,
was a two-story, 100' x 200' brick building completed at a cost of
approximately $36,000. It contained sixteen 18' x 30' rooms on the
second story for the regiment's ten companies and related support
services, as well as a large drill shed on the first story. The building
was dedicated on 24 February 1868; the opening ceremonies were
followed by an elaborate ball. Twelve years later, a large and fashionable administration building was added to the Virginia Street elevation of the 1868 armory. The 1868 and 1882 buildings were lost to fire
just as the third, and final, Virginia Street Armory was nearing completion in 1886.

Chapter 3

Armories Built in New York City during the 1870s and in Upstate New York during the 1870s and 1880s

The outbreak of the Civil War in 1861 brought an abrupt end to the statewide arsenal building program begun in 1858. The years following the Civil War were relatively quiet for the militia for several reasons. First of all, war-weary Americans had had their fill of the military; they directed energy and resources toward rebuilding their war-crippled communities and resuming their lives amid a climate of social and political uncertainty. Secondly, America plunged into a major economic depression after the Civil War, culminating in the infamous Panic of 1873; there was little money in New York State or anywhere else to undertake large, public construction projects during the 1870s and early 1880s. Many National Guard units stagnated; even the strongest, most prestigious prewar militia units now struggled to survive. Those that did persist kept a low profile, downplaying their military function and focusing instead on the quieter aspects of their fraternal associations. Despite the social, economic and political turmoil of the post–Civil War era, eighteen new armories (including the Seventh Regiment Armory in Manhattan) were erected in New York City during the 1870s and Upstate New York during the 1870s and 1880s.

In strictly chronological terms, the Seventh Regiment Armory falls in the middle of this group. However, because of its unique character when built and its immediate influence on armory construction in New York City in the 1880s (chapter 5), the Seventh Regiment Armory is discussed individually in chapter 4. The seventeen armories catalogued in this chapter continued arsenal/armory building trends that had been established before the Civil War. Specifically, despite their military function, they were virtually indistinguishable from large-scale civic buildings of the period. All were of masonry construction,

and all were located in or near the centers of their respective communities. In terms of architectural design and decoration, most of these 1870s/80s armories were like earlier militia facilities in their lack of stylistic cohesiveness. However, several differences distinguished them from the earlier facilities. Whereas most pre–Civil War arsenals served as headquarters for various regional divisions of the militia, the post–Civil War armories were built for specific units. More importantly, the 1870s/80s armories all contained ground-level drill sheds, a feature rarely found on pre–Civil War arsenals or armories. Unlike earlier arsenals and armories, most of which were funded by the state during organized building campaigns, most of these 1870s/80s armories were paid for by the units or by their respective city or county governments.

The seventeen 1870s/80s armories can be divided into three sets. The first set, comprising six regimental armories built in New York City and Upstate New York during the 1870s, contains three in Brooklyn, and one each in Oswego, Syracuse and Auburn. In Brooklyn, the Clermont Avenue Armory for the Twenty-third Regiment and the Flatbush Avenue Armory for the Thirteenth Regiment were new buildings; the third, the North Portland Avenue Armory, began as a state arsenal in 1858 but was enlarged and remodeled in the late 1870s for the Fourteenth Regiment. The second set, comprising separate company armories built in Upstate New York in 1879, contains one each in Newburgh, Watertown and Kingston. The third group includes three regimental armories (all in Buffalo) and five smaller armories built upstate in Binghamton, Troy, Oneonta, Walton and Elmira during the 1880s.

The Brooklyn, Oswego, Syracuse and Auburn armories embodied a variety of styles, although the influence of the Second Empire

The seventeen armories discussed in this chapter are loosely grouped into three sets according to size, location and date of construction. The first set, including the Syracuse Armory (1873) (left), contains six regimental armories built in New York City and Upstate New York during the 1870s. The second set, including the Watertown Armory (1879) (bottom left), comprises three nearly identical separate company armories designed by John A. Wood and built in Upstate New York in 1879. The third set, including the Elmira Armory (1886–88) (below), contains eight armories (for regiments or separate companies) built in Upstate New York during the 1880s. Other than the three armories designed by Wood, armories in this chapter embody a broad range of stylistic features; notwithstanding their telltale drill sheds, most could easily be mistaken for generic civic buildings of the period. All historic postcards from the collection of the author.

predominates. Most of the armories in this set featured symmetrical, tripartite façades articulated by bold center towers and corner bastions. The three separate company armories built in Upstate New York in 1879 comprised a more homogenous group. All were designed by John A. Wood, who practiced first in Poughkeepsie and later in New York City between 1864 and the early 1890s. In terms of design and decoration, Wood's armories embodied features associated with medieval Gothic military architecture, the most salient of which were crenelated parapets and machicolated cornices. As such, they harkened back to the two 1840s arsenals built in New York City (the Downtown Arsenal, 1844, and the Central Park Arsenal, 1848) and several ca. 1858 arsenals designed by H. N. White. They also foreshadowed the more consistent use of the medieval Gothic mode for armories built in New York City during the 1880s and 1890s and armories built upstate during the 1890s. Two of Wood's armories, those in Newburgh and Watertown, were small-scale replicas of Charles W. Clinton's design for Manhattan's Seventh Regiment Armory, which was under construction by 1877. No evidence has surfaced to prove that Wood actually consulted with Clinton, but the resemblance between Wood's armories and the Seventh's armory is uncanny enough to suspect that Wood must have been privy to Clinton's plans or drawings.

The eight armories built upstate during the 1880s were similar to those built in the 1870s, although the influence of the Romanesque Revival style predominates. Three of these eight were built for regiments: the second and third Virginia Street armories (1882 and 1884–1886), both erected for the Seventy-fourth Regiment in Buffalo, and the Sixty-fifth Regiment Armory (1884), also in Buffalo. Two were built for separate companies, although they also contained divisional headquarters: the Elmira Armory (1886–1888) was built for the Thirtieth Separate Company and the Walton Armory (1886) was built for the Thirty-third. The Oneonta Armory (1885) was built for a separate company. The Troy and Binghamton armories (1884–1886 and 1880s, respectively) each housed a battery and a separate company.

The following catalog entries are organized in roughly chronological order.

1872–73 CLERMONT AVENUE ARMORY (TWENTY-THIRD REGIMENT)
         BROOKLYN, KINGS COUNTY

Clermont Avenue between Myrtle and Willoughby avenues
Architect: Mundell

Other armories for the unit:
1830s   Gothic Hall, Adams Street
1891–95   Twenty-third Regiment Armory, Bedford Avenue

The origin of the Twenty-third Regiment dates to April 1861, when a home guard unit (first named Relief Guard, Company G, Thirteenth Regiment and then City Guard Reserve) was formed shortly after the Thirteenth Regiment was mustered into federal service during the Civil War. Members of the home guard unit immediately began planning the formation of an official regiment of their own, independent of the Thirteenth. By January 1862, components of the City Guard Reserve included portions of the former Brooklyn Greys, Carrol Hill Guards, South Brooklyn Independent Guards, Captain Bent's Company, Union Rifles, Guard Lafayette, Union Greys, Washington Home Guard, Clinton Guards, Independent Zouaves and Excelsior Guard.[1] In January 1863, the various units of the City Guard Reserve were renamed companies A through K, and the Twenty-third Regiment was officially recognized. The Twenty-third served briefly at the front during the Civil War in early 1863, but it is more often remembered for its service during the New York City Draft Riots of July 1863. During the mid- to late 1860s, the regiment was quartered at Gothic Hall, an 1830s building converted by the Thirteenth Regiment for use as an armory.

In 1871, primarily through the efforts of its commander, Colonel Rodney C. Ward, the Twenty-third Regiment obtained a $160,000 legislative appropriation for the construction of a new armory. The cornerstone for the building, located on Clermont Avenue between Myrtle and Willoughby avenues in the Fort Greene/Clinton Hill section of Brooklyn, was laid by Mayor S. S. Powell in October 1872. The building was designed by William A. Mundell and displayed features derived from both the Gothic Revival and Second Empire styles. The regiment moved into its new quarters on 30 September 1873.

During the Great Railroad Strike of 1877, the Twenty-third was stationed at Hornellsville (Steuben County), the hotbed of labor trouble in New York State. In July 1882, the regiment was among the first units to attend the newly opened state training camp, Camp Smith, near Peekskill (Westchester County). The Twenty-third Regiment vacated the Clermont Avenue Armory in 1895 and relocated to its new armory at 1322 Bedford Avenue. The Clermont Avenue Armory was occupied by a series of Brooklyn units during the next half-century, most notably the Third (Gatling) Battery. The building was radically altered around 1909–1911, virtually obliterating all traces of the 1873 façade. Vacated by the National Guard in the mid-1970s and abandoned in the late 1980s/early 1990s, the former armory is severely deteriorated.

Clermont Avenue Armory, 1872–73. Photograph (ca. 1910s) courtesy of the New York State Military Museum.

This photograph of the Clermont Avenue drill shed shows the Third (Gatling) Battery, which occupied the armory after the Twenty-third Regiment moved to its new armory on Bedford Avenue in 1895. Photograph (dating from the second decade of the twentieth century) courtesy of the New York State Military Museum.

1874–75   FLATBUSH AVENUE ARMORY (THIRTEENTH REGIMENT)
             BROOKLYN, KINGS COUNTY

Flatbush Avenue at Hanson Place
Architect: unknown

Other armories for the unit:
1830s   Gothic Hall, Adams Street
1858   Henry Street Armory
1892–94   Thirteenth Regiment Armory, Sumner Avenue

The Thirteenth Regiment, the earliest components of which date
to 1827, was officially organized in 1847. Several components of
the regiment fought on the front during the Civil War, but the
Thirteenth is better remembered for its service in New York City
during the Draft Riots of 1863. Eight years later, the Thirteenth
served during the Orange Riots of 1871. Shortly thereafter, the rapidly
expanding unit requested a replacement for its cramped Henry Street
facility; the county responded with sufficient funds to erect an imposing new armory on Flatbush Avenue. The cornerstone of the new
armory was laid in July 1874, and the building was finished the following year. The Thirteenth officially took possession of the armory in
October 1875.

     The Thirteenth flourished during the last quarter of the nine-
teenth century, particularly for its role in domestic security during the
last quarter of the nineteenth century. For example, Henry R. Stiles
reported in his 1884 history of Brooklyn that the Thirteenth assisted
authorities on several occasions:

> It was ordered out to prevent the threatened lynching of the
> murderer of Mr. Van Voorhis, a popular builder in South
> Brooklyn. . . . When the duties consequent upon the terrible
> catastrophe at the Brooklyn Theatre (December, 1876) had

nearly exhausted the police, the 13th volunteered its services,
and remained on guard at the Morgue, and the buildings
on Adams Street, where the remains of the burned were
collected. . . . On July 23, 1877, the Regiment was ordered
under arms by the Governor, together with all the State
troops, and the prompt action of Governor [Lucius]
Robinson, undoubtedly, preserved the State from the devasta-
tion which befell Pennsylvania and Maryland in the destruc-
tive railroad riots of that year.[2]

The Thirteenth also brought international attention to the
National Guard when, on 22 May 1879, the regiment traveled to
Montreal, Canada, to assist in the celebration of Queen Victoria's
birthday:

> The reception by our Canadian neighbors was unprecedent-
> edly enthusiastic and hospitable. The Regiment participated
> in the sham-battle and the grand review by the Governor-
> General (the Marquis of Lorne) and the Princess Louise, and
> the banquet tendered the officers at the Windsor House . . .
> will long be remembered for the generous utterance of the
> speakers respectively, concerning the cordial relations exist-
> ing between the United States and Great Britain and her
> colonies. A magnificent flag—one side Canadian, the other
> American, the gift of the ladies of Montreal—is treasured
> with peculiar pride.[3]

The Thirteenth remained in its armory on Flatbush Avenue
until 1894, when it moved to new quarters on Sumner Avenue. The
Flatbush Armory was demolished in the early twentieth century to
make way for the Long Island Railroad Station.

Flatbush Avenue Armory, 1874–75. Historic postcard courtesy of Gayle N. Carpenter, DMNA.

North Portland Avenue at Auburn Place
Architect: unknown

Other facilities for the unit:
1830s   Gothic Hall, Adams Street
1858   Henry Street Armory
1891–95   Fourteenth Regiment Armory, Eighth Avenue

The North Portland Avenue Armory, originally built in 1858 as a state arsenal for the Second Division, was remodeled and expanded in 1877–1878 for use by the Fourteenth Regiment. (See chapter 2, p. 60 for a picture of this facility.) The nucleus of the regiment was the Brooklyn Chasseurs, formed during the early nineteenth century; the Fourteenth achieved official regimental status in 1847. Early homes of the Chasseurs/Fourteenth included Gothic Hall (1830s) and the Henry Street Armory (1858), both of which it shared with Brooklyn's Thirteenth Regiment. One unsubstantiated source also suggests that "by the end of the Civil War," the Fourteenth shared quarters with the city's fire department in a building known as the Armory and Firemen's Hall.[4]

The unit appears to have had a relatively uneventful early existence but very quickly achieved national acclaim after being mustered into Civil War service on 23 May 1861. Clothed in bright red Zouave uniforms, members of the "Fighting Fourteenth" were dubbed the Red-Legged Devils by Confederate soldiers. The regiment occupied the North Portland Avenue Armory until 1895, when it moved to its new armory on Eighth Avenue. Scant surviving records indicate that the North Portland Avenue building served as storage space for Brooklyn's militia until a new state arsenal was built on Second Avenue in South Brooklyn in 1926. The date of the loss of the armory is unknown.

1873   EAST SIDE ARMORY (FORTY-EIGHTH REGIMENT)
        OSWEGO, OSWEGO COUNTY

East First Street

Architect: attributed to White

Other armories in Oswego:

1835   Old Market House, Water Street
1906–08   Oswego Armory, West First Street

Oswego's Forty-eighth Regiment began as the Oswego Guards during the early nineteenth century. Between the 1830s and 1873, Oswego's militia was quartered at the Old Market House on Water Street. In 1858 Oswego was supposed to have received a new state arsenal to house several components of the Sixth Division; for reasons unknown, the arsenal was never built. In 1873 an armory was built for the Forty-eighth Regiment. Major Horatio N. White was, at the time, listed as the engineer of the Twenty-fourth Brigade, to which the Forty-eighth Regiment was attached. Although not yet verified, the East Side Armory is attributed to White, who also designed five ca. 1858 arsenals in Upstate New York. According to a contemporary report:

[The armory is] a very fine, substantial brick building with a Mansard roof and tower, situated on East First Street between Oneida and Mohawk [streets] . . . and facing the Oswego River, a few rods away. It is 170' long x 100' deep. The

East Side Armory, Oswego, 1873.
Photograph (ca. 1900) courtesy of the
Oswego County Historical Society.

greater part of this building is occupied by a drill room, 70' x 170', and extending to the roof. In front of this the lower story is occupied by separate rooms for each of the several companies; the second story by other company rooms, and by regimental and brigade headquarters; the third story by a separate troop of cavalry. . . . The arms and uniforms of the men are kept in their respective company rooms. Remington breech-loading rifles with bayonets are the weapons of the infantry; sabres and Remington carbines those of the cavalry. Numerous prizes are displayed in the various rooms, attesting to the prowess of Oswego County men [in various contests and competitions with rival regiments] within the past few years.[5]

During the third quarter of the nineteenth century, the Forty-eighth served during the Great Railroad Strike of 1877, the Oswego lumber wharves riots in 1882, the Buffalo Switchmen's Strike of 1892 and the longshoremen's strike against the Standard Oil Company in Oswego in 1894. The regiment was reduced to a separate company in 1892. Oswego's militia occupied the 1873 armory until 1906, when it moved to new quarters on West First Street. After it was vacated by the National Guard, the East Side Armory was converted by a private developer for use as commercial space. Extensive alterations to the building include the loss of the Mansard roof and center and corner towers.

1873   SYRACUSE ARMORY (FIFTY-FIRST REGIMENT)
        SYRACUSE, ONONDAGA COUNTY

West Jefferson Street
Architect: White

Other arsenals/armories in Syracuse:
1858–59   Syracuse Arsenal, West Jefferson Street
1906–07   West Jefferson Street Armory
1941–43   East Genesee Street Armory

Not to be outdone by Oswego's Forty-eighth Regiment, the Fifty-first's archrivals who had recently begun construction on a new armory in Oswego, the Syracuse militia immediately embarked on a plan for an even bigger and better armory of its own. Designed by H. N. White

Syracuse Armory, 1873. Photograph (ca. 1900) courtesy of the Onondaga Historical Association.

85

Syracuse troops posing in front of their armory. Above the main entrance is a distinctive ogival arch, a detail found on few (if any) other historic armories in New York. Photograph (late nineteenth century) courtesy of the New York State Military Museum.

and completed in 1873 on Jefferson Park on the site of the old arsenal (1858), the new armory was distinguished by a monumental, five-story central tower, an ogival-arched sally port and bold triangular and round-arched windows. The unit lost its regimental status in 1881; Company D was retained and redesignated the Forty-first Separate Company. The 1873 armory was razed in 1906 and replaced with a new armory, designed by State Architect George L. Heins.

1873   AUBURN ARMORY (FORTY-NINTH REGIMENT)
        AUBURN, CAYUGA COUNTY

---

57 Water Street
Architect: Hamblin

The history of the militia in Cayuga County dates back to at least the early nineteenth century, as recounted in detail by Henry Hale in his 1869 *History of Auburn*. After commenting on the deplorable condition of militia units in nearby towns such as Aurelius, Hale goes on to describe the three companies in Auburn:

[They are in] tolerably good condition. . . . One of these, a company of light-horse, independent, appears to have been the first military organization that was formed in this village. It was raised in 1804, by Captain Trowbridge Allen. . . . The company was handsomely uniformed with dark blue coats trimmed with red, buff vests and pants, cavalry boots, and crested head-pieces profusely ornamented with plumes and horse-hair. Being composed of fine men—minutemen, by the way—it was deservedly popular.[6]

In 1829 Cayuga County's militia (including the Willard Guards and the Guard and Continentals of Auburn and units from the nearby communities of Locke, Genoa, Scipio and Brutus) were combined to form the Thirty-third Regiment under the command of Colonel William H. Seward. At this time, the regiment's battery possessed a gunhouse on the north side of Water Street, near the railroad. By the late 1830s, the Thirty-third appears to have been quartered on the fourth floor of the John H. Beach Block (a four-story stone commercial building) on State Street. In 1847 the Thirty-third was redesignated the Forty-ninth Regiment.

In 1859 the Forty-ninth moved to a new armory at the southeast corner of Dill and State streets (two blocks east of the battery's gunhouse). According to Hale, the Dill Street facility was "a strong and capacious building of brick, containing a drill room in the second story, seventy-five feet long by forty feet wide, and, in the first story, three company meeting rooms and the headquarters of the [Forty-ninth] Regiment, S.N.G. Two brass six pounders are posted here. A bill is now pending in the legislature to authorize the sale of this property, and the erection of a new armory in another quarter of the city."[7]

By the early 1870s, the Forty-ninth had outgrown this facility and a new one was built in 1873 on Water Street between the New York Central rail corridor and State Street.[8] It was built of Cayuga County limestone by Ocobock and Sisson of Auburn. Designed by G. Hamblin, the new armory was a flamboyant Victorian building with eclectic decorative features. Around 1881 the Forty-ninth Regiment was reduced and redesignated the Second Separate Company. The Second was attached to the Third Regiment during the Spanish American War and the 108th Regiment during World War I. In 1958 the National Guard vacated the 1873 armory; it was demolished in 1971 as part of Auburn's urban renewal campaign.

Auburn Armory, 1873. Additional information exists that suggests the roofs on the corner towers were, at some point, replaced with crenelated parapets. Photograph (ca. 1900) courtesy of the Cayuga County Museum.

467 Broadway (at Hoffman Street)
Architect: Wood

Other armories in Kingston:
1932   Kingston Armory, North Manor Road

The earliest roots of Kingston's militia are believed to date to 1776, when a company under the command of Captain Henry Schoonmaker served in the Revolutionary War. Little else is known about the early history of the area's citizen soldiers. By 1874 Kingston once again organized a unit, which was called out in 1875 to help disperse rioters at the nearby cement works in Rosendale; the following year, it was called out to suppress a mob in Rondout.[9] In 1881 the unit was officially reorganized as the Fourteenth Separate Company. In 1879 the Fourteenth moved into the Broadway facility and remained there until 1932, when it relocated to its new armory on North Manor Road. The city acquired the old armory in 1931 and converted it into a recreational facility. It still serves as a focal point of neighborhood activity.

Kingston Armory, 1879. Historic postcard courtesy of the author.

145 Broadway
Architect: Wood

Other armories in Newburgh:
1931–32   Newburgh Armory, South William Street

The history of Newburgh's militia dates back to the late eighteenth century, when the village, a bustling river port along the Hudson River, raised two companies for inclusion in a regiment from southern Ulster County during the Revolutionary War. The regiment boasted a unit of minutemen, commanded by Colonel Thomas Palmer of Newburgh. The regiment disbanded after the war; during the last years of the eighteenth century and the first three quarters of the nineteenth century, there were no militia units in Newburgh. It was not until 1878, when the Seventeenth Battalion was organized in Newburgh, that the city had its own unit. The Seventeenth consisted of five companies: A, B, C, D and E. The battalion ceased to exist on 11 January 1882 when three of its companies (B, C and D) were mustered out; the former Company A simultaneously reorganized as the new Fifth Separate Company and the former Company E became the new Tenth Separate Company.[10]

The Fifth and Tenth separate companies were very active in the civic life of Newburgh during the late nineteenth and early twentieth centuries. For example, a historical account of Newburgh's centennial celebration in 1883 is filled with detailed glimpses of the militia during the festivities. One of the high points of the day was a grand parade, which featured various hook and ladder companies (both local and regional), the Old Newburgh Continentals, Poughkeepsie's Fifteenth Separate Company, Hudson's Twenty-third Separate Company, Manhattan's Seventh Regiment and Brooklyn's Thirteenth and Twenty-third regiments. As recounted by the *Daily Journal*:

[T]he fine marching of the [militia] brought out a perfect furor of cheering and applause. The eager throng of people wavered upon the sidewalk, in many cases pushing each other out in the street to the great risk of life and limb. . . . The fine uniforms of the soldiers furnished a rare and beautiful sight. Their bayonets glistening in the sunlight helped to make them look every inch the well equipped soldiers they were. . . . The scene presented was such as has never before been witnessed in this part of the country, and it will undoubtedly be impressed upon the minds of all who were privileged to witness it so forcibly that the parade on the occasion of the Newburgh Centennial will stand as one of the most impressive and grand sights they have ever seen.[11]

Crowd control turned out to be quite a problem during the parade; ironically, several armed troops who were official members of the parade itself actually used their weapons during the procession to assist the police in maintaining order.[12] Later that evening, while stranded at the train station due to lack of transportation, members of the Seventh Regiment—some accompanied by "lady friends"—whiled away the time dancing on the depot's platform to music provided by the unit's band. According to an observer, "they at least appeared to enjoy the delay."[13]

In 1932 the National Guard vacated its armory on Broadway for a new facility on South William Street on the fringes of the city. The building enjoyed a few short-lived reuses but was abandoned completely by the 1970s. The building was rescued from the brink of demolition in 1996 and completely and handsomely restored in 1997 to house several county government agencies.

Newburgh Armory, 1879. Historic postcard courtesy of Gayle N. Carpenter, DMNA.

1879   WATERTOWN ARMORY (THIRTY-NINTH SEPARATE COMPANY)
        WATERTOWN, JEFFERSON COUNTY

190 Arsenal Street
Architect: Wood

The Watertown Armory, completed in 1879 for use by what later became the Thirty-ninth Separate Company, served Jefferson County's militia until 1964. The building was acquired by the city from the National Guard and demolished shortly thereafter as part of Watertown's urban renewal campaign.

Watertown Armory, 1879.
Photograph (ca. 1950) courtesy
of the New York State Military Museum.

1882   VIRGINIA STREET ARMORY (SEVENTY-FOURTH REGIMENT)
         BUFFALO, ERIE COUNTY

Virginia Street at Fremont Place (formerly North William Street, later
   Elmwood Avenue)
Architect: Beebe

Other arsenals/armories for the unit:
1858   Broadway Arsenal
1868   Virginia Street Armory, Virginia Street at North
                   William Street
1884–86   Virginia Street Armory, Virginia Street at Elmwood
                   Avenue
1896–99   Connecticut Street Armory

Since 1868 the Seventy-fourth Regiment (organized in 1854) had
been housed in an armory on Virginia Street. In 1881 the regiment
began to agitate for new quarters, claiming that the old armory was
inadequate. In 1882 a three-story, 42' x 100' administration building,
designed by M. E. Beebe, was added to the front of the 1868 armory;
the companies vacated the upper story of the old building and moved
into the new administration building in mid-1882 amid great ceremony. In order to generate revenue on a continuing basis, the Seventy-
fourth rented out its drill shed, when not in use by the regiment, as a
public skating rink. As a community service gesture, the Seventy-
fourth also allowed the Buffalo Latin and English School to use its
facility free of charge. The Seventy-fourth occupied the 1882 facility
for four years; in 1886 it moved into a new armory that was erected in
front of the 1882 building.

*Virginia Street Armory, 1882.
Evidence in the form of a poor copy
of an 1882 invitation to the grand
opening of the new Virginia Street
Armory inspired this interpretive
drawing (2006) by Mark L.
Peckham, OPRHP.*

91

Sixty-fifth Regiment Armory, 1884. This ca. 1900 photograph shows the Classically inspired armory built for the Sixty-fifth Regiment in 1884. Barely visible in the background at the rear (right-hand) corner of the drill shed is the 1858 arsenal. Courtesy of the Buffalo and Erie County Historical Society.

1884   Sixty-fifth Regiment Armory
         Buffalo, Erie County

Broadway between Potter and Milnor streets
Architect: unknown

Other arsenals/armories for the unit:
1858   Broadway Arsenal
1902–07   Masten Avenue Armory
1932–33   Masten Avenue Armory

The Sixty-fifth Regiment Armory, a massive Romanesque/Italian Renaissance edifice, was built in front of, and attached to, the old state arsenal (1858) on Broadway. Buffalo's Sixty-fifth and Seventy-fourth regiments had shared the 1858 facility until 1868, when the Seventy-fourth moved out to its own quarters on Virginia Street. In 1882 the Seventy-fourth Regiment built a new armory in front of its 1868 armory. In a battle of one-upsmanship, members of the Sixty-fifth set out to build an even bigger, fancier armory. In 1884 the Sixty-fifth's new facility, which incorporated features of the Romanesque and Renaissance Revival styles, was ready for occupancy.

    The Sixty-fifth occupied the 1884 armory until a new armory was erected in 1907 on Masten Avenue. When the regiment vacated its old quarters, the city of Buffalo acquired the facility and converted it into an auditorium. Known as the Broadway Auditorium, the former armory was Buffalo's premier civic center during the first half of the twentieth century, providing a venue for boxing and wrestling matches, marathon bicycle races, lacrosse tournaments and collegiate and high school basketball games. In 1947 the city converted the building into a storage facility for its public works department. The following year, the 1858 arsenal was destroyed by fire. The 1884 edifice was completely remodeled in the 1950s.

1884–86   Virginia Street Armory (Seventy-fourth Regiment)
          Buffalo, Erie County

Virginia Street at Elmwood Avenue (originally North William Street, subsequently Fremont Place)
Architect: R. A. Bethune and L. Bethune

Other arsenals/armories for the unit:
1858   Broadway Arsenal
1868   Virginia Street Armory, Virginia Street at North William Street
1882   Virginia Street Armory, Virginia Street at Fremont Place
1896–99   Connecticut Street Armory

Apparently not satisfied with their 1882 facility, particularly after the Sixty-fifth opened its new armory in 1884, members of the Seventy-fourth Regiment once again demanded a new armory. Surprisingly, the county acquiesced and provided funding for the project. The cornerstone for the Seventy-fourth's new headquarters was laid on 4 July 1885 as part of a massive, citywide Independence Day celebration. The new facility was built in front of the 1882 armory. It was designed by R. A. Bethune and L. Bethune and featured a 61' x 120' administration building and a 116' x 120' drill shed. The Seventy-fourth moved in in January 1886 and held a formal dedication in March 1886.

    One month before the formal dedication of the new armory, the old armory (including the 1868 drill shed and M. E. Beebe's 1882 armory) burned to the ground. The Seventy-fourth remained in the 1886 facility until 1899, when it relocated to its new armory on Connecticut Street. According to currently available information, the Virginia Street Armory (see next page) was converted for use as a convention center; it later became the Elmwood Music Hall and survived well into the twentieth century.

Virginia Street Armory, 1884–86. This drawing, courtesy of the Buffalo and Erie County Historical Society, shows the Seventy-fourth Regiment's second of two additions to its original 1868 armory. The aforementioned first addition, completed in 1882, is barely visible in the background at the left-hand corner of the drawing: the rear elevation of the 1886 drill shed, one and one-half stories tall, was attached to the front façade of the 1882 administration building.

1880s   STATE STREET ARMORY (SIXTH BATTERY AND TWENTIETH
              SEPARATE COMPANY)
         BINGHAMTON, BROOME COUNTY

202–208 State Street
Architect: unknown

Other armories in Binghamton:
1904–06   Binghamton Armory, Washington Street
1932–34   Binghamton Armory, West End Avenue

The State Street Armory, located on one of Binghamton's busiest commercial thoroughfares, was built for the Sixth Battery and Twentieth Separate Company. The nucleus of the Sixth Battery was formed in 1870, although the battery itself did not receive official recognition until 17 December 1881. The Twentieth Separate Company, an infantry unit, was formed in 1878. Designed in the Romanesque Revival style with medieval Gothic–inspired features, the armory featured crenelated parapets, machicolated cornices and bold corner towers. During their tenure in the State Street Armory, both units helped maintain order along rail lines in Broome and Tioga counties during the Buffalo Switchmen's Strike of 1892. The battery and company vacated their State Street facility around 1906 for a new armory on Washington Street. The 1880s armory was partially altered after 1906, when the building was converted for commercial use.

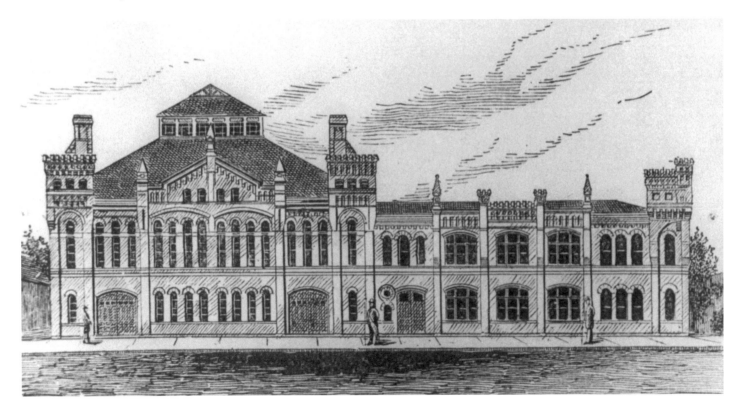

Binghamton Armory, 1880s. Rendering courtesy of the Broome County Historical Society.

Ferry Street
Architect: Brown and Dawson

Other armories in Troy:
1830s   Fulton Market Armory
1902   Troy Armory, Ferry Street
1918–19   Troy Armory, Fifteenth Street

The Troy Armory on Ferry Street was built for the Sixth Separate Company, established in February 1878, the Twelfth Separate Company, established in March 1876, the Twenty-first Separate Company, established in February 1877, and the short-lived Fourth Battery.[14] The Sixth Separate Company, although not officially organized until 1878, dates back to the formation of the Troy Citizens' Corps in 1835. During the early decades of its existence, the corps was housed in the Fulton Market Armory (1830s). In 1898 the Sixth became Company A, Second (later 105th) Infantry Regiment. The post-1870s history of the Twelfth and Twenty-first separate companies is less clear.

Designed by Brown and Dawson, the Troy Armory appears to be the only pre-1900, non–New York City armory in the state to attract attention in any of the numerous architectural journals. An illustrated article appeared in the 21 June 1884 issue of *American Architect and Building News*, one of the most esteemed professional publications in the field in the late nineteenth century. As a rare example of such contemporary critical review, it is worth quoting extensively:

> This building is now being built on the corner of River and Ferry Streets, and has a frontage of 130' on Ferry Street and 150' on River Street. . . . It consists in the main of two portions, the one three or more stories high covering the Ferry-Street front, 50' x 130', is called the administration building, and contains the different rooms for national guard purposes, such as meeting and wardrobe rooms, storage and dressing rooms, [and] squad drill, division-staff and band rooms. The other portion covering the remainder of the lot, 100' x 130', is a drill-room, covered with a curved roof supported on iron trusses springing from the level of the main floor, and resting on heavy piers. This room is lighted by a skylight and by windows in [the] gable ends. At the line of the second floor of the administration-room a gallery is built the entire length of the drill-room, giving seating room for an audience of some three hundred persons. The floor of this room is Georgia pine, and is laid on sleepers resting on a concrete pavement, except at the River-Street end where there is a basement that, owing to the grade of the street, is mostly above ground, and is used for an artillery-room and rifle-range.
>
> The exterior has a rock-faced basement of Schenectady stone, with walnut [water]-table and finish of Red Albion stones. The walls above are faced with selected common brick, with stone finish of the Blue Portage stone; some moulded or carved brick and terra-cotta, with stone bands completing the finish. The roofs are covered with black slate. The interior is entirely finished without plaster, the brick-work being pointed and stained or colored, and the timber-work is finished to show construction, and oiled. Some little decoration will be used in painting the trusses of the drill-room. The contracts for the building amount to $42,225 exclusive of the plumbing, steam and gas fittings.[15]

In 1901 Troy's militia assisted Albany's Tenth Battalion in suppressing a streetcar riot in the state's capital; in 1913 Troy's units were called out to help save lives and guard property during a period of flooding on the Hudson and Mohawk rivers. The armory was enlarged and extensively altered around 1902 to the design of State Architect George L. Heins (see chapter 8).

Within the floor plan:

Principal Floor
A. Drill Room
B. Company Room
C. Officer's Room
D. Q.M.S'R.
E. Lavatory
F. Armorer's Rm
G. Orderlys Rm

Basement Floor
H. Artillery Rm
I. Rifle Range
J. Urinals & W.C'
K. Lavatory
L. Furnace Rm
M. Firing Rm
N. Cellars

Principal Floor Plan   *Basement Floor Plan*

Troy Armory, 1884–86. This illustration of Brown and Dawson's design for the Troy Armory accompanied a lengthy article in the 21 June 1884 issue of American Architect and Building News. *While armories built in Brooklyn and Manhattan during the 1880s and 1890s received extensive coverage in both popular and scholarly magazines, newspapers and journals at the national level during the period, it is worth noting that the Troy Armory is one of the very few late nineteenth-century armories built in Upstate New York that received any attention at all in the national press.*

Academy Street at Fairview Avenue
Architect: unknown

Other armories in Oneonta:
1904–05   Oneonta Armory, Academy Street

The first militia company in the Oneonta area was formed in 1859 under the leadership of Major General S. S. Burnside, formerly of Worcester, Massachusetts. Between the early 1860s and early 1880s, the unit rented quarters on Main Street between Dietz and Ford streets and drilled in the Stanton Opera House. The unit was officially recognized as the Third Separate Company in July 1875. In 1885 the state appropriated $9,000 for the construction of a two-story brick armory on Academy Street after several leading businessmen pooled their funds and financed the purchase of a suitable parcel. The cornerstone was laid on 1 June 1885 and completed shortly thereafter. The building was demolished in 1904 to make way for a new armory.

Oneonta Armory, 1885. Photograph courtesy of the Greater Oneonta Historical Society.

1886   WALTON ARMORY (THIRTY-THIRD SEPARATE COMPANY)
   WALTON, DELAWARE COUNTY

Stockton Avenue

Architect: Randall and Gilbert

Other armories in Walton:

1895–96   Walton Armory, Stockton Avenue

The Thirty-third Separate Company was formed in May 1879, about one year after a group of men from the Walton area had formed an independent militia unit. In 1883 the state legislature appropriated $9,000 for the erection of an armory for the Thirty-third; the cost of the site, $1,200, was underwritten by the community. The architects were Randall and Gilbert of Walton. The contract of $8,492 for construction was awarded to Sullivan, Cook and Aldrich of nearby Owego (Tioga County), and ground was broken in April 1886. Members of the Thirty-third of Walton, the Third Separate Company of Oneonta and the Sixth Battery of Binghamton, along with 8,000 guests, attended the groundbreaking ceremony, which was overseen by the Grand Master of the regional Masonic District. The building was completed later that year; a grand opening ball was held on 28 December 1886. The interior was reported to have been rather lavish, particularly for the period. Compared to other 1880s armories, the Walton Armory was relatively small in scale and modest in decoration.

Within eight years, construction of a new armory, designed by State Architect Isaac G. Perry, was begun on the parcel adjacent to the 1886 building. When the Thirty-third moved out of its old armory and into its new one, the 1886 building was converted for use as a school and a grange hall. Both armories survive and both are privately owned.

Walton Armory, 1886.
Photograph (late 1800s) courtesy of
OPRHP (SHPO, NR files).

Elmira Armory, 1886–88. The armory, a three-story, red brick building, designed by the firm of Pierce and Bickford, appears in the middle ground in this historic postcard from the collection of the author. Several years after the completion of the armory, the firm was retained to design a new city hall. Completed in 1895, the National Register–listed City Hall appears in the foreground of the postcard.

1886–88 ELMIRA ARMORY (THIRTIETH SEPARATE COMPANY) ELMIRA, CHEMUNG COUNTY

307 East Church Street
Architect: Pierce and Bickford

Before the Civil War, Elmira was the headquarters for several units of the Sixtieth Regiment and the southern components of the Seventh Division. However, when the state embarked on its 1858 arsenal building campaign, nearby Corning was chosen to receive a new arsenal to meet the needs of the militia in the Southern Tier. In the 1880s, when the state began to plan the construction of a new armory for the Seventh Division, Corning was abandoned and Elmira reemerged as the focal point of militia activity in Steuben and Chemung counties. The new armory, designed by Joseph H. Pierce of the regionally renowned firm of Pierce and Bickford, was completed in 1888. In addition to serving divisional needs, the Elmira Armory also housed the Thirtieth Separate Company (established in 1874). The facility was decommissioned by the National Guard in the 1970s and acquired by Chemung County for use as office and storage space. As this book goes to press, the armory is in grave danger of collapse.

Chapter 4
The Seventh Regiment Armory

The construction of the Seventh Regiment Armory (1877–1881) on Manhattan's Upper East Side marked a major turning point in New York State's arsenal and armory building programs. Designed by Charles W. Clinton, with luxurious interiors by Louis Comfort Tiffany and Stanford White, the edifice was a testament to the esteemed position of the National Guard as "trustworthy guardians of law and order."[1] By virtue of its size, architectural sophistication and prominent location on one of Manhattan's busiest thoroughfares near some of the city's most fashionable neighborhoods, coupled with its association with New York's most prestigious militia unit, the Seventh Regiment Armory became the prototype for the new building type throughout the state and, ultimately, across the nation.

Early Nineteenth-century History of the Regiment

The origin of the Seventh Regiment dates to 1806, when four companies of volunteer militiamen in Manhattan were joined to form the Second Battalion. Attached to the Eleventh Regiment in 1812, the battalion was the first unit from New York State to volunteer for service during the War of 1812. On 24 August 1824, one week after parading in New York City in honor of the arrival of the Marquis de Lafayette, the four companies were reorganized and the newly formed unit adopted the name National Guards in deference to Lafayette's *Garde Nationale de Paris*.[2]

During the next two years, the National Guards expanded to include ten separate companies, at which point the unit achieved regimental status; in 1826 the unit was redesignated the Twenty-seventh Regiment, Artillery. As early as 1825, the regiment was called upon to assist in preserving domestic order: the unit was on duty at the public execution of James Reynolds.[3] During the antebellum era, the Twenty-seventh (redesignated the Seventh Regiment on 27 July 1847) became one of Manhattan's most prestigious and exclusive fraternal organizations. Sometimes proudly and fondly and sometimes derisively known as the Silk Stocking regiment, the unit comprised young men from some of Manhattan's richest and most socially prominent families. In addition to winning acclaim for suppressing localized disputes such as the Election Riot (1834), the Astor Place Riot (1849) and the Staten Island Quarantine Riots (1858), the regiment was often the most popular participant in both somber ceremonies and festive celebrations. Sometimes, the unit was called upon by various local, state or national entities to augment specific events; just as often, the unit hosted its own public appearance in the form of military reviews or parades.

The Seventh Regiment Armory, completed in 1881, is depicted in an 1893 engraving by Charles Frederick William Meilatz. Image courtesy of the Museum of the City of New York.

Pictured on the front cover of the 24 May 1856 issue of Leslie's, the Seventh Regiment is described in the accompanying article as "the finest volunteer corps in the United States." The caption identifies the costumes of the five militiamen in the front row as follows: Private, Captain, Colonel, Captain of Engineers, Sergeant, all in full dress.

The 1 June 1856 issue of Leslie's covered the Seventh's military review and subsequent parade up Broadway. As noted in the 24 May 1856 issue, the regiment's "appearance in the streets is always hailed with enthusiasm. . . . The ladies, too, who are always charmed with the pomp and circumstance that is necessary for war, generally manage to turn out in more than usual loveliness on the appearance of the Seventh Regiment; and we cannot blame the dear creatures, if their hearts do palpitate as they witness the moving masses of stalwart and noble men, indicating so much strength, and suggesting so much protective power."

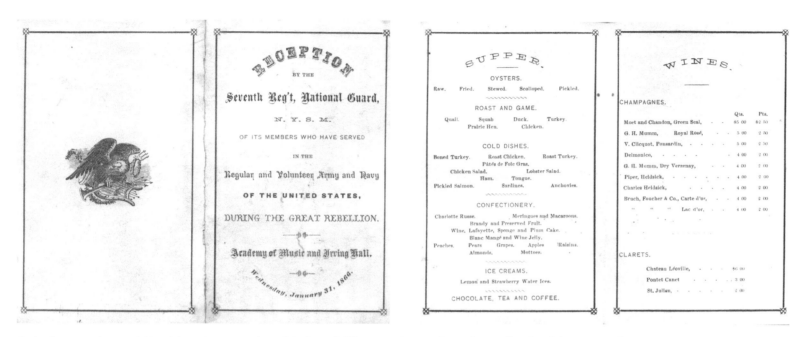

RECEPTION

BY THE

Seventh Reg't, National Guard,

N. Y. S. M.

OF ITS MEMBERS WHO HAVE SERVED

IN THE

Regular and Volunteer Army and Navy

OF THE UNITED STATES,

DURING THE GREAT REBELLION.

Academy of Music and Irving Hall.

Wednesday, January 31, 1866.

SUPPER.

OYSTERS.

Raw. Fried. Stewed. Scolloped. Pickled.

ROAST AND GAME.

Quail. Squab. Duck. Turkey.
Prairie Hen. Chicken.

COLD DISHES.

Boned Turkey. Roast Chicken. Roast Turkey.
Pâtés de Foie Gras.
Chicken Salad. Lobster Salad.
Ham. Tongue.
Pickled Salmon. Sardines. Anchovies.

CONFECTIONERY.

Charlotte Russe. Meringues and Macaroons.
Brandy and Preserved Fruit.
Wine, Lafayette, Sponge and Plum Cake.
Blanc Mangé and Wine Jelly.
Peaches. Pears. Grapes. Apples. Raisins.
Almonds. Mottoes.

ICE CREAMS.

Lemon and Strawberry Water Ices.

CHOCOLATE, TEA AND COFFEE.

WINES.

CHAMPAGNES.

	Qts.	Pts.
Moet and Chandon, Green Seal,	$5 00	$2 50
G. H. Mumm, Royal Rosé,	5 00	2 50
V. Clicquot, Ponsardin,	5 00	2 50
Delmonico,	4 00	2 00
G. H. Mumm, Dry Verzenay,	4 00	2 00
Piper, Heidsick,	4 00	2 00
Charles Heidsick,	4 00	2 00
Bruch, Foucher & Co., Carte d'or,	4 00	2 00
Lac d'or,	4 00	2 00

CLARETS.

Chateau Léoville,	$6 00	
Pontet Canet	3 00	
St. Julien.	2 00	

As for the more private activities of the regiment, members of the Seventh (like every other unit during the period) gathered for a variety of social or cultural events such as formal dinners or outings to musical soirees. Pictured here is a menu for a dinner reception held in honor of members of the Silk Stocking regiment who served during the Great Rebellion. Courtesy of the New York State Military Museum.

The Regiment during the Civil War and Gilded Age

On 15 April 1861 the Seventh, under the command of Colonel Lefferts, responded to President Abraham Lincoln's call for volunteers and enlisted en masse at the outbreak of the Civil War. The regiment was ordered back from the front in July 1863 to help quell the New York City Draft Riots. In June 1864 Lefferts was replaced by Colonel Emmons Clark, the unit's most illustrious leader.[4] Ten years later, when the Seventh's Tompkins Market Armory on the Lower East Side was damaged by fire, Clark petitioned local and state military and government officials to finance the construction of a new armory. Because of the economic depression following the Panic of 1873, public funding was not forthcoming; all the unit managed to obtain was

the city's agreement in 1874 to subsidize a twenty-one-year lease of a large parcel of land on Fourth (later Park) Avenue. Members of the unit decided to underwrite the cost of the building themselves, hoping that donations from sympathetic businessmen and fellow capitalists who were concerned about protecting their property rights would augment their budget. Financial assistance was slow in coming; it was not until late 1876 that Charles W. Clinton, a veteran of the Seventh's Company K, was retained to design the building.[5]

Excavation and foundation work began in April 1877. Three months later, when the Great Railroad Strike of 1877 paralyzed much of the nation for several weeks, the National Guard emerged as the savior of the middle and upper classes' social and economic way of life. Now recognized as a vital component of domestic security, the Seventh Regiment was able to capitalize on its sudden prestige and to exploit the widespread fear of class warfare. By fall 1877, the regiment had raised enough money from private donors to expedite the project. The corner-stone was laid on 13 October. That day, Clinton's design appeared in a full-page article in *Harper's Weekly* about the project that praised the Seventh for its distinguished fifty-year history, particularly for its role in preserving domestic peace and its gallant service during the Civil War.

Seventh Regiment Armory completion photo. Courtesy of the New York State Military Museum.

The exterior shell as well as the interior structural elements and room configurations of the three-story, Mansard-roofed administration building were completed by late 1878. Built of load-bearing brick walls trimmed with granite beltcourses, sills, lintels and cornice work, the building was distinguished by a raised and battered stone founda-tion, a five-story central tower and three-and-one-half-story corner bastions. By fall 1879, the state-funded, 200' x 300' drill shed, whose clerestoried roof was supported by eleven elliptical wrought-iron arches designed by Charles MacDonald of the Delaware Bridge Company, was done.

The 14 May 1881 issue of Leslie's *carried an article about the first of several annual musical festivals held in the drill shed of the Seventh's armory during the early 1880s. Accompanying the article was this rendering, which meticulously portrayed the elliptical wrought-iron arches installed by the Delaware Bridge Company. Courtesy Kirsten Moffett Reoch, Director, Seventh Regiment Armory Conservancy.*

In mid-November 1879, the Seventh held a three-week bazaar to raise funds to furnish and decorate the interior spaces of the administration building. By late 1880, most of the interior spaces, including a grand entrance hall with divided staircase, a veterans' room, a library, a ladies' reception room, a board of officers' room and a colonel's room (all on the first story) as well as twelve individual company meeting rooms (on the second story) were decorated and furnished. Famous designers hired to decorate various spaces included George C. Flint and Company, Associated Artists, Pottier and Stymus, Christian Herter of the Herter Brothers and L. Marcotte and Company. A private gala opening was held in September 1880 in honor of the project's most generous donors, and a formal inauguration ball, open to the public, was held on 15 December 1880.

The cover of the 13 December 1879 issue of Harper's Weekly *provided an artist's interpretation of patrons attending the Seventh Regiment's Great Fair that was held to raise funds so that members of the regiment's individual companies could furnish their respective meeting rooms. The accompanying article on page 971 claims that "to describe the gorgeous appearance of these [companies'] booths or even a few of the more wonderful articles displayed in them, would be a task of prodigious difficulty." Nonetheless, the author goes on to discuss, among other things, the tens of thousands of dollars' worth of silverware and jewelry offered for sale; an "Art Gallery" containing paintings as fine as those found in any museum in the world; and diamond-encrusted necklaces and bracelets—as well as a "small, but beautifully made yacht"—offered as raffle prizes.*

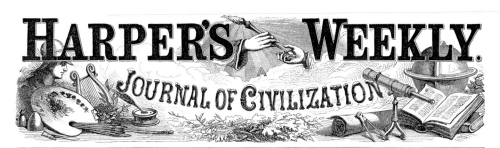

HARPER'S WEEKLY.
JOURNAL OF CIVILIZATION

VOL. XXIII.—No. 1198.] NEW YORK, SATURDAY, DECEMBER 13, 1879. [SINGLE COPIES TEN CENTS. $4.00 PER YEAR IN ADVANCE.

Entered according to Act of Congress, in the Year 1879, by Harper & Brothers, in the Office of the Librarian of Congress, at Washington.

The most significant interior space, the Veterans' Room, was not completed until 1881. This room was the creation of the renowned designer Louis Comfort Tiffany in collaboration with his cooperative of designers and artisans (Associated Artists) and archi-tect Stanford White. Reflecting the influence of the American Aesthetic Movement, the exotic décor features an eclectic blend of medieval, Persian, Japanese and Celtic motifs.

The 25 June 1881 issue of Harper's Weekly *offered a full-page drawing of the Veterans' Room, designed by Louis Comfort Tiffany, Stanford White and Associated Artists, a consortium of artists including, among others, Candace Wheeler and Augustus Saint-Gaudens.*

Wainscot

Old Venetian crane in fireplace

Columns of mantelshelf

Armchair

An article about the Veterans' Room and Library in the Seventh Regiment Armory appeared in the July 1881 issue of Scribner's Monthly. *Shown here are a few of the sketches of the Veterans' Room from that publication.*

Almost equally impressive was the library, also designed by Associated Artists in collaboration with Stanford White. It features a barrel vaulted ceiling sheathed with a basket-weave pattern, massive built-in mahogany cabinets and a chainlink chandelier. No less luxurious, but far too cumbersome to describe individually, are all the other spaces on the first and second story, each one seemingly competing to out-do the other.[6]

Detail of a column in the Veterans' Room. Photograph (1995) by Merrill E. Hesch, OPRHP.

Rendering of the Library in the Seventh Regiment Armory, also presented in the July 1881 issue of Scribner's Monthly.

Each of the twelve companies in the regiment paid for the decoration of its own company meeting room. The mantelpiece in the Sixth Company meeting room of the Seventh Regiment Armory is shown here in this mid-twentieth-century photograph from the archives of the Library of Congress (Prints and Photographs Division, Historic American Buildings Survey, #HABS, NY, 31–NEYO, 121–76).

The Entrance Hall of the Seventh Regiment Armory, designed by George C. Flint and Company in the Renaissance Revival style, is distinguished by elaborate oak woodwork, a grand staircase and bronze torchères. Courtesy of the Library of Congress (Prints and Photographs Division, Historic American Buildings Survey, #HABS, NY, 31–NEYO, 121–15).

The Board of Officers' Room of the Seventh Regiment Armory, designed by the Herter Brothers in the Renaissance Revival style, features elaborate mahogany woodwork and finely crafted stenciling. Photograph (ca. late 1800s) courtesy of Kirsten Moffett Reoch, Director, Seventh Regiment Armory Conservancy.

The Seventh Regiment Armory immediately attracted the attention of the city's social and economic elite. Manhattan's finest young men, particularly those fascinated with the pomp and circumstance of the military and captivated by romantic illusions about the previous generation's involvement in the Civil War, came in droves seeking membership. The allure of quiet hours smoking cigars, reading or playing cards by a roaring fire or of a stimulating evening of billiards or bowling with their comrades was irresistible. Only occasionally were women included in regimental events, such as gala balls complete with close-order drill demonstrations and late-night suppers. Other notable recreational or cultural events held at the armory, either open to the public or for the exclusive enjoyment of the members and their guests, included lawn tennis, annual music festivals and athletic competitions. As such, the Seventh Regiment Armory was one of the first armories to serve as a civic center, a function that would later characterize all armories.

This full-page illustration, entitled "An Evening at the Seventh Regiment Armory— a Drill and a Court-Martial," appeared on page 229 of the 3 June 1882 issue of Leslie's. *Courtesy of the New York State Historical Association.*

From an article entitled "Lawn Tennis in the Seventh Regiment Armory," in Harper's Weekly, *10 December 1881, 823–24.*

This illustration of a music event held at the Seventh Regiment Armory appeared in "The New York Musical Festival," in Harper's Weekly, *21 May 1881, 332–33.*

The lively and good-natured rivalry among companies within the Seventh Regiment is depicted here in this tug-of-war. Members of the various companies often staged athletic and/or military exercises for the entertainment of both themselves and the general public, although most events were by invitation only. From "The Seventh's Athletic Club," Harper's Weekly, *8 April 1882, 220.*

The Seventh Regiment during the Twentieth Century

In 1899 Colonel Lefferts was succeeded by Colonel Daniel Appleton, who led the Seventh until 1916. During Appleton's tenure, the regiment served at the Croton Dam Riot in 1900. The armory was remodeled and expanded between 1909 and 1914 by the New York City firm of Robinson and Kunst. A fourth story was added, and the 1881 tower was removed.

The Seventh Regiment was federalized for service at the outbreak of World War I under the designation 107th Infantry (Twenty-seventh Division), U.S. Army. In 1931 a fifth story was added to the armory and a number of interior alterations were undertaken by the A. H. Davenport Company.

In 1940 the 107th was renamed the 207th Coastal Artillery, which, by 1957, was attached to the Forty-second Infantry Division. In 1968 the 207th became the First Battalion, Forty-second Infantry Division. (Veterans of all these units continue to identify themselves as veterans of the Seventh Regiment.) Although still the benchmark against which all other armories are measured, the building has been deteriorating at an alarming rate during the past several decades due to drastically reduced state and federal funding. The National Guard maintains a small presence in the facility, in the form of the 107th Support Group, but as of early 2006, plans are underway for the armory to be acquired by a consortium of private developers (including several preservation-related, not-for-profit organizations) who intend to restore the building.

This ca. 1914 photograph shows the Seventh Regiment Armory after the 1909–1914 expansion and remodeling program undertaken by the New York City firm of Robinson and Kunst. Most notably, the belfry above the center tower was removed and a fourth story was added. Photograph courtesy of the New York State Military Museum.

In 1931, a fifth story was added to the Seventh Regiment Armory, as depicted in this 1935 sketch by Vernon Howe Bailey. Courtesy of the Museum of the City of New York.

Earlier Homes of the Seventh

Befitting its reputation as one of the state's earliest and most important units, not to mention the personal wealth of many of its members, the Seventh Regiment was one of the very few units to possess its own headquarters during the antebellum era. Between 1839 and 1848, the Silk Stocking regiment occupied rented rooms on the second floor of Centre Market (1830s), a multipurpose commercial facility in lower Manhattan (see p. 46 in chapter 2). In 1848 it moved to the newly built Central Park Arsenal on Fifth Avenue at East 64th Street. Although officially built for the use of the entire First Division, the Central Park Arsenal was soon usurped by the Seventh Regiment. In 1857 the unit moved to quarters above the newly completed Tompkins Market Armory on Third Avenue at the Bowery (see p. 122).

Central Park Arsenal, 1848. This tinted lithograph, entitled "State Arsenal in Central Park, 57th St. Troops Leaving for the War," was done by Sarony, Major and Knapp for the 1862 D. T. Valentine's Manual of New York City. Although vacated by the militia in 1859 when the city took over the arsenal for incorporation into its newly created Central Park, the arsenal served as an informal center of military activity during the early years of the Civil War. Reproduction of lithograph courtesy of the New York State Military Museum.

The Tompkins Market Armory (1857–60) is depicted on the right-hand side of this lithography by Sarony, Major and Knapp for publication in D. T. Valentine's Manual (1861). The Cooper Union appears in the foreground of the left-hand side of the illustration, and the Bible House is shown in the background at the far left. Copy courtesy of The Cooper Union.

Chapter 5

Armories Built in Brooklyn and Manhattan during the 1880s and 1890s

In Brooklyn and Manhattan, the late nineteenth-century heyday of the National Guard is reflected in nearly a dozen large, regimental-sized armories, all of which embodied the functional and design characteristics of the type as had been established by the Seventh Regiment Armory in 1879. All were military fortresses, monumental civic buildings and luxurious clubhouses for members of the militia. Each building consisted of an imposing administration building with an attached rear drill shed. Above all else, these armories were conceived and designed as fortresses intended to preserve the physical and social safety of the middle and upper classes and to ensure the survival of their lifestyles and values during the late nineteenth-century era of labor-capital conflict. A sense of security was provided in the appearance of the armories, the descriptions and evaluations of the armories in the press and the actions of the guardsmen themselves. In a series of articles published in the *Brickbuilder*, Lieutenant Colonel J. Hollis Wells wrote:

[An armory] should be so arranged as to be easily protected from the mob. There should be enfilading towers with narrow windows so arranged for rifle fire that streets at or near these exits may be cleared. . . . The building generally should, therefore, be designed in a simple, straightforward manner, combining many of the features of a medieval fortress or castle. . . . The roofs of armories should be easy of access for the troops, and parapets and platforms should be arranged for riflemen so that they may control all surrounding streets and

buildings. . . . All exterior doors and windows at or near the level of the street should be protected with heavy iron grilles and gates, and double sets of heavy, hardwood doors, hung on especially strong hinges, opening out, are necessary. . . . If possible, an armory should be equipped with a heating, power and lighting plant so as to be absolutely independent of all outside connections which might be destroyed in time of riot and insurrection.[1]

Wells's sentiments, although not published until after the turn of the twentieth century, echo similar opinions expressed during the 1880s and 1890s. For example, an article in the April 1888 issue of the *Seventh Regiment Gazette* reported that

anarchists and socialists [of eastern European origin or descent] are responsible for the appearance of novel and imposing [armories] in most of the chief cities of the country, which must remind them of the feudal castles of their native Europe. Militia armories nowadays are often formidable strongholds, stoutly built of stone and iron, pierced with portholes for musketry and cannon, and capable of sustaining a sudden onslaught or siege.[2]

Moses King, in his 1893 *Handbook of New York City*, wrote of the recently completed Twelfth Regiment Armory in Manhattan:

This watercolor painting, believed to date from ca. 1888, is an artist's rendering of the Eighth Regiment Armory (1888–89) in Manhattan. The original is in the archives of the New York State Military Museum.

[It] is a castellated structure in the Norman style of architecture, and has a solid fortress-like character, with its medieval bastions, machicolations and narrow slits in corbeled galleries, and grille-work at the windows. At each street corner are flanking towers, with loop-holes and arrangements for howitzers, or Gatling guns, on the top. Around the entire roof is a paved promenade, protected by a parapet with many loop-holes, constituting a valuable defensive position.[3]

King described the Twenty-second Regiment Armory, also in Manhattan, in similar terms:

It is, to an exceptional degree, a defensive structure, with re-entering angles, loop-holes for cannon and musketry, a bastion for heavy guns on the northwest corner, a machicolated parapet, and a sally port and portcullis.[4]

The daily and weekly newspapers and popular journals of the period also emphasized the role of armories as defensive fortresses. An article in an 1892 issue of *Harper's Weekly* remarked that the soon-to-be built Seventy-first Regiment Armory in Manhattan is "a massive structure, at once dignified and suggestive of its purpose, is strong enough to withstand the attack of any ordinary unorganized street mob, and could be easily defended against such an enemy."[5] Two years later, an article in the same magazine critiqued the nearly complete Thirteenth Regiment Armory in Brooklyn:

The façade is strong, simple, grim, aggressive, in keeping with the purpose of the building. The strength and massiveness of the structure catch the eyes of people a mile away. . . . There is a reminiscence of the Bastille in that façade, and suggestion of the French feudal castles of the eleventh and twelfth centuries.[6]

Other contemporary accounts deemphasized the warlike function and appearance of the armories and focused on the architectural and engineering challenges of executing the massive drill sheds for training purposes. Still others stressed the importance of armories as comfortable, even luxurious, clubhouses designed to retain existing membership and to attract new members. For example, an 1892 issue of *Harper's Weekly* reported that

[the new home of the Thirteenth Regiment in Brooklyn] will contain a magnificent suite of parlors, grand gymnasium, library, and other conveniences and accommodations not deemed necessary in armories erected 25 years ago. The basement will contain bowling alleys . . . and tub and plunge baths commodious enough to accommodate a whole company at once. In fact, the entire building will be one grand lyceum, where, aside from their duties as soldiers, the members may spend a day or evening at almost any kind of healthful and pleasant recreation.[7]

In an 1895 issue of *Outing*, a popular men's journal, Captain E. E. Hardin of the U.S. Army emphasized the comfort and congeniality of armories as inviting places of respite for the militia:

In all of the armories the rooms are more or less handsomely furnished, according to the means of the occupants, for all the ornamental parts of the rooms must be paid from the funds of the companies; but the men take pride in their quarters, and they are generally made very comfortable and attractive. Many of the rooms contain handsome bronzes, the trophies of the companies' skill with the rifle. . . . Nearly every company room contains a piano and means for playing games, and these, with the gymnasium and athletic sports practiced in the armory, do much toward attracting young men. . . . [The armories are] open to members at all reasonable hours and offer a pleasant place to pass the leisure time, at billiards, bowling, shuffleboard, or in gymnastic exercises. Very strictly enforced rules exist against the use or presence of liquor in the armories, and nothing like rowdyism is tolerated.[8]

The only difference between the Manhattan and Brooklyn armories during this period was the source of funding and oversight. The Manhattan armories were erected under the auspices and rigorous control of the New York City Armory Board, created in April 1884.[9] The carefully maintained and preserved records of the New York City Armory Board, succinctly summarized in *The Armory Board, 1884–1911*, provide a wealth of information about armories built in Manhattan during the 1880s and 1890s. In contrast, at least prior to 1898, Brooklyn's armories were erected without the direction of any such cohesive or dictatorial body. In fact, even though the city or county underwrote the cost of many of Brooklyn's armories during the 1890s, in many cases it is difficult to ascertain which group of local officials was responsible for overseeing construction projects. Few documents about Brooklyn's late nineteenth-century armories have been located, and they are so filled with discrepancies that it is difficult to paint an accurate picture of the individual facilities. After 1898, when the purview of the New York City Armory Board expanded to cover Brooklyn, information about the borough's armories is far more consistent and reliable.

The following catalogue entries are arranged as follows: alphabetically by city location (those in Brooklyn and those in Manhattan) and roughly chronologically within each location.

1883–84   FORTY-SEVENTH REGIMENT ARMORY (FORTY-SEVENTH
                  REGIMENT)
              BROOKLYN, KINGS COUNTY

---

355 Marcy Avenue (between Heyward and Lynch streets)
Architect: Mundell

The earliest components of what later became the Forty-seventh Regiment were organized as "home guard" units in 1862 during the Civil War; several of these companies served briefly at the front in 1862 and 1863, but returned to New York City to assist in suppressing the Draft Riots in July 1863. In its postwar years, the regiment helped subdue rioters during the Great Railroad Strike of 1877 and the Brooklyn Trolley Strike of 1895.

Between 1862 and 1864, the Forty-seventh Regiment was housed in rented quarters on Fifth Street in a building called the Odeon.[10] In 1864 a site on Fourth and North Second streets was selected for the erection of a permanent armory for the regiment, and the cornerstone was laid on 14 July 1864. Little is known of this facility. By 1883 the regiment appears to have outgrown its quarters on Fourth and North Second streets, and a new site on Marcy Avenue was acquired. The building, begun in 1883 and completed in 1884, was designed by William A. Mundell. According to a contemporary account, the new armory was built at a cost of $125,000; "it is of brick, with stone trimmings; it is 200 x 204 feet, with eight company rooms, each 19 x 42 feet, and a drill room, 130 x 128 feet. In the basement are eight rifle galleries, each 204 feet long."[11] The Forty-seventh took formal possession of its new armory in October 1885. Other than the Twenty-third Regiment Armory (1891–1895) on Bedford Avenue, the Marcy Avenue Armory was the only state-sponsored armory built in Brooklyn during this period. All others were funded and operated by the city or Kings County.

In 1899 the armory was greatly expanded by the addition of a massive second drill shed designed by State Architect Isaac G. Perry. Extending all the way back to Harrison Street on the east, the expansive new drill shed nearly tripled the overall size of the existing facility. Typical of Perry's designs for armory buildings during the late nineteenth century, the 1899 drill shed is distinguished by soaring corner towers with crenelated parapets and a massive hipped roof with a double clerestory.

Reorganized several times between ca. 1920 and the mid-1930s, the Forty-seventh was redesignated under the following titles: the Fifty-third Pioneer Infantry, the Forty-seventh Mountain Engineers, the Twenty-seventh Division Train Q.M.C. and the 102nd Quartermaster Regiment. The facility is still occupied by the National Guard.

Forty-seventh Regiment Armory, 1883–84. Historic postcard from the collection of the author; graphic enhancements by James P. Warren, OPRHP.

Drill shed of the Forty-seventh Regiment Armory, 1883–84. Photograph (ca. 1910s) courtesy of the New York State Military Museum.

1892–94   THIRTEENTH REGIMENT ARMORY (THIRTEENTH REGIMENT) BROOKLYN, KINGS COUNTY

---

357 Sumner Avenue (now Marcus Garvey Boulevard) between
  Putnam and Jefferson avenues
Architect: Daus

Other armories for the unit:
1830s   Gothic Hall, Adams Street
1858   Henry Street Armory
1874–75   Flatbush Avenue Armory

The Thirteenth Regiment, the roots of which date to the early nineteenth century, was housed in the Flatbush Armory (1874–1875) until 1894, when it moved to its new home on Sumner Avenue. One of the most thoroughly castellated fortresses of the 1890s, this facility attracted much attention in the contemporary press. For example, it was one of several armories proposed for construction in Brooklyn that were reviewed in the 9 August 1890 issue of *Harper's Weekly*:

The architect, R. L. Daus, designs it to recall the manner of the thirteenth century in feudal France; but the severe character of that era will . . . be relieved by many light and ornamental details. . . . The main entrance, on Sumner Avenue, built of huge granite blocks, will be covered by an arch of 28 feet span, which will be flanked by two large defensible

Thirteenth Regiment Armory, 1892–94.
This rendering of the recently completed
building appeared in the 28 April 1894
issue of Harper's Weekly.

towers 28 feet in diameter and height. One of these round towers is crowned with an observatory, while the other has coupled to it and corbelling out of it a graceful turret 28 feet higher, to serve as an outlook. Between the towers and above the entrance, at the height of the second story, will be a terrace 16 feet wide and 45 feet long, guarded by a rampart wall, where a handful of soldiers could make the entrance impregnable. Eight smaller towers will defend the exposed angles of the administration building and drill halls. . . . The

most striking feature of this splendidly equipped building . . . will be the main drill hall, 300 by 200 feet, covered with arched iron trusses of 200 feet span, and having on three sides wide galleries, the whole to be lighted by a lofty and capacious skylight in the centre of its arched roof.[12]

Two years later, the 16 July 1892 issue of *Harper's Weekly* provided a detailed description of the building as it was under construction, noting that the "material used in its construction is granite

Drill shed of the Thirteenth Regiment Armory, 1892–94. Photograph (ca. 1910s) courtesy of the New York State Military Museum.

for the substructure, with the building in brick with stone trimmings. It . . . was originally not to cost more than $300,000 exclusive of ground, but necessary changes will probably bring the cost up to over $400,000. It is being paid for by the county of Kings."[13] Two years later, at a final cost of nearly $700,000, the armory was finally completed. In its 28 April 1894 issue, *Harper's Weekly* noted that

> the Administration Building occupies the entire front of the building. It is [200 feet wide and] 180 feet deep. It has [a] basement and four stories, counting a mezzanine. In the basement are the rifle-galleries, firing rooms, squad drill-rooms, boiler and engine rooms, and large lavatories. A swimming-bath will soon be added, and the regiment expects to build a dozen bowling-alleys at its own expense. On the first story the company-rooms are situated six on each side, while in the center of the building is the Memorial Hall, which is used as a company drill-room. Its dimensions are 55 by 120 feet. The company rooms are 22 by 50 feet in dimensions. The ceilings are 14 feet high. Each company-room contains captain's and sergeants' rooms, and private stairs leading to the locker-room above, which is situated in the mezzanine story. . . . Officers' quarters are in the second story; they are large and excellent. The rooms of the council and the Veteran Association are especially fine, and are 44 by 50 feet each in size. The gymnasium, also on the second floor, is 50 by 80 feet. The third story contains mess-hall, kitchen and lecture-room.[14]

The regiment took possession of the building on 23 April 1894. The building was vacated by the National Guard in the 1970s and subsequently served as a shelter for homeless men.

1891–95   TWENTY-THIRD REGIMENT ARMORY (TWENTY-THIRD REGIMENT)
BROOKLYN, KINGS COUNTY

1322 Bedford Avenue (between Atlantic Avenue and Pacific Street)
Architect: Fowler and Hough with Perry

Other facilities for the unit:
1872–73   Clermont Avenue Armory

The Twenty-third Regiment, organized at the outbreak of the Civil War, was housed in the Clermont Avenue Armory between 1873 and 1895, when it moved to its new armory on Bedford Avenue. In 1889 the regiment received a $300,000 appropriation from the state legislature. Halstead P. Fowler, a principal in the local firm of Fowler and Hough and a member of the regiment, was selected to design the building under the supervision of State Architect Isaac G. Perry.[15] The design of this armory, a monumental, Romanesque Revival–style building with medieval Gothic features, served as a model for numerous other armories designed by Perry in Upstate New York during the 1890s. However, it is not clear whether Perry influenced Fowler or Fowler inspired Perry. An artist's rendering appeared in the 9 August 1890 issue of *Harper's Weekly*; the accompanying article reported that

> the new home of the Twenty-third Regiment . . . is to be built on the block bounded by Atlantic and Bedford avenues and Pacific Street. . . . The frontages on Pacific Street and Atlantic Avenue will be over 500 and 400 feet respectively. . . . The main entrance, on Bedford Avenue, will be through a heavy ornamental stone archway, on the key-stone of which will be sculptured the regimental coat of arms and motto. This entrance, which will be 35 feet wide, will be closed by a heavy steel portcullis, worked by hydraulic pressure. On each side of the arch rise two circular towers,

Twenty-third Regiment Armory, 1891–95. Photograph (ca. 1910s) courtesy of the New York State Military Museum.

70 feet high and 19 feet in diameter, surmounted by parapet walls and [turrets]. They will be four stories high and contain officers' quarters and other offices. . . . The most imposing feature of the building will be the main tower, which will rise at the corner of Pacific Street and Bedford Avenue to a height of 136 feet. . . . The outer walls of the entire building will be of such thickness as to render the building practically a fortress, like the similar massive and picturesque structure of the Thirteenth Regiment.[16]

The cornerstone was laid on 14 November 1891. The following summer, an article in *Harper's Weekly* described the work in progress:

[I]t is a castellated structure in the medieval style of Norman architecture. . . . As to its utility and impregnability there can be no doubt. . . . The material employed in construction is heavy blocks of red-brown freestone, laid in ashlar courses for the first story, with pressed brick and terra-cotta ornamentation to match for the rest of the building.[17]

The building was completed four years later. During the early twentieth century, the Twenty-third became the 106th Infantry. Vacated by the National Guard in the 1980s, the building subsequently became a city-owned homeless shelter. The once lavish interior appointments, including the WPA-era officers' lounge, have been nearly lost due to deterioration, vandalism and alteration.

1891–95   FOURTEENTH REGIMENT ARMORY (FOURTEENTH REGIMENT)
           BROOKLYN, KINGS COUNTY

1402 Eighth Avenue (between 14th and 15th streets)
Architect: Mundell

Other armories for the unit:
1830s   Gothic Hall, Adams Street
1858   Henry Street Armory
1877–78   North Portland Avenue Armory

In 1891 the Fourteenth Regiment, officially organized in 1847, purchased a parcel of land for $79,000 just west of Prospect Park in a quiet, middle-class residential community in Brooklyn's Park Slope neighborhood. William A. Mundell, who had earlier designed the Clermont Avenue Armory (1873) for the Twenty-third Regiment and the Marcy Avenue Armory (1884) for the Forty-seventh Regiment, was selected to design the Fourteenth's new building. Construction began in 1891 but was stalled between 1892 and 1893 due to financial difficulties. The cornerstone was finally laid on 6 December 1894 and the armory was ready for occupancy in August 1895. The final cost of the building was $650,000, more than twice the amount originally budgeted. Thoroughly castellated in style, the armory is a massive, brick and Warsaw bluestone fortress dominated by multistoried towers and stalwart bastions.

Fourteenth Regiment Armory, 1891–95. Photograph (ca. 1910s) courtesy of the New York State Military Museum.

The lavish interior features a spacious entrance hall, which is dominated by a handsome double staircase with fluted Corinthian columns, a large and elaborate stained-glass window attributed to Louis Comfort Tiffany (which, in the late 1990s, was moved to the Staten Island Armory), turned balusters and paneled newel posts surmounted by bronze torcheres. Massive chestnut trophy cases line the hallways. On the second story, the most impressive space is the officers' room, which features chestnut paneled walls, a coffered ceiling adorned with elaborate pressed metal and supported by fluted Corinthian columns and a marble fireplace with a massive, carved chestnut overmantel.

Descendants of the Fourteenth (and later occupants of the armory) include the 187th Infantry, the 955th Field Artillery, and the 244th Medical Group. Vacated by the National Guard in 1996 and turned over to the city, the building subsequently served as a homeless shelter.

Double staircase and stained-glass panel by Louis Comfort Tiffany in the entrance hall of the Fourteenth Regiment Armory. Photograph (1996) by Merrill E. Hesch, OPRHP.

1886–87	TWELFTH REGIMENT ARMORY (TWELFTH REGIMENT) MANHATTAN, NEW YORK COUNTY

Columbus Avenue between West 61st and West 62nd streets
Architect: J. E. Ware

The Twelfth Regiment Armory was the first facility overseen by the New York City Armory Board. Plans for the Twelfth's armory began in 1884, when a site on Columbus Avenue between West 61st and West 62nd streets (encompassing twenty city lots) was purchased for $208,000. A competition was held and the plans submitted by James E. Ware were selected.[18] (Ware had been a member of the Seventh Regiment when its armory was being planned and built in the late 1870s.) Construction began in 1886 and was completed in 1887; the building was formally dedicated on 27 April 1887.

Twelfth Regiment Armory, 1886–87. Photograph (ca. 1910s) courtesy of the New York State Military Museum.

As described in King's *Handbook*, "the building is a castellated structure in the Norman style of architecture, and has a solid fortress-like character, with its medieval bastions, machicolations and narrow slits in corbelled galleries. . . . [On the interior] the salmon-tinted walls, solid brick fire-places and wrought-iron work in gas fixtures and railings are wholly artistic."[19] The final cost of the project was nearly $300,000.

This unit was organized initially on 21 June 1847 as the Eleventh Regiment; one month later, the unit was redesignated the Twelfth Regiment.[20] In 1849 the regiment assisted local authorities on the occasion of the Astor Place Riot. It also served during the Civil War, both at the front and in Manhattan during the Draft Riots of 1863. During the tumultuous era of labor-capital conflict, the Twelfth Regiment was called out to restore order during the Orange Riots (1871), the Great Railroad Strike (1877), the Buffalo Switchmen's Strike (1892) and the Brooklyn Trolley Strike (1895).

The unit occupied several temporary quarters before moving into its armory on Columbus Avenue. According to an article in the 2 August 1871 *New York Times*, the Twelfth was first housed above the "Natural School" on Fourth Street at Broadway; as of 1870, it occupied a building on Broadway at West 34th Street. During the twentieth century, the Twelfth became the 212th Artillery Regiment. The 1886–1887 armory was razed in 1958 to make way for Lincoln Center.

1888–89   EIGHTH REGIMENT ARMORY (EIGHTH REGIMENT)
MANHATTAN, NEW YORK COUNTY

Park Avenue between East 94th and East 95th streets
Architect: Thomas
Other armories for the unit:
1912–17   Kingsbridge Armory, Kingsbridge Road (Bronx)

The cornerstone for the Eighth Regiment Armory was laid with great fanfare on 20 October 1888, and the facility was officially completed in 1889. A grand reception was held on 30 January 1890. The building also provided quarters for the Second Battery, which later acquired its own armory on Franklin Avenue in the Bronx. A particularly

notable feature of the Eighth Regiment Armory was the large, balustraded terrace nestled between the two front towers, which, according to the souvenir booklet handed out at the armory's grand opening in January 1890, "will form a place for the defense of the front and of the main door, whereby the regiment could, in case of need, march out under cover of fire above."[21] The terrace also offered an ideal stage for drill practices, which could be readily observed and admired by passersby on busy Park Avenue.

King's *Handbook* described the interior of the new building as follows:

> In the 94th-Street tower the first story is fitted up as a reception room; and in the corresponding room of the 95th-Street tower is the Board of Officers' room. These rooms are 47 feet in diameter, and 21 feet high. In the same story, in the gable, are the library, reading-room and officers quarters, substantially furnished. The companies have the entire second floor of the building. Here are ten meeting-rooms, measuring about 23 by 33 feet, and 18 feet high, plainly furnished with desks and chairs. On the third floor are 12 rooms, besides the quarters of the band and drum-corps. The fourth floor in the 94th-Street tower has been fitted up as a gymnasium; and in the 95th-Street tower on the same floor, is the regimental clubroom.[22]

The Eighth Regiment of Manhattan (later redesignated the Eighth Coastal Artillery District of the Bronx) was created on 27 July 1847. Antecedents of the Eighth include the Washington Greys, formed on 1 May 1784 under the command of Captain Jacob Sebring, and the Third and Fourth regiments. The Washington Greys achieved early recognition when members of the unit were called out to suppress a group of rioters. The Doctors' Riot of 1788 broke out in Manhattan when a medical student dangled a cadaver's arm out the window of his school and shouted to a group of boys playing on the street below, "look at your mother's arm!" Coincidentally, the mother of one of the boys had recently died; hysterical, the boy ran to his

This drawing of the Eighth Regiment Armory (1888–89) appeared in the Souvenir of the Grand Opening of the New Armory of the Eighth Regiment *that was published in honor of the ceremony on 30 January 1890. Image courtesy of the New York State Military Museum.*

The Souvenir of the Grand Opening of the New Armory of the Eighth Regiment *also included this bucolic rendering of Civil War–era munitions, suggesting that the horrors of the war between the states had faded in the memory of the subsequent generation. Image courtesy of the New York State Military Museum.*

father's factory and reported the incident. The father and his coworkers left the factory and stormed the medical students, convinced, in an era notorious for grave robbing, that the arm indeed could have belonged to the boy's mother. A riot broke out among the factory men and the would-be doctors, and members of the Washington Greys were summoned to the scene, effectively dispersing the rowdies.[23] The following year, the unit participated in the inaugural ceremony of George Washington on 30 April 1789.

On 22 March 1809, Captain Sebring's Washington Greys united with several other companies to create a battalion of artillery under the command of Major Martin Boerum. On 9 October 1809, Boerum's unit was joined by a battalion under the command of Major Jermain, thereby creating the Fourth Regiment, NYS Artillery. The unit was redesignated the Third Regiment on 13 June 1812; it served at Fort Gansevoort and Fort Greene, defending New York Harbor during the War of 1812. In 1824 the Third marched in honor of the Marquis de Lafayette.

The Third (later Eighth) Regiment was called out to quell rioters during the Abolition Riots (1834), the Stonecutters' Riot (1835), the Stevedore Riots (1836), the Croton Water Riots (1840), the Astor Place Riot (1849) and the Staten Island Quarantine Riot (1858). A letter to the editor of the *New York Herald*, entitled "In Defense of the New York Military," praised the volunteer militia in general and the Eighth Regiment in particular during an 1857 disturbance:

It has been said that the military of New York, unlike the Fire Department, were of no utility and in their existence only a waste of time and money. But . . . this sophistry [has] been exploded. During the late [Sixth Ward] Riots [in July 1857] they have proved themselves to be a most valuable citizen organization. The police, in its inexperience and disorganized state, were unable to quell the disturbance that existed on the 4th and 5th of July, and but for the timely aid which was rendered by the military there is no way of knowing where these scenes of bloodshed would have ended. Too much importance cannot be ascribed to our citizen soldiery.[24]

The Eighth Regiment received national attention as the first militia unit to respond to the Quarantine Riot on Staten Island in September 1858. The disruption began when neighbors of the State Quarantine Station (for victims of yellow fever), fearing for their health, revolted against the medical facility and burned several hospital buildings to the ground. The Eighth Regiment, later joined by other New York City regiments, set up camp near the hospital ruins and effectively contained the violence, its "presence being sufficient to keep in order the refractory citizens of Richmond County" and to "cool the fiery blood of the rioters."[25]

In addition to strike duty during the mid-nineteenth century, the Eighth also participated in a variety of social and civic events that demonstrated the unit's pomp and circumstance. In 1850 they paraded at the obsequies of President Zachary Taylor, and in 1858 they served as special escort and Guard of Honor for the disinterred remains of President James Monroe.

Members of subunits of the Eighth Regiment fought at the front during the Civil War; they also helped quell the Draft Riots of 1863. Postwar riot duty included suppression of the Orange Riots of 1871, the Great Railroad Strike of 1877 and the Brooklyn Trolley Strike of 1895.

In 1894–1895 a new armory for Squadron A was built on Madison Avenue behind and attached to the rear of the Eighth Regiment's Park Avenue facility; the drill shed between the two administration buildings was shared by the two units. (See also the Squadron A Armory.) The Eighth remained at the joint facility until 1913, when it moved to its not-quite-finished Kingsbridge Armory in the Bronx. Squadron A (and its successor units) remained at the Madison Avenue complex until 1969, when the National Guard sold the property to the city. In 1971 the city demolished the entire facility, except the front façade of Squadron A's 1895 administration building, and built Intermediate School 29. The old façade now serves as a wall behind the school's playground.

The archives of the Eighth Regiment contain a surprisingly detailed chronicle of the various locations occupied by the unit since the mid-nineteenth century. Its first home was the Centre Market (1830s; see chapter 2) at the corner of Grand and Centre streets, previously occupied by the Seventh Regiment. The Eighth shared Centre Market with several other local regiments, including the Sixth (later the Ninth) Regiment and the Seventy-first Regiment, between the early 1850s and ca. 1871.[26]

In late 1871 the Eighth Regiment moved to a large commercial block at 226 West 23rd Street between Seventh and Eighth avenues. The entire building, which the unit shared with several commercial enterprises, was destroyed by fire on 17 February 1878; the regiment

Between 1871 and 1878, the Eighth Regiment was housed on the upper floors of this six-story commercial building on West 23rd Street. Courtesy of the New York State Military Museum.

Between 1887 and 1889, the Eighth Regiment was housed in the former home of the Seventy-first Regiment on Broadway at West 36th Street. The inscription in the cornice of the right-hand cross-gable says: "Seventy-first Infantry, N.G.S.N.Y." A temporary sign, added at the base of the tripartite window below the Seventy-first's inscription, reads "Armory, 8th Regiment, N.G.S.N.Y." Courtesy of the New York State Military Museum.

lost virtually everything. After the fire, the regiment spent two years in a large, private house on Seventh Avenue between West 34th and West 35th streets; drills were held in the nearby State Arsenal (1858) at the corner of Seventh Avenue and West 35th Street. Around 1880 the unit moved to a loft over the Old Broadway Stage stables at Ninth Avenue and West 27th Street.

In 1884, during its seven-year tenure above the stables on Ninth Avenue, the Eighth acquired a large parcel, comprising thirty-two city lots, on Park Avenue on Manhattan's Upper East Side for approximately $350,000. In 1885 the plans of John R. Thomas were accepted, and by 1887 a contract (in the amount of $284,000) for construction was let to Isaac A. Hopper.[27] That year, the Eighth temporarily took up residence in the Seventy-first Regiment's old armory on West 36th Street at Broadway while its new armory was under construction.

1889–92   TWENTY-SECOND REGIMENT ARMORY (TWENTY-SECOND REGIMENT)
MANHATTAN, NEW YORK COUNTY

Western Boulevard (later Broadway) and Columbus Avenue between
 West 67th and West 68th streets
Architect: Leo

Other armories for the unit:
1863   Twenty-second Regiment Armory, West 14th Street
1911   Fort Washington Avenue Armory

Since 1863 the Twenty-second Regiment (organized in 1861) had been housed in an aging facility on West 14th Street near Sixth Avenue. By 1882 the regiment began agitating for new quarters; in fact, between 1882 and 1884, several of its most influential members were key players in the creation of the New York City Armory Board in an effort to obtain funding for a new armory.

George Wood Wingate's 1896 *History of the Twenty-second Regiment of the National Guard of the State of New York from Its Organization to 1895* provides a detailed account of the unit's nearly eight-year battle to raise sufficient capital to finance its new armory. On 8 February 1884, after nearly two years of fruitless efforts to solicit donations from local public and private sources, a special committee of unit members traveled to Albany and approached the New York State Military Affairs Bureau, the New York State Senate and Assembly, and even Governor Grover Cleveland himself, in search of state funding. Although impressed with the Twenty-second Regiment's spokesmen, state officials responded only by legislating the creation of a New York City Armory Board to study the problem and to determine which New York City regiments needed new armories.

Members of the Twenty-second Regiment then proceeded to persuade the commissioners of the Armory Board that theirs was, in fact, the most needy regiment; their efforts paid off, and the commissioners almost immediately authorized the purchase of a site bounded by Western Boulevard (later Broadway), Columbus Avenue and West 67th and West 68th streets. Embracing twenty-two city lots, the site cost $265,000. In early 1885, the regiment procured a $300,000

Twenty-second Regiment Armory, 1889–92. Photograph (ca. 1910s) courtesy of the New York State Military Museum.

appropriation from the Armory Board; the next three years were wasted as members of the unit and the board bickered over the selection of an architect. The first plans had been prepared by noted New York City architect George B. Post. A colonel in the militia, a Civil War veteran and a former commander of the Twenty-second Regiment, Post may have donated his professional services on behalf of the unit. Unfortunately, Post's plans proved far too elaborate for the $300,000 budget. Subsequently, members of the regiment tried in vain to convince the board to increase the original appropriation; they even entertained members of the board at an elaborate dinner at the famous Delmonico's on 19 December 1885, "not, of course, with any thought of bribery."[28] But board members stood firm on their original appropriation.

Subsequently, scaled-down plans were prepared by the regiment's Captain John P. Leo and approved by the Armory Board in March 1888. Contracts for construction were let in early 1889 and the cornerstone was laid on 30 May 1889 as recounted by Wingate:

> The occasion being Decoration Day, the regiment had paraded in the morning, having as its guests the officers and men of the First Pennsylvania Regiment, which paraded under its escort. After the parade the Twenty-second entertained its Pennsylvania friends in its [West] 14th Street Armory, and in the afternoon both regiments formed and marched to the site of the new armory, where the cornerstone was laid. . . . The day was bright and beautiful itself, but inexpressibly bright to those faithful officers who then saw the result of their six years of arduous and unselfish labors taking a practical form. The occasion was still further celebrated by a dinner at the Casino in Central Park, at which the officers entertained the officers of the First Pennsylvania and the distinguished civil and military authorities who had participated in the ceremonies of the day.[29]

The unit moved into its partially constructed facility in April 1890; the armory was finally finished in 1892 at a cost of $280,000. In his *Handbook*, King stated:

[The building is] a granite-trimmed brick fortress, in the general style of the fifteenth century. It is, to an exceptional degree, a defensive structure, with re-entering angles, loopholes for cannon and musketry, a bastion for heavy guns on the northwest corner, a machicolated parapet, and a sally port and portcullis. The main entrance on the Boulevard will allow the free passage of batteries and cavalry. The main building contains the offices, library, etc., a handsome reception-room, two stories high, kitchen, gymnasium and messroom on the third floor, and a hospital and medical department in the tower. . . . The drill room is 235 by 175 feet, with a high arched roof and large central skylight. On the north side of this room are ten company locker rooms, for uniforms and arms; and above these are ten company parlors, nicely furnished and with galleries, each capable of seating 50 persons.[30]

During the next few years, the Twenty-second helped suppress riots in Buffalo during the Switchmen's Strike of 1892 and in Brooklyn during the Trolley Strike of 1895. In 1902 the regiment, originally an infantry unit, was reorganized as the Twenty-second Regiment Corps of Engineers. In 1911 the unit left its 1892 facility for a new armory on Fort Washington Avenue. The old armory on Broadway was razed in 1929.

1892–94   SEVENTY-FIRST REGIMENT ARMORY (SEVENTY-FIRST
           REGIMENT)
           MANHATTAN, NEW YORK COUNTY

Park Avenue between East 33rd and East 34th streets
Architect: Thomas

Other armories for the unit:
1904–06   Seventy-first Regiment Armory, Park Avenue

The origin of the Seventy-first Regiment, officially organized in August 1852, dates from October 1850, when four independent companies were joined to form the American Rifles. The Seventy-first

Seventy-first Regiment Armory, 1892–94. This sketch of the proposed armory for the Seventy-first appeared in the 27 February 1892 issue of Harper's Weekly.

served in several local disturbances, including the Dead Rabbits Riot of 1857 and the Staten Island Quarantine Riots of 1858. It also fought at the front during the Civil War and helped quell the New York City Draft Riots of 1863. During the turbulent years of the late nineteenth century, the regiment helped control crowds during the Orange Riots of 1871, the Great Railroad Strike of 1877, the Buffalo Switchmen's Strike of 1892 and the 1895 Trolley Strike in Brooklyn.

Between the early 1850s and late 1880s, the Seventy-first occupied a series of armories, including the Centre Market Armory (see chapter 2); a two-story Romanesque building on Broadway between West 44th and West 45th streets; a three-story brick building on West 32nd Street near Sixth Avenue; and a two-story, Italianate-style

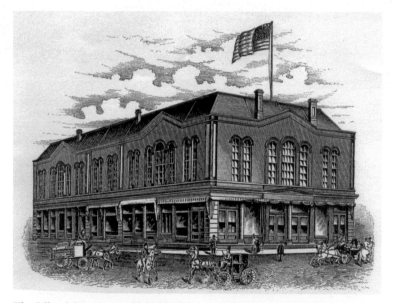

The Official Souvenir, published by the Seventy-first Regiment for the 20 April 1894 grand opening of its new armory, included this rendering of its former armory on Broadway at West 36th Street.

commercial building on Broadway between West 35th and West 36th streets.

In 1884 the Seventy-first Regiment was among the first units to petition the newly created Armory Board for new quarters. However, it was not until 1891 that the board finally authorized the purchase of a site on Park Avenue between East 33rd and East 34th streets for approximately $446,000. The building was designed by John R. Thomas, who had, several years earlier, designed the Eighth Regiment Armory, farther north on Park Avenue. Construction began in 1892 and was described in a July 1892 issue of *Harper's Weekly*:

> It is a massive structure, at once dignified and suggestive of its purpose. It is to be built of rough granite, with a tile roof, and, while it has not the defensive strength of a fort to resist modern artillery, it is strong enough to withstand the attack of any ordinary unorganized street mob.[31]

The contractor, P. Gallagher, received approximately $348,000 upon completion of the armory in 1894. A portion of the armory was assigned to the Second Battery, which later relocated to an armory of its own in the Bronx. The armory was destroyed by fire in February 1902; a new armory was promptly built on the site.

1894–96   NINTH REGIMENT ARMORY (NINTH REGIMENT) MANHATTAN, NEW YORK COUNTY

West 14th Street between Sixth and Seventh avenues
Architect: Cable and Sargent

The Ninth Regiment was officially organized in June 1859, although its nucleus is believed to be the Sixth Regiment, formed in 1799. According to currently available information, the Sixth appears to have been formed by consolidating two earlier New York City units, the Grenadiers and the Fusiliers.[32] The Ninth served during the Civil War as a component of the Eighty-third New York Volunteers. In

Ninth Regiment Armory, 1894–96. Photograph (ca. 1910s) courtesy of the New York State Military Museum.

Drill shed of the Ninth Regiment Armory. Photograph (ca. 1910s) courtesy of the New York State Military Museum.

state service, the unit performed at the Abolition Riots (1835), the Orange Riots (1871), the Great Railroad Strike (1877), the Buffalo Switchmen's Strike (1892), the Brooklyn Trolley Strike (1895) and the Albany Trolley Strike (1901).

In 1891, seven years after first petitioning the New York City Armory Board for permanent quarters, the Ninth Regiment was finally authorized to acquire a site on West 14th Street for the erection of a new armory. The two-year battle to acquire this property illustrates the amount of power enjoyed by the Armory Board during the 1880s and 1890s. Between 1863 and 1890, the city rented a parcel on West 14th Street upon which the Twenty-second Regiment had built an armory. When the Twenty-second left its West 14th Street facility in 1890 for a new armory on Western Boulevard, the owners of the property offered to sell it to the Armory Board for about $300,000. The

board accepted, but just before the deal was closed, the owners increased the selling price. Not to be toyed with, the board proceeded to have the property seized through eminent domain; much to the chagrin of the would-be sellers, they found themselves in receipt of a mere $225,000 via the condemnation process. As succinctly summarized in the 1891 annual report of the Armory Board, the property was indeed secured, "thus proving to the owners of the old armory site that a too vigorous 'boosting' of land values was . . . an error in judgment."[33]

A competition for the design of the new armory was held in 1894 and a proposal by the firm of W. E. Cable and E. A. Sargent was selected from nineteen competing entries.[34] Cable's earlier membership in both the Seventh Regiment and Squadron A may have given him an edge over his competitors. On 10 October 1894, the Armory Board awarded James D. Murphy a contract for $298,000 to construct the armory; the cornerstone was laid on 7 December 1894. The building, extending all the way back to West 15th Street, was finished two years later. The Ninth, originally an artillery unit, later became an infantry regiment. During the early twentieth century, it was converted into a coastal defense artillery unit and renamed the Ninth Artillery District. In 1924 it became the 244th Artillery. The unit's armory was razed in 1969 to make way for the new Forty-second Division Headquarters.

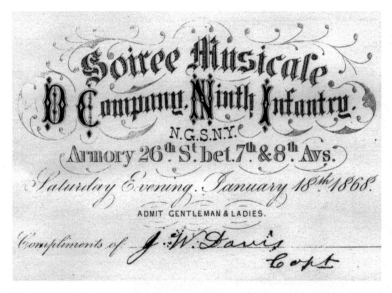

The Ninth Regiment, like virtually every other unit during the Gilded Age, was a fraternal club as well as a military organization. Members of the regiment (or of the individual companies within the unit) hosted or attended a broad range of recreational and cultural events. Some were for the enjoyment of only the unit members and their guests, while others were open to the general public. This ticket for D Company's "Soiree Musicale" was good for one gentleman and an unspecified number of female guests. Courtesy of the New York State Military Museum.

1894–95   SQUADRON A ARMORY (SQUADRON A)
MANHATTAN, NEW YORK COUNTY

Madison Avenue between East 94th and East 95th streets
Architect: Thomas

The roots of Squadron A date to 1884, when a group of wealthy young gentlemen interested in riding formed a private unit called the First New York Hussars or First Dragoons. On 3 April 1889, the unit became Troop A and was mustered into the New York National Guard and attached to the First Brigade.[35] The cavalrymen were called to serve in the Buffalo Switchmen's Strike of 1892, and in 1893 they served as Governor Roswell P. Flower's escort at the inauguration of President Grover Cleveland in Washington, D.C. They also played a significant role in subduing the Brooklyn Trolley Strike of 1895, as reported in the March 1895 issue of *Outing*: "Troop A proved that the cavalry arm is a necessary adjunct to the militia service; their scrupulously kept horses, stable and equipment speak volumes for their veteran commander and their work was splendidly accomplished."[36] The unit's stellar reputation throughout the last fifteen years of the nineteenth century contributed greatly to the proliferation of cavalry troops during the next decade.[37]

During the early 1890s, Troop A rented quarters at Dickel's Riding Academy at 136 West 56th Street.[38] By 1893 the unit was deemed worthy of an armory of its own and John R. Thomas, who had earlier designed armories for both the Eighth and the Seventy-first regiments in Manhattan, was commissioned to draw up plans for the new cavalry armory. Since the unit was, at the time, just a troop rather than a full squadron, the board decided to attach the new facility to the rear of the Eighth Regiment Armory (1889; Park Avenue). The two units would share the modified drill shed.

Contracts for the new building were let in 1894; John E. Johnson was awarded approximately $132,000 to undertake the project. While the armory was under construction, the troop expanded into a full squadron, thus necessitating a number of changes to the partially built facility. The change-orders were carried out by James

Squadron A Armory, 1894–95. Photograph (ca. 1910s) courtesy of the New York State Military Museum.

147

Drill shed of the Squadron A Armory. Photograph (ca. 1910s) courtesy of the New York State Military Museum.

R. F. Kelly and Company.[39] The building was completed in late 1895; the formal opening of the facility occurred on 31 January 1896 and was celebrated with a formal reception and elaborate ball.

By 1903 Squadron A felt it had already outgrown its new quarters and petitioned the Armory Board for a bigger and better armory. Instead, the Eighth was selected to receive a new facility, to be located on Kingsbridge Road in the Bronx. Squadron A was forced to make use of its existing facility on Madison Avenue. The cavalrymen expanded into the Eighth Regiment's vacated administration building on Park Avenue and occupied the entire complex until 1969.

In 1971 the Squadron A Armory (that is, the administration buildings on Madison and Park avenues and the shared drill shed) was slated for demolition to make way for Intermediate School 29. At the eleventh hour, after nearly the entire complex had been razed, the front (Madison Avenue) façade of the Squadron A facility was salvaged for use as the rear wall of the school's playground.

Chapter 6

Upstate Armories Designed by Isaac G. Perry between 1888 and 1899

In Upstate New York, the late nineteenth-century preeminence of the National Guard is reflected in nearly thirty armories designed by State Architect Isaac G. Perry between 1888 and 1899. Perry was a self-trained architect who achieved regional renown in New York, New Jersey and Pennsylvania during the second half of the nineteenth century for the design of large-scale public buildings. His first major commission, won in 1857 for the design of the New York State Inebriate Asylum in Binghamton, catapulted him to the forefront of his field and placed him in great demand for the next several decades. In 1883 reform-minded Governor Grover Cleveland selected Perry to oversee the completion of the New York State Capitol in Albany. In his new role as capitol commissioner, Perry spent most of the 1880s getting the contentious building program at the capitol back on track. By the late 1880s, his purview encompassed all state-funded building programs and he was informally entitled New York State Architect.[1]

The expansion of Perry's duties coincided with the increase in size and prestige of many of the state's National Guard units. During the 1870s and 1880s, many regiments in New York's major urban centers (such as Manhattan, Brooklyn, Buffalo, Syracuse and Oswego) acquired new armories. Not to be outdone by their comrades, members of many units in the state's smaller cities and villages clamored for comparable buildings of their own. By the late 1880s, the New York State Armory Board (created in 1884) was able to begin to honor these requests for several reasons. First, the board was able to call on the services of the newly empowered state architect and second, a flourishing state economy had created significant budget surpluses. More importantly, the National Guard was already at the peak of its popularity and prestige in terms of widespread public support: neither the company leaders nor the board members were obliged to persuade the state legislature that the National Guard was a worthy recipient of government largess.

Perry designed and/or oversaw the construction of twenty-seven armories in Upstate New York.[2] As a group, they can be evaluated in several ways: first, in comparison with contemporary armories built in Manhattan and Brooklyn and second, by comparing and contrasting the individual armories with each other. Most obviously, Perry's armories are smaller than the New York City armories because they were built for separate companies rather than regiments.[3] The motivation for their construction was also very different. Most armories erected (or at least begun) in New York City during the 1880s were built in direct response to the middle and upper classes' fear of class warfare. New York City militiamen and their leaders, bolstered by alarmist accounts published in widely read newspapers and magazines, were quick to exploit the paranoia and succeeded in obtaining large sums of money to build their fortress-like facilities. Upstate communities, however, were relatively remote from the perceived threat. Disputes between workers and owners/managers in most upstate cities were fewer in number and shorter in duration than those in Manhattan and Brooklyn. Despite occasional articles in the upstate press that echoed the panic-stricken tone found in other contemporary publications, government and military officials outside New York City were far more restrained in their interpretation of labor-capital conflict. For example, in his annual report for 1887, Adjutant General Josiah Porter completely refrained from inflammatory rhetoric in his attempt to impress upon the state legislature the need for more armories:

> The armory lies at the basis of our State system in military matters. In establishing a National Guard organization, almost the first thing to be considered is how to get a drill room . . . and there must also be a place where their arms, equipment, ammunition and uniforms can be safely kept. . . .

The Connecticut Street Armory in Buffalo, constructed in 1896–99, is still owned and occupied by the National Guard. Built for the Seventy-fourth Regiment, it is one of the largest, most finely appointed armories designed by State Architect Isaac G. Perry during the last decade of the nineteenth century. This painting, executed in 1896 by Hughson Hawley, currently hangs in the lobby of the building. Courtesy of DMNA.

More than this, the armory should be commodious and comfortable, as well as attractive in appearance and in its furnishings, in order to induce young men having military inclinations to enter the service.[4]

With the blessing of Governor David B. Hill (1885–1891) and Governor Roswell P. Flower (1892–1894), Porter spearheaded one of the state's most aggressive armory building programs. By the end of 1888, appropriations for eleven new armories had been made[5] and preconstruction design and/or actual construction work had begun on at least three new facilities: the Hoosick Falls, Mount Vernon and Catskill armories. Like all construction projects, some proceeded more quickly and smoothly than others; the Catskill Armory, for example, was completed the year after its initial appropriation, while others, such as the Poughkeepsie and Middletown armories, took four to five years to complete. The remainder of the armories designed by Perry during the 1890s followed the same general pattern: acquisition of public money from the legislature, the selection of a site and the erection of the building itself. The building programs occurred in waves, usually dependent upon the political and economic cycles of the period at both the local and state levels. For example, major appropriations were made in 1888, in 1893 and again in 1896. Small amounts of funding were available in the intervening years, but these were mostly in the form of amendments to existing allocations. As soon as one group of armories was finished and the economic forecast was positive, funding for another wave was approved. By the turn of the century, twenty-seven new facilities had been added to the National Guard's holdings.

Architectural Features

Perry's armories share many similarities. In terms of function, all served as military headquarters, fraternal clubhouses and civic monuments proclaiming the importance of the militia. All consisted of administration buildings with attached drill sheds and all were of load-bearing masonry construction. All were located in or near the center of their respective communities, and all occupied nearly the full extent of their lots. In terms of design and decoration, Perry continued to use the medieval Gothic mode popularized in New York City during the 1880s, but he also employed his personal favorite, the Richardsonian Romanesque idiom. Reflecting the influence of that style, most of Perry's armories are generally asymmetrical in form and horizontal in massing. They feature round-arched door and window openings (especially massive, Syrian-arched sally ports), polychromatic building materials and multigabled, often slate-clad roofs (especially on the administration buildings) pierced by wall dormers, cross gables or turrets. The administration buildings of many of Perry's armories, particularly those built in the mid- to late 1890s, are dominated by multistory corner towers; massive, tripartite arcades sheltering recessed porches and/or balconies; and elaborate decoration in the form of stone carvings, molded terra-cotta cartouches and/or mosaic tiling. Borrowing from medieval military architecture, Perry also employed multistoried towers, crenelated parapets, machicolated cornices, iron portcullises and tall, narrow windows protected by iron grilles. Many of his later armories feature tripartite arcades sheltering recessed porches and/or balconies and a profusion of carved stone, terra-cotta or tile-mosaic detailing. In contrast, several of his earliest armories, including those in Catskill, Mohawk and Geneva, are slightly smaller in scale and less exuberant in form and detailing. These earlier ones, lacking exaggerated asymmetry, crenelated parapets and soaring corner towers, are not unlike civic or large residential buildings of the period.

The interiors of Perry's administration buildings exhibit a variety of decorative features, including a profusion of oak woodwork in the form of elegant wainscoting and paneling, coffered ceilings, door and window trim and furniture crafted in the shops of Gustave Stickley. Fireplaces, usually embellished with glazed tiles and cast-iron fire backs, are often surmounted by elaborate overmantels with massive, beveled mirrors and/or decorative murals. Pressed-metal ceilings and elaborate lighting fixtures are also characteristic. The first and

The rear tower of the Ogdensburg Armory's administration building (1898) illustrates another example of polychrome masonry, in this case, light and dark Potsdam sandstone. Also of note are the tower's crenelated parapet, the roughly hewn lintels and sills above and below the windows, the iron grilles on all basement and first-story windows and the drill shed's stone-capped buttresses that articulate the tripartite windows.

This group of photographs, taken by the author between 1995 and 2006, illustrates a variety of exterior features found on Perry's armories.

The Washington Avenue Armory in Albany, built in 1889–93 (above left and right) for the Tenth Battalion, is one of Perry's largest, most elaborately detailed armories. For example, carved brownstone trim articulates the sally port and elaborate tile mosaics surmount many of the iron-grilled windows. Underutilized and neglected for more than a decade, the armory has recently undergone a remarkable restoration for use as a center of recreation and entertainment in Albany. Since late 2005, the armory has served as home to the Albany Patroons basketball team.

Characteristic of Perry's use of materials and methods of construction, the Whitehall Armory (1899) is built of polychromatic masonry, in this case, limestone and brick. Note the battered stone foundation of the tower and the tripartite arcade that shelters the first-story entrance porch and the second-story balcony.

As portrayed in this 1890s photograph, the company meeting room in the Poughkeepsie Armory (1891–92) featured a coffered ceiling sheathed with pressed tin; a fireplace surrounded by glazed tiles and an oak overmantel with a large, beveled mirror; handsomely crafted oak furniture (both freestanding as well as built-in); hardwood floors; and cove molding, picture rails and stenciled friezes. With the exception of the removal of most of the historic furniture, the interior spaces in the armory survive virtually intact. Photograph courtesy of the New York State Military Museum.

The illustrations to the left and above show a variety of details typically found inside the administration buildings of Perry's armories. Unless otherwise noted, the photographs were taken by the author between 1995 and 2006.

(Above) Like most of Perry's armories, the Saratoga Armory (1889–91) features a grand entrance hall with elaborate oak wainscoting, a sweeping staircase with a finely crafted oak newel post and banister and a fancy, pressed-tin ceiling.

(Left) Many of the ceilings in the entrance halls and parlors of Perry's armories are sheathed with pressed tin, as seen in this detail of the ceiling in the lobby of the Poughkeepsie Armory (1891–92).

second stories of most of Perry's armories feature grand entrance halls, spacious staircases, at least one large company meeting room and several smaller rooms for use as offices, libraries, club rooms and officers' quarters. Basements contain mess halls, rifle ranges, bowling alleys, pools and/or storage facilities.

All of Perry's drill sheds were rectangular; most featured regular fenestration with paired or tripartite groups of tall windows articulated by buttresses. The interiors of the drill sheds usually featured exposed brick walls and ceilings of beaded wainscoting. Balconies at either the front or the rear of the drill shed contained spectator seating and/or company locker rooms. Occasionally, elegant curved staircases provided access to the rear balconies, while the front balconies were reached via the second-story lobby or stair hall of the administration building.

A variety of features commonly associated with Perry's drill sheds is found in this group of photographs.

The side elevations (left) of most of Perry's drill sheds feature paired or tripartite windows trimmed with decorative stone or brickwork and articulated by pilasters, as seen here at the Whitehall Armory (1899). Photograph (1995) by the author.

Because most of Perry's armories occupied entire city blocks (above, top), their rear elevations were often finely crafted for the public's viewing pleasure. This late nineteenth-century photograph of the Ogdensburg Armory (1898) shows the broad gable end of the drill shed with tripartite groups of tall, narrow, round-arched windows neatly trimmed with stone voussoirs. Of particular note is the large round tower at the rear corner of drill shed that contains a spiral staircase to the locker room in the balcony. Photograph (ca. 1898) courtesy of the Ogdensburg Public Library, Dow Collection. Special thanks to the late Persis E. Boyesen, former Ogdensburg City Historian.

Hornell Armory (1894–96) (above, bottom). Like all other late nineteenth- and early twentieth-century armories, Perry's drill sheds feature exposed steel truss work. Photograph (1996) by David Lamb Photography.

Ceremonies and Press Coverage

The level of community interest and involvement in armory building is reflected in the festive groundbreaking, cornerstone-laying and ribbon-cutting ceremonies that celebrated the erection of virtually every upstate armory. The following examples, which deal with the Twenty-second Separate Company's new armory in Saratoga and the Seventy-fourth Regiment's facility on Connecticut Street in Buffalo, provide a brief glimpse of the typical fanfare and press coverage that accompanied the construction of Perry's armories. On 22 November 1889, the *Daily Saratogian* reported that

> the ceremonies of laying the corner stone of the armory . . . proved to be one of the most auspicious occasions that has ever occurred in Saratoga. Business was practically suspended, and the schools were dismissed to give everyone an opportunity to attend the impressive and imposing ceremonies. The manner in which everyone, old and young, misses and masters, ladies and gentlemen, embraced the opportunity, demonstrated the pride they feel in our unexcelled local militia.[6]

In closing, the keynote speaker at the ceremony observed that the new armory was to be erected across the street from the Union Free School of Saratoga Springs (since replaced by a firehouse) and remarked:

> Verily public education is no less a defense to popular liberty than the military establishment. Generations of schoolboys have debated the question whether the pen or the sword were mightier without having definitively settled the vexed question; but give me a land where the powers of the pen and the sword unite to maintain the rights and liberties of the people and I shall have a country into which tyranny can never enter, where preparation for war will insure peace, where the government of the people, by the people, for the people shall never perish, so long as the Almighty Ruler of the universe gives this planet for a residence to the children of men.[7]

Similarly, the groundbreaking ceremony for Buffalo's new Seventy-fourth Regiment Armory on Connecticut Street on 7 November 1896 inspired equally eloquent rhetoric:

> We are actors today in a ceremony which is both impressive and significant. Our hearts thrill with joy and satisfaction at the thought that this building is the finest devoted to military purposes in the State of New York. Representing an investment of over half a million dollars, I believe it to be justly regarded as one of the noblest and handsomest edifices in the country and a great and enduring ornament to the City of Buffalo.[8]

The cornerstone laying of the Seventy-fourth Regiment Armory on 4 July 1898 was cause for still another celebration. This time the

The laying of the cornerstone for the Connecticut Street Armory (1896–99) in Buffalo was cause for a community-wide celebration. Photograph (1898) courtesy of the New York State Military Museum.

Freemasons took center stage amidst the festivities. In closing his address, Grand Marshal Sullivan declaimed:

> The peace-inculcating society of Freemasons unites with [the National Guard] in celebrating a most warlike event; the members of the Seventy-fourth Regiment stand about this cornerstone today the very embodiment and representation of death-dealing war. . . . Nevertheless, the Grand Lodge of one of the most peaceful societies has been summoned to inaugurate this building, and to anoint its cornerstone with those emblems of peace, the corn of nourishment, the wine of refreshment and the oil of joy. . . . May the house that is here to rise long stand as a monument of our national strength. May all whose enlistment shall bring them here be as manly and as admirable as the present membership of the Seventy-fourth Regiment. And may the God of Battles bring all nations to universal peace below and everlasting peace above.[9]

Equally impressive were the formal dedications, ribbon cuttings and balls held to celebrate the official opening of each new armory. For example, in February 1897 the *Niagara Falls Daily Cataract* reported on the upcoming dedication of the Tonawanda Armory:

> The new armory of the Twenty-fifth Separate Company of Tonawanda will be dedicated with a grand reception and ball next Monday. . . . The armory, when completed, will, with its interior fixtures, rank as the finest Separate Company in the state. It is not unlike the armories at Hornellsville, Niagara Falls and other cities throughout the state, that have been built during the past three or four years, and in accordance with modern military designs. That is as far as the drill hall, locker rooms, gun racks, etc., is concerned, but it is generally believed that the interior decorating and furnishing of this armory is better than in any of the armories of its class. . . . The building complete will cost upwards of $85,000.[10]

One hundred years later, Perry's surviving armories are as imposing and awe inspiring as the day they were built. Whereas many earlier and later National Guard facilities (both upstate and in New York City) blend in with or are overwhelmed by subsequent development, Perry's armories remain imposing monuments in their local streetscapes.

1889–93   WASHINGTON AVENUE ARMORY (TENTH BATTALION) ALBANY, ALBANY COUNTY

---

195 Washington Avenue
Architect: Perry

Other arsenals/armories in Albany:
1799   Albany Arsenal, Broadway
1858   Albany Arsenal, Hudson Street
1914   New Scotland Avenue Armory

The Tenth Battalion, created in 1881 from the former Tenth Regiment, vacated the old Albany Arsenal (1858) on Hudson Street in 1891 and moved into its new quarters on Washington Avenue. One of Perry's earliest, largest and most luxurious armories, the Washington Avenue facility is distinguished by a variety of Richardsonian Romanesque–inspired elements, including massive, round-arched openings, a four-story corner tower, a profusion of turrets and cross gables, polychrome mosaic ornamentation and carved brownstone details.

Most of the battalion remained in the armory until well into the twentieth century. (Cavalry Troop B left in 1914 for a separate armory on New Scotland Avenue.) By the second decade of the twentieth century, the unit was once again expanded to regimental status, and the Tenth Regiment was resurrected. Company A (formerly the Albany Zouave Cadets) became the Twenty-sixth Separate Company, Company B (formerly the Washington Continentals) became the Thirty-fifth Separate Company, Company C became the Thirty-eighth

Washington Avenue Armory, Albany, 1889–93. Photograph (ca. 1910s) courtesy of the New York State Military Museum.

Washington Avenue Armory, Albany, 1889–93. A group of unidentified men sit around a table in the Company A Meeting Room. Photograph (ca. 1910s) courtesy of the New York State Military Museum.

Washington Avenue Armory, Albany, 1889–93. Corner tower. Photograph (2005) by the author.

Washington Avenue Armory, Albany, 1889–93. Two details of the inglenook in the Company A Meeting Room. Photographs (2005) by the author.

Separate Company and Company D became the Forty-fifth Separate Company. During its tenure in the Washington Avenue Armory, the battalion served during the Spanish American War, World War I and, as the 106th Infantry Regiment, during World War II.

The National Guard vacated the armory in 1991 and turned it over to the New York State Education Department. The building was later acquired by a private developer.

1895   AMSTERDAM ARMORY (FORTY-SIXTH SEPARATE COMPANY)
       AMSTERDAM, MONTGOMERY COUNTY

Florida Avenue at DeWitt Street
Architect: Perry

The Forty-sixth Separate Company was officially organized on 3 September 1883. The company was initially housed at Montgomery County's expense on the top floor of the Behr Block in Amsterdam for $700 per year. Three years after moving into its new armory, the Forty-sixth was redesignated Company G of the newly formed Second (later 105th) Infantry Regiment. The armory was closed in 1993 and sold to a private concern.

Amsterdam Armory, 1895.
Historic postcard from the collection
of the author.

1896–99	CONNECTICUT STREET ARMORY (SEVENTY-FOURTH REGIMENT)
	BUFFALO, ERIE COUNTY

184 Connecticut Street (between Niagara Street and Prospect Avenue)
Architect: Perry

Other arsenals/armories for the unit:

1858	Broadway Arsenal, Broadway
1868	Virginia Street Armory, Virginia Street at North William Street
1882	Virginia Street Armory, Virginia Street at Fremont Place
1884–86	Virginia Street Armory, Virginia Street at Elmwood Avenue

With the possible exception of the Twenty-third Regiment Armory (1891–1895) in Brooklyn, the Connecticut Street Armory was by far the largest and most lavish armory built during Perry's tenure as state architect. Actually, however, the building was designed by Captain Williams Lansing, the commander of the Seventy-fourth Regiment's Company F, who worked under Perry's supervision.

The Seventy-fourth Regiment was organized in 1854. Early homes of the regiment included the Broadway Arsenal (1858) and three separate armories on Virginia Street (1868, 1882 and 1884–1886). In 1894 the state's adjutant general remarked in his annual report that the eight-year-old armory on Virginia Street was not adequate for the Seventy-fourth's needs. Thus began the regiment's five-year battle to obtain a new armory.[11] The key players in the unit's struggle to obtain the building of its dreams were aptly

Connecticut Street Armory, Buffalo, 1896–99. Photograph (ca. 1900) courtesy of the Buffalo and Erie County Historical Society.

161

Connecticut Street Armory, Buffalo, 1896–99. Detail of the sally port during construction of the armory. This is one of a series of photographs taken between 1896 and 1899. The collection is on file at the New York State Military Museum.

Connecticut Street Armory, Buffalo, 1896–99. Aerial view of the armory. Photograph (ca. 1940) courtesy of the Buffalo and Erie County Historical Society.

described in the 2 January 1898 issue of the *Buffalo News* as having "led many a daring charge and bewildering skirmish against the legislative hosts in the cause of the armory."[12] The first skirmish, begun in October 1894 and not won until June 1896, involved the selection and acquisition of the city-owned Old Prospect Avenue Reservoir. On 12 May 1896, one month before the city deeded the site to the state, Governor Levi P. Morton finally signed a bill appropriating $400,000 to build the armory, $25,000 of which was granted immediately and $375,000 of which was supposed to be disbursed in early 1897.

Contracts were immediately let for the laying of the foundation walls, and ground was broken amid great pomp and circumstance on 7 November 1896. Much to the chagrin of everyone involved in the project, the legislature released only $75,000 for 1897 and declared that the remaining $300,000 would be divided into two $150,000 payments in 1898 and 1899. To complicate matters further, all proposals submitted in response to the state's solicitation for construction bids, which called for a cut-stone, fireproof building, far exceeded the budget and the lowest bid was for $600,000. It appeared that a scaled-down, brick version of the original proposal would have to be substituted.

However, a small group of individuals, led by Captain Lansing, refused to give up the idea of a magnificent stone building as first envisioned; the group spent the last three months of 1897 negotiating and compromising with both Perry and the hopeful contractor to bring the proposal within budget. Finally, a revised bid was accepted and, on 31 December 1897, the firm of C. Berrick's Sons of Buffalo was awarded a contract for $335,585 to build an armory of Medina sandstone. Captain Lansing was appointed superintendent of construction.

The cornerstone for the new building was laid on Independence Day, 1898. The building was nearly complete by mid-1899, with the exception of interior embellishments, which the state refused to underwrite in order to keep the costs within the original budget. Consequently, the burden of finishing the armory fell upon the regiment itself. In order to earn money, the regiment held a two-week fundraiser in its cavernous drill shed, gymnasium and "Great Hall." Tens of thousands of visitors patronized the Pan American Bazaar between 23 October and 6 November 1899, enjoying dozens of dazzling booths and larger-than-life exhibits and attractions, including a giant replica of a portal from a Bombay palace, a 118'-long, 30'-high

Connecticut Street Armory, Buffalo, 1896–99. Taken during the construction of the armory, this photograph (from the aforementioned series) shows the laying of the raised foundation.

reproduction of San Juan Hill (complete with faithful reenactments of the storming troops) and a 30'-high replica of a European castle filled with displays of medieval armor and weapons. The bazaar culminated with a formal military ball.

The Seventy-fourth retained its original designation until World War I, when it was consolidated with Fenton's Guard from nearby Jamestown and the Twenty-fifth Separate Company of Tonawanda to form the 174th Infantry Regiment. Headquarters for the 174th remained at the Connecticut Street Armory. In 1982 a fire nearly destroyed the drill shed. Several years and seven million dollars later, the exterior walls and towers of the drill shed were faithfully restored to their original condition. The interior features were pragmatically restored with modern, economical materials (primarily concrete blocks) and the massive, iron-trussed, barrel-vaulted roof was replaced with a nearly flat roof. The facility is still occupied by the National Guard.

Connecticut Street Armory, Buffalo, 1896–99. A devastating fire in 1982 nearly destroyed the drill shed. Photograph courtesy of the New York State Military Museum.

Catskill Armory, 1888–89. Like some of Perry's earlier armories, the Catskill Armory was more like a small civic or large residential building than a castellated fortress. When built, the front corner tower was capped with a conical roof. During the early twentieth century, the conical roof was replaced with a crenelated parapet that more clearly signified the building's function as a military facility. A similar trend was seen on the Geneva, Mohawk, Niagara Falls and Saratoga armories, all of whose conical tower roofs were replaced with crenelated parapets. Historic postcard courtesy of the author.

1888–89 CATSKILL ARMORY (SIXTEENTH SEPARATE COMPANY)
CATSKILL, GREENE COUNTY

78 Water Street
Architect: Perry

The Sixteenth Separate Company was organized in October 1879; three years later the unit was called to Coxsackie to suppress a riot among Italian laborers on the New York, West Shore and Buffalo Railroad. The Sixteenth Separate Company was one of the first upstate units to receive a new armory designed by Isaac G. Perry. Completed in 1889, it was constructed by a local contractor named George W. Holdridge. It is one of several Perry-designed armories dating from the late 1880s/early 1890s that stand out for their modest scale and ambiguous character. Although signature Perry elements such as asymmetrical form, corner towers and the use of Romanesque-inspired ornament are evident, these buildings lack the over-scaled massing and features clearly derived from "fortress-like" constructions that signify the link between design and function in many of Perry's later armories. Instead, these armories are sturdy yet stylish buildings that could just as easily accommodate a variety of public, civic or residential uses.

During the early twentieth century, the Sixteenth Separate Company became Company E, Tenth Regiment. By 1913 the company appears to have been extremely dissatisfied with its 1889 facility. "[T]he location is about the worst in town," wrote the company's commanding officer in a letter to the State Armory Board of Commissioners on 20 November 1913. "If anything proper is ever done here it would be to sell this property and purchase a proper lot on a respectable street. . . . [The current building is] of no value for any other purpose but a garage." The complaint apparently fell on deaf ears; the building remained in use for the next half-century. It was vacated by the National Guard in 1963 and subsequently demolished.

**1892–93 Cohoes Armory (Seventh Separate Company)
Cohoes, Albany County**

Hart Street (current legal address: 41 Columbia Street)
Architect: Perry

Organized as the Third Separate Company in early 1876, the unit was officially redesignated the Seventh Separate Company in late 1877. Completed at the relatively early date of 1893, the Cohoes Armory is

Drill shed of the Cohoes Armory, 1892–93. Photograph (ca. 1910s) courtesy of the New York State Military Museum.

Cohoes Armory, 1892–93. Photograph (ca. 1910s) courtesy of the New York State Military Museum.

much more like Perry's later armories with its massive sally port and five-story corner tower. In 1898 the company was reorganized as a component of the Second Regiment for service during the Spanish American War; upon mustering into federal service during World War I, the Cohoes unit was redesignated Company D, 105th Infantry Regiment. The armory was vacated by the National Guard in 1964; it was acquired by a private developer and converted for use as retail commercial space.

1892 GENEVA ARMORY (THIRTY-FOURTH SEPARATE COMPANY)
GENEVA, ONTARIO COUNTY

300 Main Street
Architect: Perry

The Thirty-fourth Separate Company was organized in January 1880. Twelve years later the unit received a new armory designed by Perry.

Like several other late 1880s/early 1890s armories designed by Perry, the Geneva Armory was relatively small and nonmilitary in appearance. The link between design and function that characterized many of Perry's later and/or larger armories was missing; the Geneva Armory was not unlike a public or civic building of the 1890s. In 1906 Perry's armory was altered and greatly expanded to the design of State Architect George L. Heins (see chapter 8). The facility is still occupied by the National Guard.

Geneva Armory, 1892. Historic postcard from the collection of the author.

Geneva Armory, 1892. This photograph of the main parlor was taken before 1906 when the armory was greatly enlarged and remodeled by State Architect George L. Heins. Courtesy of the New York State Military Museum.

During the nineteenth century, the state occasionally allowed community organizations to use armories as meeting spaces, usually because there were no other sheltered facilities in the respective locations that could accommodate large-scale public events. For example, a charity fair was held in the Geneva Armory (1892) in 1893. The use of armories as civic centers proliferated after World War I. Photograph (1893) courtesy of the Geneva Historical Society.

1895 GLENS FALLS ARMORY (EIGHTEENTH SEPARATE COMPANY) GLENS FALLS, WARREN COUNTY

147 Warren Street
Architect: Perry

Initially organized in 1876, Warren County's militia unit was officially designated the Eighteenth Separate Company in 1877. For many years, the Eighteenth rented temporary quarters in the Glens Falls Music Hall. The unit's first and only permanent armory, completed in 1895, is typical of Perry's mid-1890s designs in its multistory tower and bold, arcaded façade sheltering a deeply recessed porch and balcony. In terms of its layout, however, it is atypical of Perry's work: it is one of only three armories whose drill sheds are attached to the side, rather than

Glens Falls Armory, 1895. Historic postcard from the collection of the author.

167

Glens Falls Armory, 1895. Officers of the Eighteenth Separate Company pose for a formal portrait. Undated photograph courtesy of the New York State Military Museum.

rear, of the administration buildings. (The others are in Hornell and Jamestown.) In 1898 the Eighteenth was redesignated Company K and attached to the newly created Second Regiment, which, at the outbreak of World War I, was redesignated the 105th Infantry Regiment. The armory is still occupied by the National Guard.

1888–89   HOOSICK FALLS ARMORY (THIRTY-SECOND SEPARATE
                    COMPANY)
              HOOSICK FALLS, RENSSELAER COUNTY

Church Street at Elm Street
Architect: Perry

The earliest volunteer unit in Hoosick Falls was formed on 23 September 1835. The Thirty-second Separate Company was officially organized in March 1885; in 1898 it became Company M of the newly created Second Regiment, which, at the outbreak of World War I, was redesignated the 105th Infantry Regiment. The facility is now shared by the local National Guard unit and village government officials.

Hornell Armory, 1894–96. Unlike most of Perry's armories, whose drill sheds are attached to the rear of the administration buildings, the drill shed of the Hornell Armory is attached to the side. Historic postcard from the collection of the author.

1894–96   HORNELL ARMORY (FORTY-SEVENTH SEPARATE COMPANY)
              HORNELL (FORMERLY HORNELLSVILLE), STEUBEN COUNTY

---

100 Seneca Street
Architect: Perry

The Forty-seventh Separate Company, comprising militiamen from the Southern Tier's Canisteo Valley, was incorporated in 1891 under the command of Captain Harry McDougall. The unit was furnished with a temporary drill shed in a building at Main and Pardee streets. In 1892 members of the Forty-seventh served during the Switchmen's Strike in Buffalo. The following year, the state appropriated $32,000 for the construction of the new armory. Work on the brick and Warsaw bluestone building was begun in 1894 and completed in 1896. Andrew Douglas of Binghamton was the contractor. Eleven years later, the unit was redesignated Company K and attached to Central New York's Third (later 108th) Infantry Regiment. The facility is still occupied by the National Guard.

Hoosick Falls Armory, 1888–89. Historic postcard from the collection of the author.

Hudson Armory, 1898. Historic postcard from the collection of the author.

1890–92   JAMESTOWN ARMORY (THIRTEENTH SEPARATE COMPANY)
JAMESTOWN, CHAUTAUQUA COUNTY

South Main Street
Architect: Perry

Other armories in Jamestown:
1932   Jamestown Armory, Porter Avenue and Front Street

The Thirteenth Regiment was mustered into the National Guard in 1875. In honor of Reuben E. Fenton, a Jamestown citizen who was New York's governor during part of the Civil War, the unit was dubbed Fenton's Guard.[15] Like several other militia units in the state, the Thirteenth was organized by like-minded men of common ethnicity: in this case, Swedish. Members of the unit even adopted the blue

1898   HUDSON ARMORY (TWENTY-THIRD SEPARATE COMPANY)
HUDSON, COLUMBIA COUNTY

Fifth and State streets
Architect: Perry

The Twenty-third Separate Company was officially organized in May 1878. Twenty years later the unit received a new armory designed by Perry. Remarkably similar to Perry's armories in Whitehall, Tonawanda and Ogdensburg, the Hudson armory featured a raised and battered stone foundation, a tripartite, arcaded entrance pavilion and a four-story corner tower surmounted by a crenelated parapet. In 1900 the unit achieved local recognition for assisting in the enforcement of a smallpox quarantine in nearby Stockport.[13] Much of the armory's drill shed was destroyed by fire in 1921; extensive repairs were not completed until nearly ten years later.[14] Decommissioned by the National Guard during the late 1970s, the building is now privately owned.

Jamestown Armory, 1890–92. Historic postcard from the collection of the author.

Jamestown Armory, 1890–92. The Thirteenth Regiment (later Company E, 174th Infantry) posing in front of its armory. Like the Glens Falls and Hornell armories, the Jamestown Armory features a side, rather than a rear, drill shed. Photograph (ca. 1910s) courtesy of the New York State Military Museum.

and yellow uniform worn by the official bodyguards of Charles XII of Sweden as their distinctive garb. Until they acquired their permanent quarters on South Main Street in 1892, the members of the Thirteenth occupied a series of rented spaces, including Jones's Hall on East Third Street, the old Congregational church at the southwest corner of Main and Fifth streets and the opera house on East Second Street.[16] The Thirteenth (later Company E, 174th Infantry) remained in the South Main Street facility until 1932, when it moved to its new facility on Porter Avenue. The 1892 building was subsequently demolished.

116 West Main Street
Architect: Perry

Several sources indicate that a state arsenal was built in Malone as early as 1812. According to J. W. Lewis in his 1880 *History of Clinton and Franklin Counties*, it "was located in the east part of the arsenal park, near the present residence of Hon. William A. Wheeler. It was a two-story stone building." When the arsenal was sold around 1850, the profits were used to improve a state-owned parcel in Malone that was known as the "arsenal green and parade ground." By 1852 the green had been graded, ringed with newly planted trees and "neatly and tastefully enclosed. . . . This beautiful park is crossed by the Northern Railroad, which here required a deep cutting, but the two sides have been united by a foot-bridge."[17]

Malone Armory, 1891–92. Historic postcard from the collection of the author.

The Twenty-seventh Separate Company was officially organized in 1878. For nearly twelve years, until the completion of its new armory in 1892, the Malone militia met in a commercial block on the south side of West Main Street, between Harrison Place and Academy Street, and drilled on the local parade ground. The company was an immensely popular local entity from its very inception, as evidenced in an 1879 issue of the daily *Malone Palladium*:

> The first really public introduction of our military company to our people was on Thursday last, and the impression it left was of admiration and even enthusiasm. . . . The parade, in the individual carriage of the men, in their handsome uniforms, and in their manoeuvres in column, seemed perfect, and would have done credit to an organization of longer service and more constant practice. Their bearing was soldierly, their drill indicated precision, and they themselves testified to the splendid material which constitutes the company.
>
> The reception at the armory in the evening was among the finest events of the kind Malone has ever witnessed. The reception-room itself, harmonious in decoration and arrangement, was made more tasteful still by festoons of evergreens, drapings of flags, and hanging of pictures. . . . The floor was covered with cotton, and, spotless white, was as attractive as the dancers afterward found it to be suitable for their purpose. Add to this a brilliant illumination, glittering uniforms, and the handsome toilets of the ladies, and the picture was one which compelled admiration and promoted enjoyment.[18]

During the first quarter of the twentieth century, the Twenty-seventh Separate Company (which, by then, had become Company K, Second Infantry Regiment) won acclaim for putting down rioters at the Aluminum Company of America in nearby Massena in 1911 and for marching in the inaugural parade for President Woodrow Wilson in Washington, D.C., in 1913. The unit was also called out to guard the Croton Aqueduct in 1917, when pro-German sympathizers threatened (and even attempted) to sabotage New York City's primary source of water. The armory was vacated by the National Guard in 2003.

Highland Avenue at Wickham Avenue
Architect: Perry

The militia in western Orange County dates back to the War of 1812, when the Wallkill Republican Blues were called to serve in the campaign against the British in northern New York. A second militia unit, the Middletown Light Guard, was organized at some point before the outbreak of the Civil War. The Twenty-fourth Separate Company was officially organized on 17 March 1887. The following year the state legislature approved an appropriation for the construction of a new armory for the unit, and a site at the intersection of Highland and Wickham avenues was acquired on 17 December 1888. Work was delayed for several years, pending the appropriation of additional money. Between 1887 and 1891 the unit occupied temporary quarters in a large local building known as the Casino. When the Casino was destroyed by fire in 1891, strenuous efforts were made to get the building program for the new armory back on track. Their efforts were immediately rewarded: another appropriation was secured, and the cornerstone was laid in October 1891.

"Few days have been as gala in Middletown as October 28, 1891, when was laid the cornerstone for the Middletown Armory," writes Franklin B. Williams in his 1928 history of the city.[19] Participants in the grand parade included units from Newburgh, Middletown, Albany, Patterson (New Jersey) and Walton as well as the U.S. Military Academy Band from West Point, numerous Civil War veterans and the Masons. William Sherer, Grand Master of the New York Masons, laid the cornerstone and a banquet followed at the Russell House. An inauguration ball was held at the new armory on 18 November 1892.

In 1898 the Twenty-fourth became Company I, Second (later 105th) Infantry Regiment. At some point before 1931, the Middletown unit became Battery D and was attached to the 156th Field Artillery Unit. During the Great Depression, the Middletown facility was among the first state armories pressed into service for housing the homeless and unemployed.[20] On 25 November 1931, Governor Franklin D. Roosevelt

Middletown Armory, 1891–92. The Twenty-fourth Regiment (later Company I, Second [later 105th] Infantry) posing in front of its armory. Photograph (ca. 1910s) courtesy of the New York State Military Museum.

authorized use of the armory to shelter several dozen out-of-town laborers who had been stranded in the city when a paving contractor from Long Island, working in Middletown, went bankrupt and abandoned its project. During the next few days, virtually the entire community pitched in to help the guard take care of the abandoned, mostly penniless men, foreshadowing a trend that would persist throughout the Depression era. The building was vacated by the National Guard in the 1970s and converted for use as a radio station.

1891–92 MOHAWK ARMORY (THIRTY-FIRST SEPARATE COMPANY)
        MOHAWK, HERKIMER COUNTY

---

83 East Main Street
Architect: Perry

According to an undated typescript on file at the New York State Military Museum, the first militia unit in Mohawk was formed in early 1878 under the command of Captain Jacob Brazie. By the fall of that year, the unit adopted the name Remington Rifle Corps, in honor of the firm of Remington and Sons of nearby Ilion. The unit was officially organized as the Thirty-first Separate Company on 25 November 1878. The unit's first quarters were above a livery barn on Otsego Street; a few years later they moved down the street to a commercial block owned by Cyrus Woodruff. In 1881 the unit took part in the inaugural parade of President Garfield.

The Thirty-first was among the first units chosen to receive a new armory designed by Perry. The state appropriated $22,000 for the building, and the county donated the land on East Main Street. Similar to several other armories that Perry designed during his early years as state architect, the Mohawk Armory could easily have been mistaken for a civic or large-scale residential building of the period. Vacated by the National Guard in 1971, the armory now houses the local branch of the YMCA.

Mohawk Armory, 1891–92. Like several other early 1890s armories designed by Perry (including the Catskill, Geneva, Niagara Falls and Saratoga armories), the Mohawk Armory originally featured a conical roof atop its corner tower. The conical roofs on all of these armories were replaced with crenelated parapets during the early twentieth century. Historic postcard from the collection of the author.

1888–89   MOUNT VERNON ARMORY (ELEVENTH SEPARATE COMPANY)
           MOUNT VERNON, WESTCHESTER COUNTY

North Fifth Avenue at North Street
Architect: Perry

Mount Vernon's militia was initially organized in 1876 and redesignated the Eleventh Separate Company in October 1881. Seven years later, Mount Vernon was one of the first communities to be awarded a new armory. Like several other early armories by Perry, the Mount Vernon Armory features a small-scale administration building that is more civic than military in appearance. In 1900 the unit was among the first to arrive at the scene of the Croton Dam strike and successfully contained the rioters until help from several New York City regiments arrived to force the laborers' surrender. The armory was vacated by the National Guard in the 1960s. It was converted by the city into a recreation facility for senior citizens.

Mount Vernon Armory, 1888–89. Historic postcard courtesy of Gayle N. Carpenter, DMNA.

1895 NIAGARA FALLS ARMORY (FORTY-SECOND SEPARATE COMPANY) NIAGARA FALLS, NIAGARA COUNTY

901 Main Street
Architect: Perry

The first militia unit in Niagara County appears to have been the Niagara Light Guards, which formed in Lockport (the county seat) in 1876. The Forty-second Separate Company was officially organized in Niagara Falls in November 1885 under the leadership of Captain Charles B. Gaskill. As of 1887, the unit was housed in a recently built frame armory on Walnut Avenue. Eight years later the Forty-second moved to its new quarters on Main Street. The armory is still occupied by the National Guard.

Niagara Falls Armory, 1895. When built, the four-story, front corner tower was capped with a conical roof as seen here. During the early twentieth century, the conical roof was replaced with a crenelated parapet that more clearly signified the building's function as a military facility. A similar trend was seen on the Catskill, Geneva, Mohawk and Saratoga armories, all of whose conical tower roofs were replaced with crenelated parapets. Historic postcard courtesy of Gayle N. Carpenter, DMNA.

1898 OGDENSBURG ARMORY (THIRTY-FIFTH SEPARATE COMPANY) OGDENSBURG, ST. LAWRENCE COUNTY

225 Elizabeth Street (at Ford Street)
Architect: Perry

Other arsenals/armories in Ogdensburg:
1858   Ogdensburg Arsenal

This was the second facility built in Ogdensburg for the militia; the first, the still-extant Ogdensburg Arsenal, was built in 1858. Perry's 1898 armory, one of the very few armories built solely of stone (in this case, Potsdam sandstone), is still occupied by the National Guard.

Ogdensburg Armory, 1898. The arcaded front façade of the Ogdensburg Armory overlooks Elizabeth Street, a residential sidestreet in the city. The side elevation overlooks Ford Street, a major east-west thoroughfare. Hence, the side elevation serves as the "main" façade. Photograph (ca. 1898) courtesy of the Ogdensburg Public Library, Dow Collection. Special thanks to the late Persis E. Boyesen, former Ogdensburg City Historian.

Ogdensburg Armory, 1898. Front arcade under construction. Photograph (ca. 1898) courtesy of the Ogdensburg Public Library, Dow Collection.

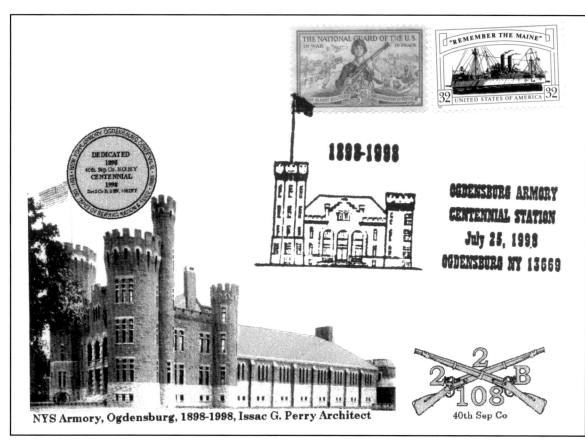

THE NATIONAL GUARD OF THE U.S.
IN WAR · IN PEACE
THE OLDEST MILITARY ORGANIZATION IN THE U.S.

"REMEMBER THE MAINE"
32 UNITED STATES OF AMERICA 32

1898-1998

OGDENSBURG ARMORY
CENTENNIAL STATION
July 25, 1998
OGDENSBURG NY 13669

DEDICATED 1898
40th Sep Co. N.G.N.Y
CENTENNIAL 1998
Det 2 Co B, 2 BN, 108 INT

2 2 B
108
40th Sep Co

NYS Armory, Ogdensburg, 1898-1998, Issac G. Perry Architect

Ogdensburg Armory, 1898. During the 1990s, DMNA hosted a series of centennial celebrations at most of the Perry armories still in state ownership. Ranging from small dedication ceremonies to large-scale parades and lavish black-tie dinners, these celebrations illustrate DMNA's commitment to preserving and protecting these monuments to the role of the militia in American military history. For example, on 25 July 1998, a community-wide parade along Ford Street was the highlight of Ogdensburg's centennial celebration of its armory. Photograph courtesy of the author (bottom, right). Six-year-old Allie Dermont watches as local National Guardsmen gather on the Elizabeth Street elevation of the armory before lining up in the parade. Photograph courtesy of the author (below, left). Fancy envelopes with commemorative stamps were offered to the public that day. Courtesy of DMNA (left).

177

1889–91   OLEAN ARMORY (DRILL SHED ONLY) (FORTY-THIRD
               SEPARATE COMPANY)
           OLEAN, CATTARAUGUS COUNTY

North Barry and North streets (later Times Square)
Architect: Perry

Other armories in Olean:
1919   Olean Armory, Times Square (new administration
                building attached to Perry's drill shed)

The Forty-third Separate Company was organized in March 1887. Shortly thereafter, the unit acquired a large, Second Empire–style residence (dating from the third quarter of the nineteenth century) and converted it for use as an administration building. The unit then received state funding to build a drill shed behind and attached to its new headquarters. About three decades later, the Second Empire building was demolished and replaced with a new administration building to the design of State Architect Lewis F. Pilcher (see chapter 8). Perry's drill shed was retained. Pilcher's administration building and Perry's drill shed are still occupied by the National Guard.

N.Y. STATE ARMORY, OLEAN, N.Y.

Olean Armory, 1889–91. Perry's drill shed is seen on the right in this historic postcard from the collection of the author. On the left is the late nineteenth-century residence that the Forty-third Separate Company converted for use as its administration building.

1891–92 POUGHKEEPSIE ARMORY (FIFTEENTH SEPARATE COMPANY)
POUGHKEEPSIE, DUTCHESS COUNTY

Market Street (at Church Street)
Architect: Perry

The city's earliest militia unit, the Poughkeepsie Invincibles, served during the Revolutionary War under the command of Captain Jacobus Frear.[21] Another early militia unit served under Matthew Vassar. During the Civil War era, the city's volunteers were known first as the Poughkeepsie Drill Guards and then as Ellsworth's Grays. The city militia's first armory, as of 1865, was in an old carriage factory; its second armory was on the upper floors of the newly completed Kirchner Building (1872) on Main Street.

The Fifteenth Separate Company was officially recognized in 1881 and ten years later it received a new armory. In 1898–1899 the unit served during the Spanish American War as Company K, First New York Volunteers. In 1905 the unit was redesignated Company K, Tenth Infantry; it later became Battery C of the 156th Field Artillery. The building is still occupied by the National Guard.

Poughkeepsie Armory, 1891–92 (top). This late nineteenth-century ink-on-linen drawing of the building had, by the late twentieth century, suffered partial deterioration. The linen was painstakingly conserved in 1998 by Marie E. Culver, paper conservator at OPRHP. The original drawing is now in the archives of the New York State Military Museum.

Poughkeepsie Armory, 1891–92 (right). This historic photograph (ca. 1890s) of the parlor in the Poughkeepsie Armory conveys the fraternal atmosphere of virtually all late nineteenth-century armories. Courtesy of the New York State Military Museum.

Saratoga Armory, 1889–91. Historic postcard from the collection of the author.

Saratoga Armory, 1889–91. This undated photograph shows the finely crafted decorative detailing found on the Saratoga Armory. Many of Perry's armories feature such carved stone, molded terra-cotta and/or tile mosaic ornamentation. Courtesy of OPRHP (SHPO, NR files).

1889–91   SARATOGA ARMORY (TWENTY-SECOND SEPARATE COMPANY)
SARATOGA SPRINGS, SARATOGA COUNTY

61 Lake Avenue
Architect: Perry

The Twenty-second Separate Company, initially known as the Citizens' Corps, was formed in Saratoga Springs in March 1878. Between the 1850s and early 1870s, Saratoga County's militia was headquartered in nearby Ballston Spa where, in 1858, a new state arsenal had been erected. It is not clear whether the Citizens' Corps of Saratoga Springs was a completely new unit or a revitalization of the old Ballston Spa–based militia.

During the 1880s, the Twenty-second occupied rented quarters in the Saratoga Springs Village (later City) Hall on Broadway. The cornerstone for the new armory on Lake Avenue was laid in 1889; according to an article in the 25 December 1889 issue of the *Saratoga Union*, the building's design "suggests dungeons and keeps, and portcullis and other thingamies." The building was ready for occupancy in 1891. The armory was partially remodeled and expanded

180

around 1906, eight years after the Twenty-second had become Company L of the Second (later 105th) Infantry Regiment. The most obvious alteration was the replacement of the original conical roof above the front tower with a battlemented parapet. The armory now houses the New York State Military Museum and Veterans Research Center.

Saratoga Armory, 1889–91. This photograph, taken at the 2002 ribbon-cutting ceremony at the New York State Military Museum and Veterans Research Center, shows the crenelated parapet that replaced the original conical roof of the front corner tower. Courtesy of DMNA.

1898–99   SCHENECTADY ARMORY (THIRTY-SIXTH AND
            THIRTY-SEVENTH SEPARATE COMPANIES)
            SCHENECTADY, SCHENECTADY COUNTY

State Street at Crescent (now Veterans') Park
Architect: Perry

Other armories in Schenectady:
1868   Schenectady Arsenal, State Street at Crescent Park
1936   Schenectady Armory, Washington Avenue

Agitation for a new armory for Schenectady's Thirty-sixth and Thirty-seventh separate companies began as early as 1880, when the two units began to outgrow their twelve-year-old arsenal at the east end of Crescent Park. In 1889 State Assemblyman Austin A. Yates of

Schenectady Armory, 1898–99. Side elevation, fronting State Street. Historic postcard courtesy of Gayle N. Carpenter, DMNA.

Schenectady, who also happened to be the current commander of the Thirty-sixth Separate Company, secured a $5,000 appropriation for the repair of the 1868 arsenal. Eight years later, Yates obtained a $60,000 appropriation for the construction of a new armory and the construction firm of Barnes, Butts and Ingalls was selected. The old arsenal was razed and, by late 1899, the new armory was finished, just in time for the jubilant return of Schenectady's militia from the Spanish American War. Upon mustering in for service in 1898, the

Thirty-sixth and Thirty-seventh separate companies became companies E and F, respectively, of the newly formed Second Regiment, which later became the 105th Infantry Regiment. In 1913 federal military officials recommended condemning the 1898 armory, but it was not until more than two decades later that a new facility (located on Washington Avenue) was built. Perry's armory was torn down in 1947.

1896–97   Tonawanda Armory (Twenty-fifth Separate Company)
Tonawanda, Erie County

---

79 Delaware Street
Architect: Perry

Tonawanda's Twenty-fifth Separate Company was established in May 1891 and attached to the Fourth Brigade. The following year the Twenty-fifth joined numerous other National Guard units in suppress-

Tonawanda Armory, 1896–97. Historic postcard courtesy of Gayle N. Carpenter, DMNA.

Schenectady Armory, 1898–99. The armory was demolished in 1947. Photograph courtesy of the Schenectady County Historical Society.

182

Tonawanda Armory, 1896–97. View of the company meeting room at the armory's centennial celebration in 1997. Photograph by David Lamb Photography.

Tonawanda Armory, 1896–97. Detail of front corner tower. Photograph (1996) by the author.

ing rioters at the Switchmen's Strike in Buffalo. In 1894 the unit procured a $32,000 appropriation for the construction of a new armory. Ground was broken in 1896 and the building was completed by early 1897. The final cost of the building was nearly $85,000, almost three times the cost of similar armories by Perry. The formal dedication of the armory took place on Washington's birthday, 22 February 1897, as recounted the next day in the local newspaper:

> The 25th Separate Company opened their new armory . . .
> last night with a very successful ball. Never before have the
> Twin cities [i.e., Tonawanda and North Tonawanda] had
> such a social function as the one last night. . . . Nearly 700
> guests were present. . . . The decorations were magnificent. . . .
> Arranged in festoons and artistically draped throughout the
> entire main hall were more colors, streamers and flags of
> America's colors. There were potted plants, palms and flowers
> about the balconies where the spectators sat, all of which
> added beauty to the already well decorated armory. . . . The
> side walls of the parlor are paneled in silk of a bright orange,

with draperies and decoration of a color to match the walls. The reading room off the parlor is finished in burlaps with Moorish designs. The corridors, upstairs and down, are of bright, buff-colored burlap with hand-painted panels. The captain's office is finished in red cheviot, with [a pressed] steel ceiling. There are red rugs, draperies and richly upholstered furniture to match. The other officers' rooms are done in green burlap of French patterns. There are 30,000 square feet of floor space in the drill hall. The floor is finished in quartered oak and the walls of the administration [building] and drill hall are trimmed with white oak. The drill hall is lighted by six arc lights and 280 incandescent lamps.[22]

During the twentieth century, the unit was attached to the 174th (former Seventy-fourth) Infantry in Buffalo. The Tonawanda Armory was vacated by the National Guard in 2003.

1893–94   UTICA ARMORY (TWENTY-EIGHTH AND FORTY-FOURTH
                     SEPARATE COMPANIES)
            UTICA, ONEIDA COUNTY

Rutger and Steuben streets, Steuben Park
Architect: Perry

Other arsenals/armories in Utica:
1862   Utica Arsenal, Bleecker Street
1929–30   Utica Armory, Parkway East

This was the second of three historic armories built for Utica's volunteer militia, which was organized during the early nineteenth century. First known as the Utica Citizens' Corps (organized in 1837) and then as the Twenty-eighth Separate Company, the city's militia was initially housed in the Chubbuck Hotel and then in the Utica Arsenal (1862). Utica's second militia unit, officially organized 1887, was the Forty-fourth Separate Company. In 1891 the legislature appropriated funds for a new armory for the two units to share; a site was acquired later that year, plans were drawn up the next year and ground was broken in 1893. The cornerstone was laid on 10 October

Utica Armory, 1893–94. Historic postcard courtesy of the author.

1893; the completed building, erected by P. J. McCaffrey of New York City, was dedicated on 22 October 1894.[23] A lavish inaugural ball was held in February 1895. As reported in the local press,

such a brilliant ball as that given by the Utica Citizens' Corps [and the Forty-fourth] Separate Company . . . has not before been seen in Utica. . . . Were they not celebrating their deliverance from that Egypt of Bleecker Street and their occupation of the promised land of Steuben Park? At last they had realized their hopes and were at home in a brand new building, complete in all appointments and an ornament to the city in which it stands. The drill hall of the new armory has no peer in Central New York.[24]

Utica Armory, 1893–94. Forty-fourth Separate Company posing in its drill shed. Photograph (ca. 1910s) courtesy of the New York State Military Museum.

During their tenure in the Steuben Park armory, the Twenty-eighth (Company A, later Company L) and the Forty-fourth (Company B) served during the Spanish American War, and in 1916 they were called upon to serve during the Mexican border disputes. Two years later they were mustered into service during World War I.

After World War I, both units were attached to the Tenth Infantry, N.Y.N.G. In 1930 Utica's cavalrymen moved to a new facility on Parkway East. Utica's infantry militia remained in the facility until the early 1950s; shortly thereafter, Perry's armory was razed by the city to make way for a parking lot.

1895–96   WALTON ARMORY (THIRTY-THIRD SEPARATE COMPANY)
          WALTON, DELAWARE COUNTY

Stockton Avenue
Architect: Perry

Other armories in Walton:
1886   Walton Armory, Stockton Avenue

The Thirty-third Separate Company was formed in May 1879. Seven years later, the unit received its first permanent quarters, a brick building on the south side of the West Branch of the Delaware River on the southern edge of the village proper. It stayed in the 1886 facility a mere ten years, until a new armory was built on the adjacent lot in 1896. Designed by Perry, the new building was constructed by a local contractor named Bussman; many laborers were drawn from the village itself. The trusses were supplied by the renowned Groton Iron Bridge Company of nearby Tompkins County. The brick came from manufactories in Cornwall and Haverstraw, and the stone for the building's trim was obtained from the James Nivins and Sons quarry in East Walton. The armory was dedicated in September 1896 in a lavish ceremony attended by visiting militia from Oneonta, Middletown and Binghamton. Vacated by the National Guard in 1965, the 1896 armory is currently privately owned.

Walton Armory, 1895–96. The juxtapositioning of the 1886 and 1896 armories in this postcard provides a graphic illustration of the radical differences between 1880s and 1890s armories in Upstate New York. The 1886 building was distinctly non-military in appearance, while the 1896 armory, with its multistoried towers, massive sally port, machicolated cornices and crenelated parapets, was the epitome of a medieval-inspired fortress. Historic postcard from the collection of the author.

Walton Armory, 1895–96. The Thirty-third Separate Company in front of its armory. Photograph (late 1890s) courtesy of the New York State Military Museum.

1899 Whitehall Armory (Ninth Separate Company)
Whitehall, Washington County

62 Poultney Street (at Williams Street)
Architect: Perry

Whitehall's first militia unit was organized in 1876 as the Second Separate Company, also known as the Burleigh Corps, under the leadership of G. Thomas Hall, a locally prominent citizen of the village. The unit was redesignated the Ninth Separate Company in 1877; that same year the Ninth served at the railroad riots in Troy. During its early years, the unit was temporarily housed in the Anderson Building on Main Street.[25] In 1898 the State Legislature approved a $42,000 appropriation for the construction of a permanent armory in the village; the county underwrote the $8,000 cost of the site. The building, lavishly appointed on the interior, was completed in 1899. It is still occupied by the National Guard.

Yonkers Armory, 1890s. Historic postcard courtesy of Gayle N. Carpenter, DMNA.

1890s Yonkers Armory (Fourth Separate Company)
Yonkers, Westchester County

Waverly Street
Architect: Perry

Other armories in Yonkers:
1918   Yonkers Armory, North Broadway at Quincy Place

The first National Guard unit in Yonkers was formed in July 1870; eleven years later it was redesignated the Fourth Separate Company.[26] In the 1890s, the unit received a new armory designed by Isaac Perry. The Fourth achieved recognition as one of the first units to respond to a strike by laborers at the Croton Dam in 1900; along with a unit from Mount Vernon, it contained the mob until several regiments from New York City arrived to put down the rioters. In 1918 the unit moved to a new armory, designed by State Architect Lewis F. Pilcher, on North Broadway and Quincy; Perry's armory was converted for use as a Polish community center.

Whitehall Armory, 1899. Photograph (ca. 1910s) courtesy of the New York State Military Museum.

Chapter 7

Armories Built in New York City between 1900 and World War I

There were seven large armories constructed in New York City between 1900 and 1917.[1] Four, including the Sixty-ninth Regiment Armory in Manhattan, the Troop C Armory in Brooklyn, the Franklin Avenue Armory in the Bronx and the Fort Washington Avenue Armory in Manhattan, rejected the castellated style and, at least momentarily, appeared to foreshadow radically new trends in armory construction. Three, including the First Battery Armory in Manhattan, the Seventy-first Regiment Armory in Manhattan and the Kingsbridge Armory in the Bronx, reflected the persistence of the castellated style. In addition to these new constructions, two older armories in Brooklyn, the Clermont Avenue Armory (1873) and the Dean Street Armory (ca. 1884), received significant modifications during the second decade of the twentieth century.

These seven armories are among nearly forty armories that were built in New York State during the first four decades of the twentieth century. The forty post-1900 armories can be divided into three general categories: large armories built for full regiments, batteries or squadrons in New York City from 1900 to 1917; small armories built for separate companies or individual troops in Upstate New York between 1900 and 1919 and designed by state architects George L. Heins, Franklin B. Ware or Lewis F. Pilcher; and armories built either for regiments in New York City or for separate companies in Upstate New York during the 1920s and 1930s. The latter two categories will be treated separately in the remaining chapters, although several generalizations can be stated about the similarities and differences between the forty early twentieth-century armories and their late nineteenth-century counterparts.

In terms of similarities, twentieth-century armories continued to serve as military headquarters, luxurious clubhouses and reminders of military strength and governmental presence. Like pre-1900 armories, post-1900 armories consisted of administration buildings with attached drill sheds and all were of masonry construction. Sources of funding and building oversight also remained the same: most New York City armories were financed and controlled by the New York City Armory Board, while non–New York City facilities remained the responsibility of the New York State Armory Board. Designers of armories in New York City were most often selected through open competitions, while armories outside of the city were designed by a state architect appointed by the governor.[2]

The main differences between late nineteenth- and early twentieth-century armories relate to methods of construction and architectural design and decoration. All pre-1900 armories were of load-bearing masonry construction. Most early twentieth-century armories employed state-of-the-art construction and engineering techniques, primarily structural steel framing sheathed with brick or stone veneers. As a group, late nineteenth-century armories are a relatively homogeneous collection of richly appointed, castellated-style fortresses embodying features associated with the medieval Gothic military mode. New York State's post-1900 armories displayed a considerably broader range of styles and levels of sophistication. Although restrained Collegiate Gothic, Tudor Gothic and Neoclassical buildings predominate, the group also includes retardetaire, castlelike extravaganzas as well as grand, Beaux Arts and sleek, modern Art Deco–style armories.

The architectural diversity among these twentieth-century armories can be attributed to several factors, the most important of which appear to be related to available funding, political patronage and the public's perception of the role of the National Guard. Underlying and influencing these factors was the changing status of the citizen soldiery after the Dick Act of 1903 and the National

Sixty-ninth Regiment Armory, 1904–06. Representing a radical departure from the medieval Gothic mode embodied in most late nineteenth-century armories, the Sixty-ninth Regiment's armory on Lexington Avenue near the Gramercy Park neighborhood of Manhattan was designed by Hunt and Hunt in the classically inspired Beaux Arts style. In 1913 the armory hosted the bold and highly controversial International Exhibit of Modern Art, forever after known as the Armory Show in worldwide art circles. Prior to this show, the centuries-old civilizations in Western Europe and the Far East were the wellsprings of virtually all significant contributions in the fine arts. After the Armory Show, the United States—particularly New York City—emerged as a new leader in the field: in an international context, American-based artists are among the most important figures in early twentieth-century art history. Image (1913) is courtesy of the Walt Kuhn, Kuhn family papers, and Armory Show records, 1882–1966 in the Archives of American Art, Smithsonian Institution.

Defense Acts of 1916 and 1920 redefined the militia as the primary reserve force of the emergent, regular U.S. Army. During the late nineteenth century, when the National Guard was the country's key domestic armed force, the New York State legislature was notably generous with its funding for armories; after 1903 legislators were reluctant to allocate funding to the National Guard until its new role became more clearly defined. Furthermore, New Yorkers were still burdened with the debt of the late nineteenth-century armories and were hesitant to spend more public money on new armory building programs.

More importantly, however, major social, economic and political changes were sweeping across America after 1900. Labor-capital conflict at the national level waned during the late 1890s for several reasons. The lower classes had been effectively silenced by a combination of military force and employers' and society's concessions to the workers' most critical demands. Laws were passed to provide eight-hour workdays, minimum safety standards and the rudiments of health, disability and unemployment benefits. Tenement laws were passed to ensure that adequate levels of heat, ventilation, light and water were supplied in low-income housing. While sporadic, small-scale riots occurred in communities throughout the country during the early twentieth century, incidents of widespread unrest declined dramatically and fear of wholesale class warfare dissipated. Consequently, the need for the militia's services as domestic peacekeepers decreased.

In an effort to reinstate itself in public favor as well as generate revenue, the National Guard undertook several nonmilitary initiatives during the early twentieth century, including promoting its armories for use as civic centers. In his 1907 annual report, the adjutant general remarked that "a more liberal use of these structures for purposes other than military will be a subject for consideration."[3] Although armories had served as community centers on a limited basis for decades, it was not until the early 1900s that they became common venues for a broad range of social and recreational activities. By the 1920s, many armories were used frequently by a wide variety of nonmilitary groups.

Noncastellated-style Armories in New York City: 1900 to World War I

The Sixty-ninth Regiment Armory in Manhattan represents one of the most radical departures from the medieval Gothic mode. Designed in 1903 by Joseph Hunt of the well-known New York City firm of Hunt and Hunt, the Sixty-ninth Regiment Armory displayed a variety of features associated with the Beaux Arts style, which so often influenced the work of that firm. Symmetrical and devoid of any affected medievalism, this armory was anything but a fortress. Writing for the *Architectural Record* in 1906, the critic Montgomery Schuyler remarked that the Sixty-ninth Regiment Armory was "of an entirely different inspiration . . . from any of its predecessors. It seems even to be a protest and token of revolt against them. It is noteworthy by the absence of the conventions of military architecture."[4] Despite Schuyler's praise of this new and refreshing approach to building a "modern armory on modern lines," he speculated that "it will [not] have much influence in inducing future designers of armories to refrain from reverting to their traditional [use of the picturesque Gothic mode]."[5]

The Troop C Armory in Brooklyn also achieved immediate acclaim, particularly in the professional architectural journals of the day, as a radically new type of armory. Designed in 1903 by Lewis F. Pilcher of the New York City firm of Pilcher and Tachau, the facility consisted of a symmetrical, two-story administration building with a massive, Tudor-arched sally port; a large, three-story gym attached to the front corner of the administration building; and a huge, multicomponent stable wing that spanned the south side of the massive, vaulted drill shed. Crenelated parapets encircled the administration building and stable wing. A multistory tower originally graced the southwest corner of the administration building.

The Troop C Armory was also noteworthy as one of the earliest, most progressive examples of a new armory subtype, the cavalry armory. Cavalry and horse-drawn artillery units had always been a part of the militia system. Until the late 1890s, however, cavalrymen had been expected not only to supply their own horses but to quarter them as well at their own expense and at their own facilities. The Squadron A Armory, constructed in Manhattan in 1895, was the first armory intended to house both the cavalrymen and their horses. The difficulties of designing such a building were evident almost immediately, particularly in terms of providing adequate ventilation and other necessities for the animals. Pilcher resolved these problems well in his design for the Troop C Armory. The stable wing was actually a series of separate wings; each small wing had windows on three elevations for cross ventilation while the fourth elevation, attached to the main drill shed, allowed for easy passage directly onto the riding floor. Furthermore, improved engineering, particularly lighter and stronger trusses, allowed for an extremely high drill shed roof with two tiers of clerestory windows, greatly enhancing lighting and ventilation.

The Second Battery Armory on Franklin Avenue in the Bronx embodied the Collegiate Gothic style, which, as the name implies, was most often employed for large-scale educational buildings. Even before its completion, the building achieved national attention in architectural circles. Writing in a 1908 issue of the *Brickbuilder*, Lieutenant Colonel J. Hollis Wells reported that

> the site suggested the effectiveness of vertical masses, and these with a carefully studied sky-line gave the expression desired. . . . The silhouette against the sky, prominent through the building's high situation, has been perhaps the most carefully studied element of the façade, and on it the success of the exterior in a great measure depends. In short, its merit is in the composition of its masses of dark red brick with little or no ornament and a sparing use of sandstone.[6]

A 1910 issue of *Architecture* praised the Second Battery Armory as follows:

> [It is] probably the best in the city of New York. . . . The architecture is of a curious and fascinating style; powerful

without being brutal, original without being bizarre. The military thought is at once apparent. . . . The composition is exceedingly picturesque and has not been carried to a point which entails a sacrifice of the dignity so essential in a public building. . . . The complete disregard for symmetry displayed throughout the building is of much interest. . . . It is a building of the very highest interest and originality.[7]

Even as the years passed, the Franklin Avenue facility continued to attract attention; a 1917 issue of *Architectural Record*, another widely circulated professional journal, included an article by Montgomery Schuyler, who called the building "an oasis in the Bronx" and deemed it "virtually the best building in the entire borough." Schuyler praised the new armory as "an exception to the rule of atrocities and violators of common architectural decency" that prevailed in the Bronx at the time.[8]

Castellated-style Armories in New York City: 1900 to World War I

Just as important as the new armories that abandoned the castellated style were the ones that reflected its persistence. The First Battery Armory in Manhattan, designed by the New York City firm of Horgan and Slattery, was a castellated fortress in the mold of Manhattan's Seventh Regiment Armory and Brooklyn's Forty-seventh Regiment Armory. In its design, symmetrical form and restrained embellishment, the armory recalled a number of English and Welsh castles of the fourteenth and fifteenth centuries.[9]

The Seventy-first Regiment's second armory was built on the ruins of its first armory (1892–1894), which had burned to the ground in 1902. The design for this medieval-inspired fortress was approved by the New York City Armory Board in 1903 at the same meeting at which the decidedly noncastellated style designs for the Sixty-ninth Regiment and Troop C armories were approved. The armory was designed by J. Hollis Wells, a member of the Seventy-first as well as an architect in the New York City firm of Clinton and Russell. In an article in the April 1906 issue of *Architectural Record,* Montgomery Schuyler observed:

> [The Seventy-first Regiment Armory is] a particularly good thing. . . . The traditions one finds in full force, all the conventions of the medieval warfare to which distance lends romantic enchantment, contrariwise to the actual and prosaic art of murder. The parapets are crenelated, though nobody is expected to shoot between the crenelles. The cornices are machicolated, though nobody expects to pour hot lead from the machicoulis. . . . The stark brick tower, with its Florentine reminiscence, or even without its Florentine reminiscence, is an oasis in our architecture.[10]

Perhaps the most prominent castlelike armory of this period is the Kingsbridge Armory (1912–1917), built in the Bronx for the Eighth Coastal Artillery District (formerly the Eighth Regiment of Manhattan). Since 1889 the Eighth Regiment had been housed in an armory on Park Avenue in Manhattan, sharing its drill shed with Squadron A, its neighbor on Madison Avenue. In an effort to obtain a separate armory of its own, the Eighth decided to seek affordable land in the then less densely developed borough of the Bronx. A design competition was held, and in 1911 a proposal submitted by Lewis F. Pilcher was selected. In an article published in the *New York Herald* that year, Pilcher reported:

> The design is of the French medieval style. . . . The administration building projects from the front of the armory and in it will be housed the lockers, co[mpany], reception and dressing rooms and regimental offices. It will be 436 feet long, 44

feet high and 44 feet wide, except at the bastions and towers, where it will be 69 feet wide. . . . The main entrance for officers and friends, between the twin 144-foot high towers, will have a monumental vestibule, with space set aside for a memorial hall flanking it. On one side will be a large office for the adjutant and [offices for] his staff [will be] on the other side. . . . Luxuries of club life, with social and athletic features, will also be enjoyed by the envied Eighth Corps in its new home. A fully equipped gymnasium for 1,200 men, with a four lap to the mile running track, will afford recreation, and less energetic gunners will find amusement in the billiard rooms and bowling alleys. The officers' club will comprise a writing room, library and mess. An immense basement driveway, where [twenty] wagons may be loaded, is available also for carriages and automobiles on gala nights.[11]

The catalog entries in this chapter are organized as follows:

Noncastellated:
1904–06	Sixty-ninth Regiment Armory, Lexington Avenue, Manhattan
1903–07	Troop C Armory, Bedford Avenue, Brooklyn
1908–11	Franklin Avenue Armory, Bronx
1911	Fort Washington Avenue Armory, Manhattan

Castellated:
1901–03	First Battery Armory, West 66th Street, Manhattan
1904–06	Seventy-first Regiment Armory, Park Avenue, Manhattan
1912–17	Kingsbridge Armory, Kingsbridge Road, Bronx
1909–11	Dean Street Armory, Brooklyn
1911	Clermont Avenue Armory, Brooklyn

1904–06   SIXTY-NINTH REGIMENT ARMORY (SIXTY-NINTH REGIMENT)
MANHATTAN, NEW YORK COUNTY

68 Lexington Avenue (between East 25th and East 26th streets)
Architect: Hunt and Hunt

The Sixty-ninth Regiment Armory, still housing the National Guard,
was built for the Fighting Sixty-ninth of Civil War fame. The history
of the unit dates back to late 1851, when several separate companies,
including the Montgomery Light Guards, were united under the com-

*Sixty-ninth Regiment Armory, 1904–06. Designed in the classically inspired Beaux Arts style, the Sixty-ninth
Regiment Armory represented a bold break from the medieval-inspired castellated style that characterized New York
State's late nineteenth-century armories. Photograph (ca. 1910s) courtesy of the New York State Military
Museum.*

*Sixty-ninth Regiment Armory, 1904–06. Because of its radically new style and its
design by one of New York City's most famous architectural firms, the Sixty-ninth
Regiment Armory drew the attention of numerous professional architectural journals
of the period. For example, this illustration of the armory's front entrance was one of
many illustrations accompanying a three-part article by J. Hollis Wells in volume 17
(nos. 6, 7 and 8: 1908) of the Brickbuilder (later called Architectural Forum).*

194

Sixty-ninth Regiment Armory, 1904–06. Interior view of the drill shed. Photograph (ca. 1910s) courtesy of the New York State Military Museum.

mand of Colonel Charles S. Roe. Most members of the regiment were first- or second-generation Irish immigrants. The regiment's Company A was singled out by state authorities for exemplary service during the Staten Island Quarantine Riots of 1858. Shortly after the outbreak of the Civil War, the Sixty-ninth Regiment enlisted en masse. After the war, the Sixty-ninth flourished as one of New York's most prestigious regiments throughout the late nineteenth century.

Despite its widespread popularity during the Gilded Age, the Sixty-ninth was the very last New York City regiment to obtain permanent quarters. It is not clear where the unit was housed during the first two decades of its existence but, by 1871 it occupied rooms above Essex Market at the corner of Grand and Essex streets. By the early 1880s, it had moved to "temporary" quarters in the old Tompkins Market Armory (1857–1860) that had recently been vacated by the Seventh Regiment. Along with just about every other New York City regiment, the Sixty-ninth began petitioning the newly created Armory Board in 1884 for a new facility. It was not until 1896 that the unit was able to acquire a site; however, several years of bickering among the unit members delayed the project. Finally, in 1903, the Armory Board approved a design submitted by Joseph Hunt of the New York City firm of Hunt and Hunt. Hunt rejected the traditional castellated style and employed, instead, the Beaux Arts vocabulary, for which his firm was well known. The cornerstone was laid on 23 April 1904; the building was completed in 1906. The consulting engineer on the project was M. Lewinson, the superintendent was J. R. French, the general contractor was J. D. Murphy Co. and the steelwork was done by Milliken Brothers. Writing in 1905, William Francis Stanton Root provided a full account of the building in his history of the regiment:

> The rifle and revolver range, kitchen and mess hall, and boiler-room are located in the basement. On the first floor are the drill hall, offices for the field, staff and board of officers; library and reception rooms. On the second floor are twelve company rooms, memorial hall, veterans' room and balconies. On the third floor are the locker-rooms, each being located over its company room, and reached by a private stairway; hospital corps room and surgeon's room and gymnasium. On the fourth floor are the quarters of the band, drum corps, quartermaster's office and storeroom, toilets and bath rooms.
>
> The drill hall roof is carried by six pairs of three-hinge riveted steel trusses. Each truss has a span of 189' 8" and a rise of 103' 4⁹/₁₆" center to center of pins. These trusses were designed for 50-lb. dead load, and 30-lb. live load per square foot of horizontal projection of the roof, and for 20-lb. per square foot dead load of the skylight, and 20-lb. per square foot of vertical projection for wind pressure. The values give a horizontal reaction of 77,300 pounds at the crown hinge, a thrust of 61,800 pounds, and a resultant reaction of 179,000 pounds at the skewback.
>
> The skylight extends the entire length of the Drill Hall, and has a width of about 40 feet on each side of the centerline, giving a dimension of about 80' x 202'. . . . All floor and roof slabs are of the Roebling standard reinforced concrete construction. All floor slabs have suspended concrete ceilings below them, and aggregate about 70,000 square feet. There is about 55,000 square feet of concrete roofing, which, with the flooring and ceilings, is made of 1: 2¹/₂: 6 Vulcanite brand Portland cement. The large brick arch at the east end of the Drill Hall is the largest in the United States. [12]

Upon mustering in for service during World War I, the unit was redesignated the 165th Infantry Regiment. The facility is still occupied by the National Guard, although its upper stories are used by the city as a homeless shelter.

1903–07   TROOP C ARMORY (TROOP C)
BROOKLYN, KINGS COUNTY

1579 Bedford Avenue (between President and Union Streets)
Architect: Pilcher and Tachau

Troop C, a cavalry unit established in 1895, was initially housed in the North Portland Avenue Armory, a facility built in 1858 as a state arsenal and later remodeled for use by the Fourteenth Regiment. Troop C was mustered into federal service in 1898 during the Spanish American War; two years later it was called into state service to suppress rioting laborers during the Croton Dam Strike. Around 1900 the cavalrymen began lobbying for permanent quarters, and a site on Bedford Avenue was acquired in 1901. The design for a new armory, submitted by the New York City firm of Pilcher and Tachau, was approved by the Armory Board in March 1903. Interestingly, one of the principals of this firm, Lewis F. Pilcher, had very close ties to one of the board's most influential advisors, Professor A. D. F. Hamlin of Columbia University's School of Architecture; Hamlin had been Pilcher's mentor when the latter was a student at Columbia in the early 1890s. The Troop C Armory was the first of many armories designed by Pilcher, who later served as the state architect.

In November 1903, contracts for construction were let to John Kennedy and Son; the building was completed in 1907. In 1904 the troop was expanded and became Squadron C; in 1911 it was consolidated with the state's other cavalry units to form the First Regiment of Cavalry. In 1921 it became the 101st Cavalry. The facility is still occupied by the National Guard.

Troop C Armory, 1903–07. Like the Sixty-ninth Regiment Armory, the Troop C Armory represented a departure from the castellated style. Photograph (ca. 1910s) courtesy of the New York State Military Museum.

Troop C Armory, 1903–07. A three-part article by J. Hollis Wells in volume 17 (nos. 6, 7 and 8: 1908) of the Brickbuilder carried several illustrations of the Troop C Armory, including this detail of the front entrance.

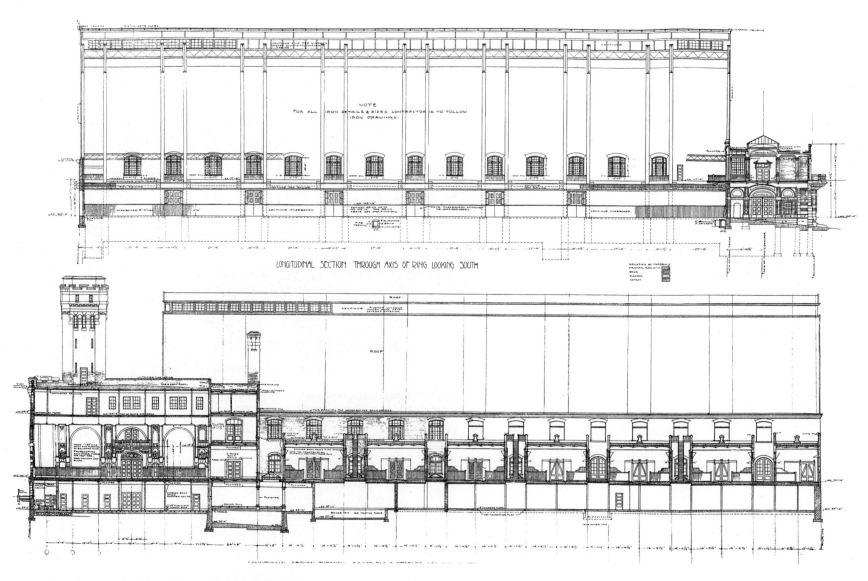

Troop C Armory, 1903–07. The 13 January 1906 issue of American Architect and Building News *carried a series of elevation drawings, including this one (Plate 1568) of the side elevation.*

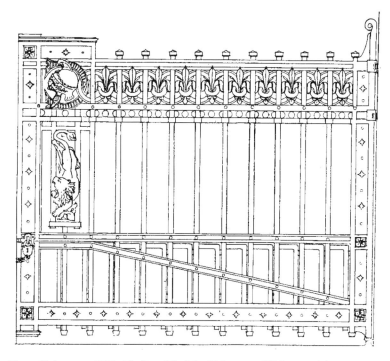

Troop C Armory, 1903–07. Page 15 of the 13 January 1906 issue of American Architect and Building News *offered this drawing of one "valve" of the portcullis across the front door of the main entrance.*

Troop C Armory, 1903–07. This construction photograph is one of a series that accompanied an article in the subsequent issue of American Architect and Building News *(20 January 1906).*

Troop C Armory, 1903–07. View of the squad room/gymnasium at the south end of the administration building. Photograph (ca. 1910) courtesy of the Brooklyn Public Library, Brooklyn Collection.

1122 Franklin Avenue (at East 166th Street)
Architect: Haight

Designed by Charles C. Haight in the Collegiate Gothic style and built between 1908 and 1911, this armory was the first permanent National Guard facility erected in the Bronx. The origin of the Second Battery dates to 1833, when the Washington Grey Troop (Horse Artillery) was first organized in Manhattan. It was attached to the Washington Greys (Infantry), which, in 1847, became the Eighth Regiment. Still attached to the Eighth Regiment, the artillery unit became known as Company I at the close of the Civil War; by 1867 the company had grown large enough to become a full battalion. In 1879 the artillery battalion separated from the Eighth Regiment and was reorganized as Battery E; on 17 December 1882 the unit was redesignated the Second Battery.

While affiliated with the Eighth Regiment prior to 1879, the artillery unit was widely recognized for its service in a variety of riots and strikes, as well as for its distinguished performance during the Civil War. The unit served during the Abolition Riot (1834), the Stevedore Riots (1836), the Croton Water Riots (1840), the Astor Place Riot (1849), the Staten Island Quarantine Riots (1858), the New York City Draft Riots (1863), the Orange Riots (1871) and the Great Railroad Strike (1877).

For several years after achieving independent status, the Second Battery shared quarters with the Seventy-first (Infantry) Regiment in the latter's newly constructed armory (1894) on Park Avenue in Manhattan. When the Seventy-first Regiment Armory was destroyed by fire in February 1902, the infantrymen immediately began planning to rebuild their armory on the foundations of the old one. The artillerymen, however, opted to strike out on their own and moved to temporary quarters at 1891 Bathgate Avenue in the Bronx; two years later they acquired a site for a new facility on Franklin Avenue near the Third Avenue elevated station in the Morrisania section of the Bronx.

Franklin Avenue Armory, 1908–11. Historic postcard courtesy of Gayle N. Carpenter, DMNA.

In 1906 the Armory Board authorized $450,000 for the new armory; the following year, Haight was commissioned to design the building. Construction began in September 1908 and was essentially done by November 1909. An additional $48,000 was provided for equipment and furnishings in 1910 and 1911. The completion date of the building is officially recorded as January 1911, although the battery had moved into the facility in June 1910. Seven years later, the facility was still appreciated by architectural critics: in the February 1917 issue of the *Architectural Record*, Montgomery Schuyler remarked that the armory was virtually the best building in the entire borough, particularly noting that there was nothing "capricious or arbitrary" about the building's structural or decorative features; they were, rather, "organic and essential." Schuyler continued with the following observations:

> The suggestions of "military Gothic" are not overdone, as they are so apt to be in similar erections. They are confined to the crenelations of the parapets . . . and the corbelling of the balcony over the archway of the side. These touches of tradition, denoting the purpose of the building, are perfectly compatible with the fact that the detail throughout is simply straightforward structural modeling which might have taken the same forms if the designer had never heard of a Gothic castle, and is the logical expression of the materials and the construction employed.[13]

In February 1908, the First, Second and Third batteries had been combined to form the First Battalion, First Artillery. The battalion headquarters, along with the entire Second Battery, were housed in the new Franklin Avenue facility upon its completion. In 1917 the former First, Second and Third batteries were once again separated; the First then became the 104th Field Artillery and the Second became the 105th Field Artillery. The Third appears to have languished altogether. The building was vacated by the National Guard in 1988 and subsequently converted by the city for use as a homeless shelter.

1911 FORT WASHINGTON AVENUE ARMORY (TWENTY-SECOND REGIMENT CORPS OF ENGINEERS) MANHATTAN, NEW YORK COUNTY

---

216 Fort Washington Avenue
Architect: Walker and Morris

Other armories for the unit:

| 1863 | Twenty-second Regiment Armory, West 14th Street |
| 1889–92 | Twenty-second Regiment Armory, Western Boulevard |

This was the third armory built for the Twenty-second Regiment, which was organized in 1861. The unit was first housed on West 14th Street in an older building that had been remodeled and expanded around 1863. Its second armory, completed in 1892, was on Western Boulevard. In 1902 the regiment, which had begun as an infantry unit, became a corps of engineers. Five years later, a site in the Washington Heights neighborhood on the Upper West Side was obtained, and the Armory Board approved the designs submitted by the New York City firm of Walker and Morris. The building cost $650,000; including the land and furnishings, the entire project totaled $1,160,000.

Upon mustering in for service at the outbreak of World War I, the Twenty-second Regiment Corps of Engineers was designated the 102nd Engineers of the newly created Twenty-seventh Division. During the late 1980s and early 1990s, the armory served as a shelter for the homeless; more recently, it was acquired by the city and converted into a multipurpose recreational facility for the community.

Fort Washington Avenue Armory, 1911. Like numerous armories in New York City, the Fort Washington Avenue Armory served as a homeless shelter in the 1980s and 1990s. In some cases, city officials leased space in the armories; in other cases, DMNA vacated entire facilities and turned them over to the city. Photograph (1996) by Merrill E. Hesch, OPRHP.

Fort Washington Avenue Armory, 1911. Unidentified clipping courtesy of the New York State Military Museum.

Fort Washington Avenue Armory, 1911. Interior lighting fixture in the lobby of the armory. Photograph (1996) by Merrill E. Hesch, OPRHP.

56 West 66th Street
Architect: Horgan and Slattery

The First Battery, a mounted artillery unit, was organized on 3 April 1867 as Battery K, First Regiment of Artillery. After 10 December 1869, the unit was known as Separate Battery K; in 1881 it was officially redesignated the First Battery. Commanded initially by a Captain Heubner and, later, by Captain Louis Wendel, the unit was predominantly German American in composition, with its own Teutonic-inspired traditions and uniforms. The unit was unofficially known as Wendel's Battery in deference to its long-term leader. The first known quarters of the unit were at 334–346 West 44th Street in a building above a saloon managed by Wendel; during this period, the battery served in the Orange Riots of 1871, the Great Railroad Strike of 1877 and the Brooklyn Trolley Strike of 1895.[14]

Wendel, who commanded the battery between 1881 and 1907, was among the most colorful and shady characters who populated the New York National Guard during the late nineteenth century. Intimately connected to Mayor Robert A. Van Wyck of Tammany Hall's notorious Democratic Party machine, Wendel was an infamous Nineteenth Ward politician who also owned a saloon and operated hotels, picnic grounds and other "places of amusement." Wendel was instrumental in getting the new armory built for the First Battery. He began petitioning the armory board for a new facility in 1884; in March 1896, the board purchased seven city lots on West 66th Street for the unit. Plans were almost immediately drawn up by the firm of Horgan and Slattery (Tammany Boss Van Wyck's controversial "City Architects"), but board members resisted accepting the firm's design until they were forced to do so in 1900.[15] Contracts for construction were awarded to Luke A. Burke, low bidder at $170,900, the following year. Work began on 23 May 1901. Although supposedly complete by May 1903, the armory was not officially opened until February 1904.

The influence of the medieval Gothic mode is reflected in the building's crenelated parapets, machicolated cornices and projecting towers and bastions. Like the Seventh Regiment Armory, the First Battery Armory is symmetrical in form and restrained in ornamentation, thus distinguishing it from the more flamboyant, late nineteenth-century castellated fortresses. As described in the New York City Landmarks Preservation Commission's designation report, the armory is like a "castle dressed up for a tournament, playful rather than severe, engaging rather than intimidating."[16]

Major John F. O'Ryan, an engineer and West Point graduate, took control of the still predominantly German unit after Wendel's departure in 1907 amid great scandal.[17] Major O'Ryan, an ardent supporter of the types of reforms occurring at the federal level in the wake of the Dick Act of 1903, transformed the battery into a top-notch, modern National Guard unit, particularly after 1908, when it joined the Second Battery of the Bronx and the Third Battery of Brooklyn to form the First Battalion, Field Artillery. By 1910 battalion headquarters were located at the Second Battery's newly built armory on Franklin Avenue in the Bronx. In 1917 the First Battalion was disbanded; the former First Battery was revived as the 104th Field Artillery, the Second was revived as the 105th Field Artillery and the Third seems to have been phased out altogether. At some point, the armory served as headquarters of the 102nd Medical Regiment; subunits of this regiment included hospital and ambulance companies in Binghamton, Corning and Ticonderoga. In 1976 the building was decommissioned by the National Guard and converted by the American Broadcasting Company (ABC) for use as a television studio.

*First Battery Armory, 1911.
Photograph (ca. 1910s)
courtesy of the New York
State Military Museum.*

First Battery Armory, 1911. Because batteries and cavalry troops used horses, the floors of their drill sheds were of dirt rather than wood. Photograph (ca. 1910s) courtesy of the New York State Military Museum.

Park Avenue between East 33rd and East 34th streets
Architect: Clinton and Russell

Other armories for the unit:
1892–94   Seventy-first Regiment Armory, Park Avenue

Since 1894 the Seventy-first Regiment (established in 1850) had been housed in an armory on Park Avenue. This building was destroyed by fire in 1902, and plans for the construction of a new armory were undertaken immediately. Although officially designed by the New York City firm of Clinton and Russell, the building was actually the creation of Lieutenant Colonel J. Hollis Wells, a member of the Seventy-first Regiment and an employee of Clinton and Russell. The contract for construction, utilizing a $650,000 allocation, was awarded to Fleischman Realty and Construction Company.[18] The building was ready for occupancy in May 1906. According to an article in the 1906

issue of the *Architectural Record*, the new building was "a particularly good thing. . . . We should be sincerely obliged to [Wells]."[19]

Two years later, an article by Lieutenant Colonel Wells was published in the *Brickbuilder*. Employing rhetoric more typical of the late nineteenth century than of the early twentieth century, Wells contended that

> [an armory] should be so arranged as to be easily protected from the mob. There should be enfilading towers with narrow windows so arranged for rifle fire that streets at or near these exits may be cleared. . . . The roofs of armories should be easy of access for troops, and parapets and platforms should be arranged for riflemen so that they may control all surrounding streets and buildings. . . . If possible, an armory should be equipped with a heating, power and lighting plant so as to be absolutely independent of all outside connections which might be destroyed in time of riot and insurrection.[20]

The armory was vacated by the National Guard around 1971 and was subsequently demolished.

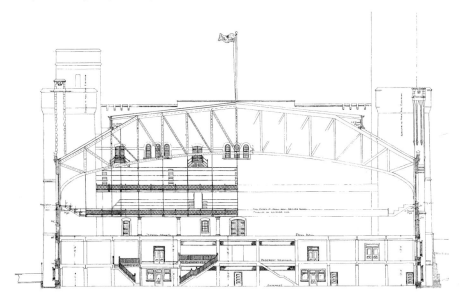

Seventy-first Regiment Armory, 1904–06. A lavish-ly illustrated article about this armory appeared in the 10 March 1906 issue of American Architect and Building News. *Shown here is a cross-section drawing of the building.*

Seventy-first Regiment Armory, 1904–06. Photograph (ca. 1910s) courtesy of the New York State Military Museum.

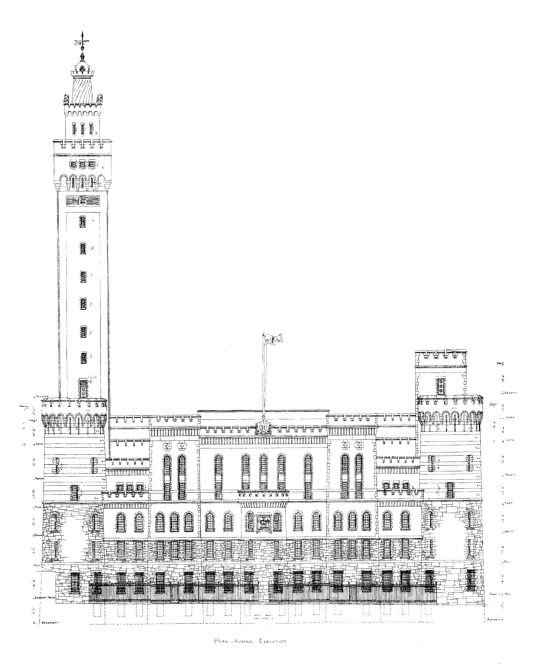

PARK AVENUE ELEVATION

Seventy-first Regiment Armory, 1904–06. This drawing of the Park Avenue elevation of the armory appeared in the 10 March 1906 issue of American Architect and Building News.

1912–17   Kingsbridge Armory (Eighth Coastal Artillery District)
Bronx, Bronx County

29 Kingsbridge Road (between Jerome and Reservoir avenues)
Architect: Pilcher and Tachau

Other armories for the unit:
1888–89   Eighth Regiment Armory, Park Avenue (Manhattan)

The origin of the Eighth Coastal Artillery District dates back to the Washington Greys, an infantry militia unit established in Manhattan during the late eighteenth century. The Washington Greys formed the core of the Eighth Regiment, which was organized in 1847. In 1889 the regiment (including an artillery unit that later became the Second Battery), acquired a new armory on Park Avenue in Manhattan. In 1895 an administration building for the newly formed Squadron A was attached to the rear (Madison Avenue) elevation of the Eighth's drill shed, and the two units were expected to share the joint hall. Within a few years, however, the cavalry squadron expanded into a full troop (Troop A), and the Eighth converted from infantry to artillery. The already cramped drill hall proved woefully inadequate for either unit, and the cavalrymen petitioned the Armory Board for a new facility of their own.

Much to the chagrin of Troop A, the board responded by authorizing the Eighth to build a new armory. During the next several years, members of the Eighth opted to relocate to the more affordable borough of the Bronx and finally obtained a large site comprising sixty city lots on Kingsbridge Road. (At the time, the site embraced the lower portion of the Jerome Park Reservoir, which was then owned by the New York City Department of Water Supply, Gas and Electricity.)

In March 1911 the New York City firm of Pilcher and Tachau was awarded the commission to design the Eighth's new armory. Construction was begun in 1912 and the Norman-inspired fortress was completed in 1917. Occupying nearly three full city blocks, the armory is the largest pre–World War II armory in America. The drill shed alone measures approximately 300 by 600 feet; it is more than three

Kingsbridge Armory, 1912–17. By far the largest armory built in New York State, the Kingsbridge Armory filled three city blocks in the Bronx. Pictured here is a detail of the front façade. Photograph (ca. 1980s) courtesy of OPRHP (SHPO, NR files).

Kingsbridge Armory, 1912–17. An unidentified man performs acrobatics on a truss while the armory was under construction. Photograph (ca. 1910s) courtesy of the New York State Military Museum.

times the size of many of New York State's regimental armories and twelve to fifteen times larger than most separate company armories.

On 10 August 1914, the Eighth Coastal Artillery District was redesignated the Eighth Coast Defense Command. Subsequently, the unit was converted into a motorized field artillery unit and, on 11 October 1921, officially designated as the 258th Field Artillery. The armory was decommissioned in 1996 and turned over to New York City for use as a homeless shelter; its fate remains in question, particularly because of its extensively deteriorated condition and enormous size.

1909–11 DEAN STREET ARMORY (SECOND SIGNAL CORPS)
         BROOKLYN, KINGS COUNTY

793–801 Dean Street
Architect: attributed to Robinson and Kunst

In its current form, the Dean Street Armory reflects the extensive alterations carried out between 1909 and 1911, when it was remodeled for use by the Second Signal Corps. The building is believed to have been designed by Robert Dixon and built around 1884 for the Third (Gatling) Battery. Virtually nothing of the 1884 armory survives; furthermore, no records have been found to suggest its original appearance.

The Third (Gatling) Battery evolved out of the Third Battery, a light artillery unit organized in 1864 and armed with howitzers. During its early years of existence, the Third Battery was housed in the old state arsenal (1858) on North Portland Avenue. In 1875 the battery turned in its howitzers for new, state-of-the-art Gatling guns and officially became the Third (Gatling) Battery. The battery, with a full array of horses and equine-related equipment, was subsequently assigned quarters in the Henry Street Armory (1858), which had just been vacated by the Thirteenth Regiment. In early 1882, seven years after the battery moved in, the city sold the Henry Street Armory to a private concern; evicted from the premises, the artillerymen relocated to Gothic Hall, a decrepit old building used by Brooklyn's militia since the 1830s. In December 1882, Gothic Hall burned to the ground. The homeless battery was reassigned temporarily to a portion of the old North Portland Avenue Armory, which had been expanded and remodeled around 1878 for use by the Fourteenth Regiment. The battery then set out to obtain permanent quarters of its own; in 1883 the Board of Supervisors of Kings County purchased a plot of ground on Dean Street between Washington and Grand avenues in Brooklyn's Prospect Heights neighborhood; by 1884 the new armory was ready for occupancy.

For reasons unknown, the battery appears to have left its new Dean Street facility around 1895 and moved into the old Clermont Avenue Armory, which had been built in 1872–1873 for the Twenty-third Regiment. (The Twenty-third vacated the Clermont Avenue Armory in 1895 and moved into its new facility on Bedford Avenue.) It is not clear how the Dean Street facility was used between 1895 and around 1909, when the building was extensively altered for use by the Second Signal Corps. The early twentieth-century renovations are believed to have been designed by Robinson and Kunst, the New York City firm that remodeled and expanded the Seventh Regiment Armory on Park Avenue (Manhattan) in 1909–1914. The armory was vacated by the National Guard around 1964 and has since housed a variety of local private and public concerns.

Dean Street Armory, 1909–11. Originally built for the Third (Gatling) Battery in 1884, the Dean Street Armory was remodeled in 1909–11 for the Second Company Signal Corps. Photograph (ca. 1910s) courtesy of the New York State Military Museum.

Clermont Avenue Armory, 1911. Originally an elegant, Second Empire edifice built in 1873 for the Twenty-third Regiment (see chapter 3), the Clermont Avenue Armory was extensively altered in 1911 to house the Third (Gatling) Battery. Photograph (ca. 1910s) courtesy of the Brooklyn Public Library, Brooklyn Collection.

1911   CLERMONT AVENUE ARMORY (FIRST BATTALION OF FIELD
           ARTILLERY)
        BROOKLYN, KINGS COUNTY

171 Clermont Avenue (between Myrtle and Willoughby avenues)
Architect: unknown

This armory was originally built in 1873 for the Twenty-third Regiment, which used it until moving to its new armory on Bedford Avenue in 1895. When the Twenty-third moved out, the facility was assigned to the Third (Gatling) Battery, which had previously been housed in the Dean Street Armory.

In 1908 the Third Battery was consolidated with the First Battery of Manhattan and the Second Battery of the Bronx to form the First Battalion of Field Artillery. Three years later, on 26 June 1911, the New York City Armory Board appropriated $150,000 for the "remodeling and reconstruction" of the Clermont Avenue facility for continued use by subgroups of the battalion.[21]

In 1917 the battalion was disbanded; the former First Battery became the 104th Field Artillery, the former Second Battery became the 105th Field Artillery and the former Third Battery seems to have disappeared altogether. The armory was vacated by the National Guard around 1965; after serving several ill-fated private ventures, the building was abandoned. As of the late 1990s, the facility was still vacant and in extremely dilapidated condition.

Members of the First Company, Signal Corps, pose for a photographer while preparing a meal in the kitchen of the Binghamton Armory. Built in 1904–06, the Binghamton Armory was one of eleven armories designed by State Architect George L. Heins during the first decade of the twentieth century. Heins was succeeded by State Architect Franklin B. Ware, who designed one armory in 1909–10, and State Architect Lewis F. Pilcher, who designed seven armories during the second decade of the twentieth century. Photograph (ca. 1910s) courtesy of the New York State Military Museum.

Chapter 8
Armories Built in Upstate New York between 1900 and World War I

Most armories built in Upstate New York between 1900 and ca. 1919 reflect the persistence of the castellated style. This group includes approximately twenty armories, all of which were built by state architects appointed by the governor. More than half were designed by George L. Heins during the first decade of the new century. Franklin B. Ware, Heins's successor, designed only one armory during his tenure. Lewis F. Pilcher, who succeeded Ware and served during the second decade of the century, designed seven armories, three of which introduced a new building type in Upstate New York, the cavalry armory. In terms of scale and architectural design and decoration, the armories of Heins, Ware and Pilcher varied dramatically, even though most of them embodied many elements of the medieval Gothic mode popularized during the late nineteenth century.

New York's Office of the State Architect

The origin of the state's Department of Architecture, officially created in 1914, dates to the early 1880s. In 1883 reform-minded Governor Grover Cleveland appointed Isaac G. Perry to oversee ongoing construction programs at the state capitol. By the mid- to late 1880s, Perry was given the responsibility of overseeing all state building programs. Although officially entitled Capitol Commissioner, Perry was commonly referred to as State Architect. Governor Cleveland and his Republican successors (governors David B. Hill, Roswell P. Flower and Levi P. Morton) began the long process of modernizing Perry's office and many other state agencies by introducing the political ideals of the Progressive movement. The old system of patronage, in which

public servants were appointed to office according to favoritism, began to be replaced with a system of professional bureaucracy, in which jobs were filled according to merit. Perry's integrity, honesty and professional expertise complemented the ruling party's goals and justified the continued expansion and prestige of the office. When Perry retired in 1899, Governor Theodore Roosevelt appointed George L. Heins to replace him and, via a legislative act, officially created the Office of the State Architect. Heins, educated at the Massachusetts Institute of Technology and in architectural partnership with Christopher LaFarge since 1886, was well known for the many churches he designed throughout the Northeast during the late nineteenth century. Heins remained in state service for eight years, serving under Republican governors Odell, Higgins and Hughes. Like Perry, Heins enjoyed an unblemished career as an honest public servant and a talented professional architect.

When Heins died in October 1907, Governor Hughes appointed Franklin B. Ware to succeed him. Ware graduated from Columbia University's School of Architecture in 1894 and entered into practice with his father, James E. Ware, in New York City. (In 1886–1887, Ware Sr. designed the Twelfth Regiment Armory in Manhattan.) Shortly before Hughes gave up his gubernatorial position in October 1910 to join the U.S. Supreme Court, the younger Ware designed his one and only state armory. The remaining two years of Ware's five-year service as state architect were tainted by scandals associated with state politics during the tenure of Democratic Governor John A. Dix (elected November 1910). Ware was removed from office in April 1912 despite the lack of any credible evidence of personal corruption. Governor Dix appointed Herman Hoefer, the hand-picked candidate of powerful New York City Democrats, as Ware's replacement. Hoefer, about whom little is known, designed no armories during his tenure.

In November 1912, Democrat William Sulzer won the gubernatorial election. He brought with him a well-established and "worthy record of accomplishment for social, economic and political reforms."[1] Upon taking office in January 1913, Governor Sulzer discovered that many of the state's departments were at best disorganized and inefficient; at worst they were corrupt. An investigation of the Office of the State Architect "disclosed graft and loose business practices."[2] Hoefer was removed from office in February 1913 and replaced by Lewis Pilcher. Educated at Columbia University's School of Architecture, Pilcher was an architect in private practice who had gained renown during the first decade of the twentieth century in New York City. In particular, he had won much acclaim for his design for the Troop C Armory (1903) in Brooklyn. During his ten-year service as state architect, Pilcher was responsible for the design of seven armories in Upstate New York, the last of which was completed in 1919.[3] When Pilcher retired in 1923, his former teacher and mentor, Professor A. D. F. Hamlin of Columbia University, published a lengthy, eulogistic article in the *Architectural Record* that credited Pilcher with salvaging the state's Department of Architecture in the wake of "the political manipulators and grafters [who controlled] what they regarded as a rich barrel of patronage, influence and boodle."[4]

The Motivation behind Armory Construction between 1900 and World War I

In addition to events occurring in state politics, a number of social and economic trends at the state and federal levels influenced armory building programs during the early twentieth century. Sporadic strikes broke out in communities across the state during the early twentieth century, but they were little more than short-term disruptions to the generally smoothly operating capitalist economy. When civil unrest erupted, the National Guard continued to lead or assist local authorities in restoring order, despite the ill-defined role of the militia in the wake of the 1903 Dick Act. For example, militia units from Yonkers and Mount Vernon, augmented by several New York City regiments, were summoned to disperse rioting laborers at the Croton Dam in 1900. Several companies of the Tenth Battalion in Albany were called out in 1901 to assist local authorities during a violent trolley strike by employees of the United Traction Company. Separate companies from Saratoga Springs, Glens Falls and Whitehall, and eventually the entire 105th Infantry, served along the Albany–Lake George rail corridor during the Hudson Valley Railroad Strike in 1902.[5] Eight years later, the 105th served in Corinth, South Glens Falls and Fort Edward during a strike by employees of the International Paper Company. Farther north, a number of local militia units, including Malone's Twenty-seventh Separate Company, Watertown's Thirty-ninth Separate Company and Ogdensburg's Thirty-fifth Separate Company, performed strike duty at the Aluminum Company of America in nearby Massena in 1911. Militia units in the central part of the state were sent to restore order during strikes at New York Mills in 1912. In the adjutant general's annual report of 1905, excerpts from a survey conducted by inspectors from the U.S. Army praised New York's militia units for their "reliability in domestic emergencies" and their continued usefulness "in quelling labor riots."[6] As evidenced by the generous funding allocated to armory construction between 1900 and America's entry into World War I, New York's citizen soldiers continued to enjoy political support even as changes at the federal level began to erode the preeminence of the militia in the nation's armed forces.

The Architectural Design and Decoration of Armories by Heins, Ware and Pilcher

George L. Heins

Heins, who designed nine new armories and remodeled two older armories, carried on the traditions of his predecessor, Isaac Perry, usually blending features of the Gothic with the Romanesque Revival styles.[7] Like Perry's later armories, many of Heins's armories featured polychromatic masonry construction, arcaded entrance pavilions and overall asymmetry accentuated by multistoried corner towers, although Heins favored octagonal rather than round towers. Unlike Perry, who employed load-bearing masonry construction, Heins used modern architectural and engineering techniques such as structural steel support systems sheathed with brick and stone veneers. Like Perry, Heins decorated the interiors of his armories with elaborate oak woodwork. However, Heins's decorations were more simply rendered, in keeping with the Arts and Crafts taste that replaced the more flamboyant Victorian vocabulary preferred by Perry.

In addition to armories for separate companies, Heins also designed or oversaw the design of two large armories for regiments, the Sixty-fifth in Buffalo and the Third in Rochester. Both were massive, medieval-inspired fortresses dominated by multistoried towers, crenelated parapets and machicolated cornices. Several professional journals, including *American Architect and Building News* and the *Brickbuilder*, gave serious critical attention to the buildings.[8] The popular press, such as *Harper's Weekly,* printed typical boosterism rhetoric. For example, the Sixty-fifth Regiment Armory was declared "the finest armory in the world."[9]

Franklin B. Ware

Ware's only armory, located in White Plains, was a small-scale replica of the East Main Street Armory in Rochester that his predecessor had designed for the Third Regiment. The White Plains Armory was praised in a lavishly illustrated article in the 31 March 1909 issue of the *American Architect*; were it not for Ware's association with the tainted Governor Dix, he might have enjoyed a long and fruitful career in public service.

Lewis F. Pilcher

Pilcher designed seven new state armories between 1914 and 1919; three were built for cavalry troops, three were for infantry troops and one was designed for military educational purposes and used as a centralized training facility for the state's militia. As a group, Pilcher's armories were more modest and restrained in both design and decorative features than their predecessors. As such, they embodied the goals of economy and efficiency espoused by adherents of the Progressive movement. None were ostentatious, romantic or overly picturesque, although most continued to make reference to the Gothic mode. Relatively unpretentious in overall character, these armories featured especially utilitarian interiors. In his 1923 article about Pilcher, A. D. F. Hamlin had nothing but praise for his former student's work:

> I think the prize of hearty and unqualified approval should go to the splendid drill-hall at Cornell University. In this noble building, constructed of the local limestone, the huge scale of the drill-shed is made evident by the contrast of scale in the

openings and in the design of the head-house. The two unequal square towers terminating the main façade, while evidently inspired by English medieval examples like Rochester castle, for instance, are thoroughly practical and modern designs, every detail of which has its *raison d'etre*. The flanks express as clearly as any French Gothic cathedral the structural scheme of the drill-shed with its huge double trusses, and this is also clearly expressed by its exposed ends with their vast areas of glass framed in the outline of the inner and lower members of the end trusses. . . . The interior fully carries out this expression of scale: its vastness is impressive when empty; it is still more impressive when one sees considerable bodies of men upon its two acres of floor space. It is a notably modern achievement in American architecture.[10]

Professor Hamlin was also impressed by Pilcher's cavalry troop armories in Albany, Rochester and Buffalo, primarily because they were relatively clean, modern and functional in design. He called them "severely simple and practical in exterior form and detail. Without any affectation of medievalism and without a single superfluous feature, they are . . . unmistakenly military in aspect, and thoroughly expressive of their function."[11] Unfortunately, these three armories did not incorporate the innovative but costly system of quartering the horses that Pilcher had employed in his design for the Troop C Armory in Brooklyn in 1903. That facility had a series of small stable wings, each housing only a few horses. In Pilcher's later cavalry armories, however, the stables were concentrated under one roof, thereby greatly reducing the cost of construction.

Pilcher's infantry armories in Troy, Yonkers and Olean were smaller and simpler than his cavalry facilities since there was no need to accommodate horses and related supplies. As Hamlin observed in his article in the *Architectural Record*:

> [T]he problem thus becomes that of combining a drill-hall with a head-house containing the company rooms, officers' rooms, lockers, toilets, etc., a rifle-range and sometimes a gymnasium. The simplest of the plans shown is that of the Troy Armory, with a head-house across the front end of a drill shed measuring 206 x 191 feet. . . . The rooms are in two stories and an attic or mezzanine, the locker-rooms and baths being directly accessible from the drill-hall with company and officers' quarters upstairs.[12]

Hamlin was less enthusiastic about the exterior decoration of the Troy Armory:

> [T]he introduction of round towers of the French fifteenth-century type to flank the very medieval entrance gates . . . is evidently motivated rather by artistic than practical consideration. That it is artistically pleasing and emphasizes the expression of military character may be conceded, and to most minds this is ample warrant for the device. The hypercritical might object that it is an archaeological affectation, a bit of stage effect out of harmony with the wholly modern character of the building, and demonstrably unnecessary as a means of expression of function.[13]

The following catalog entries are organized into three chronological groups according to the architect who designed them. Within each group, the armories are arranged alphabetically according to location.

1904–06	BINGHAMTON ARMORY (SIXTH BATTERY AND TWENTIETH SEPARATE COMPANY) BINGHAMTON, BROOME COUNTY

Washington Street
Architect: Heins

Other armories in Binghamton:
1880s   Binghamton Armory, State Street
1932–34   Binghamton Armory, West End Avenue

The Binghamton Armory on Washington Street was built for the Sixth Battery (formed in 1870 and reorganized in 1881) and the

Twentieth Separate Company (established in 1878) to replace the two units' aging facility on State Street (1880s). Heins's design for Binghamton's armory was nearly identical to his contemporaneous design for the Seventeenth Separate Company's facility in Flushing: both featured arcaded entrance porticoes and multistoried corner towers that recall the castellated-style armories so typical of Perry. Units of Broome County's militia used the 1906 facility for about three decades; in 1934 they moved to a newly completed armory on West End Avenue on the suburban fringes of the city. In 1947 the 1906 armory was acquired by the Broome County Technical Community College and converted for use as classrooms. The building housed the college until it was destroyed by fire in 1951.

Binghamton Armory, 1904–06. Nearly identical to the Flushing Armory, also built ca. 1904, the Binghamton Armory appears here in the background of this early twentieth-century streetscape. It is pictured with the Knights of Columbus building, the Elks Club and the Shrine Temple, illustrating the prominent downtown locations, often in the hearts of their respective civic or commercial cores, of many early twentieth-century armories. Historic postcard from the collection of the author.

Binghamton Armory, 1904–06. Members of the Sixth Battery, 104th Field Artillery, pose for the photographer during target practice. Photograph (ca. 1910s) courtesy of the New York State Military Museum.

1902–07 MASTEN AVENUE ARMORY (SIXTY-FIFTH REGIMENT) BUFFALO, ERIE COUNTY

Masten Avenue between Best and North streets
Architect: Heins (with Metzger)

Other arsenals/armories for the unit:

1858	Broadway Arsenal
1884	Sixty-fifth Regiment Armory, Broadway
1932–33	Masten Avenue Armory, Masten Avenue

The Sixty-fifth Regiment, Buffalo's oldest militia unit, was organized in 1818. The regiment's first permanent quarters were in the Broadway Arsenal, built in 1858 and enlarged in 1884. By the turn of the century, the rapidly expanding Sixty-fifth was in desperate need of newer and larger quarters. The new armory, begun in 1902, took nearly five years to complete. It was designed by militiaman and local architect George J. Metzger, in consultation with (and therefore officially attributed to) Heins. Occupying nearly four acres of its nine-acre site, the massive fortress, designed in an eleventh-century, Norman-inspired mode, was the epitome of the castellated style popularized in New York City during the 1880s and 1890s. The Sixty-fifth took possession of the new armory on 26 January 1907.

On 6 May 1931, about fourteen years after the Sixty-fifth was officially redesignated the 106th Field Artillery, the 1907 armory burned to the ground. The fire, which started in the armory's basement, eventually spread to a nearby church and more than a hundred houses; it was one of the worst fires in the city's history. A new facility, designed by State Architect William E. Haugaard, was promptly erected on the foundation of the old armory.

Masten Avenue Armory, 1902–07 (top, right). Photograph (ca. 1910s) courtesy of the Buffalo and Erie County Historical Society.

Masten Avenue Armory, 1902–07 (bottom, right). Covering nearly four acres of land, the massive Masten Avenue Armory sat next to the Masten Park High School (1897; replaced in 1914). Pictured in the foreground is the former Dodge Reservoir. Historic postcard (pre–1914) from the collection of the author.

Flushing Armory, 1904–05. Nearly identical to the armory built for the Sixth Battery in Binghamton, the Flushing Armory was the only armory built in New York City during the first decade of the twentieth century under the purview of the New York State Armory Board. Historic postcard courtesy of Gayle N. Carpenter, DMNA.

The Seventeenth Separate Company was officially organized in 1876, although its roots may date back to the creation of the First Regiment, Long Island Minutemen of 1776. Descendants of this unit include the Hamilton Rifles, also known as the Flushing Guards (organized in 1839). After the Flushing Guards became the Seventeenth Separate Company, the unit was housed temporarily in the old Peck and Fayerweather Store, which was located near Lawrence Street and Northern Boulevard.[14] The Seventeenth's first permanent armory, located on Amity Street (ca. 1884), served the unit until the new armory was completed in 1905. After World War I, the unit was redesignated Company I and attached to Brooklyn's Fourteenth Regiment. The National Guard vacated the building around 1999 and turned it over to the city for use as a homeless shelter.

1906   GENEVA ARMORY (THIRTY-FOURTH SEPARATE COMPANY)
GENEVA, ONTARIO COUNTY

---

300 Main Street
Architect: Heins

The Thirty-fourth Separate Company was organized in January 1880. Twelve years later the unit received a new armory designed by Perry. Ontario County's militia expanded greatly during the 1890s; by the early 1900s, members of the Thirty-fourth were clamoring for new quarters. Rather than authorizing the construction of a new building, the state legislature funded a massive expansion of the old, Perry-designed armory. Carried out by Heins, a huge new wing was attached to the south (side) elevation of Perry's administration building and the east (front) elevation of the old drill shed. Heins's addition echoed the rectangular, hip-roofed form and arcaded façade of Perry's facility, but he added a five-story tower with a bold crenelated parapet that exaggerated the military flavor of the overall design. Heins was also responsible for interior modifications to the 1892 facility. At some point, the conical roof on Perry's 1892 tower (left untouched by Heins) was replaced by a crenelated parapet. The armory is still occupied by the National Guard.

1904–05   FLUSHING ARMORY (SEVENTEENTH SEPARATE COMPANY)
FLUSHING, QUEENS COUNTY

137–58 Northern Avenue
Architect: Heins

Although located in Queens, this armory was a state-funded and state-controlled facility designed by Heins under the direction of the New York State Armory Board. It is nearly identical to several other separate company armories by Pilcher and is thus included in the group produced in Upstate New York during the first decade of the twentieth century. Like the Binghamton, Oneonta and Gloversville armories, the Flushing Armory is characterized by a raised and battered stone foundation, a monumental entrance pavilion and a five-story corner tower, features that reflected the persistence of the castellated style employed by Isaac Perry during the 1890s.

Geneva Armory, 1906. In 1906 the existing armory in Geneva, built in 1892, was greatly expanded with the addition of a large administration building designed by Heins. Attached to the south end of the old administration building, the addition dwarfed Perry's three-bay building with its modest, three-and-one-half-story, conical-roofed corner tower (see chapter 6). Several years later, the conical roof of the old tower was replaced with a crenelated parapet, a trend repeated in several of Perry's 1890s armories, including the Catskill, Mohawk and Saratoga armories. Historic postcard from the collection of the author.

1904–05 GLOVERSVILLE ARMORY (NINETEENTH SEPARATE COMPANY)
GLOVERSVILLE, FULTON COUNTY

87 Washington Street
Architect: Heins

The Nineteenth Separate Company was officially organized in November 1900 and attached to the newly created Second Regiment, which, at the outbreak of World War I, was redesignated the 105th Infantry Regiment. During the first years of its existence, the Nineteenth was quartered in a small hall on the third floor of an old

Gloversville Armory, 1904–05. The administration building of the armory is filled with intact, well-maintained, decorative interior woodwork. Photograph (1997) by the author.

Gloversville Armory, 1904–05. Historic postcard from the collection of the author.

building furnished by the county and located in Gloversville's central business district. In 1903 the state legislature appropriated $50,000 for a new armory for the unit. Work was begun in 1904 and completed in 1905. Virtually identical to the Oneonta Armory (1904–1905), the Gloversville Armory is evocative of Perry's late 1890s armories in its tripartite, arcaded entrance pavilion and its octagonal corner tower. Heins's duplication of Perry's design may be the result of cost-cutting measures favored during the Progressive Era. The building is still occupied by the National Guard.

224

Medina Armory, 1901. Photograph (ca. 1950s) on file at OPRHP (SHPO, NR files).

1901   MEDINA ARMORY (TWENTY-NINTH SEPARATE COMPANY)
         MEDINA, ORLEANS COUNTY

302 Pearl Street (at Prospect Street)
Architect: Heins

The Twenty-ninth Separate Company was organized in December 1891 under the command of Captain A. S. Ross. The origin of the militia in the area appears to date back to around 1830, when a unit called Bowen's Rifles was established under the command of Colonel Hesikiah Bowen. Bowen's unit was succeeded by Linus Beecher's Light Guards, the members of which were housed in a stone building behind the locally popular Walsh Hotel. Beecher's Light Guards later became the Pitts Light Guard.

After becoming the Twenty-ninth Separate Company in 1891, the infantry unit was housed in a temporary armory at 417 Main Street at the county's expense. Medina's only permanent armory was completed in 1901. According to a series of turn-of-the-century articles in the *Medina Tribune*, the land for the new armory was acquired in 1899 and excavation commenced the following year. The contract for construction was awarded to the local firm of Filkins and DeGraff; the final cost of the project was around $57,000.[15] In terms of design and building materials, the Medina Armory is not like the rest of Heins's oeuvre. Most of Heins's other armories are asymmetrical, castellated-style brick buildings sparingly trimmed with stone; the Medina facility is a symmetrical, restrained, Tudor Revival–style building constructed in elegant, regionally quarried Medina sandstone. Six years after moving into the armory, the Twenty-ninth Separate Company was redesignated Company F of Central New York's Third (later 108th) Infantry Regiment. Vacated by the National Guard in the 1970s, the building was converted for use as a community day-care facility and a public gymnasium.

1904–05   ONEONTA ARMORY (THIRD SEPARATE COMPANY)
          ONEONTA, OTSEGO COUNTY

4 Academy Street
Architect: Heins

Other armories in Oneonta:
1885   Oneonta Armory, Academy Street

Oneonta's militia, initially organized on 10 August 1875 as the First Separate Company, was officially designated the Third Separate Company on 8 December 1877. In 1885 a two-story brick armory with crenelated parapets was built at 4 Academy Street for the unit. In 1903 the state legislature allocated $50,000 for the erection of a new armory for the Third Separate Company. The 1885 armory was razed, and work on the new building was begun in 1904; the unit took possession of the armory in March of the following year. Identical to the Gloversville Armory and similar to the Binghamton and Flushing armories, the Oneonta Armory is a clear illustration of Perry's influence on Heins. The armory was vacated by the National Guard in 2003.

New State Armory, Oneonta,

Oneonta Armory, 1904–05. Historic postcard from the collection of the author.

Oneonta Armory, 1904–05. Members of Company G, 107th Infantry pose in front of their armory before serving in World War I. Photograph (ca. 1918) courtesy of the New York State Military Museum.

1906–08   OSWEGO ARMORY (FORTY-EIGHTH SEPARATE COMPANY)
         OSWEGO, OSWEGO COUNTY

265 West First Street
Architect: Heins

Other armories in Oswego:
1835   Old Market House, Water Street
1873   East Side Armory, East First Street

The Forty-eighth Separate Company was formed in 1892. Forerunners of the unit included the Oswego Guards, formed during the early nineteenth century and housed in the Old Market House on Water Street, and the Forty-eighth Regiment, formed during the mid-nineteenth century and eventually housed in the East Side Armory (1873). Six years after being downsized from a regiment to a separate company, the Forty-eighth was attached to Central New York's newly formed Third Regiment, initially formed in 1898 and officially reorganized in 1907. Oswego's new armory, completed in 1908 and thoroughly medieval in inspiration, is no longer owned by the state.

State Armory, Oswego, N. Y.

Oswego Armory, 1906–08. Historic postcard courtesy of Gayle N. Carpenter, DMNA.

1904–07   EAST MAIN STREET ARMORY (THIRD REGIMENT)
ROCHESTER, MONROE COUNTY

900 East Main Street
Architect: Heins

Other arsenals/armories in Rochester:
1836–37   Center Market Armory, Front and Market streets
1868–70   Rochester Arsenal, Woodbury Boulevard
1917   Culver Road Armory

The East Main Street Armory, built for the Third Regiment (including the First and Eighth separate companies and Rochester's naval militia), was one of the largest, most sophisticated armories built in Upstate New York during the period. Thoroughly castellated in style, the edifice drew the attention of several professional journals at the national level. For example, a handsome rendering was published in the 2 February 1907 issue of the *American Architect*. The National Guard vacated the building in 1990 and moved to its newly built facility on Weidner Road. The East Main Street Armory, underutilized and threatened by neglect and deterioration, is now privately owned.

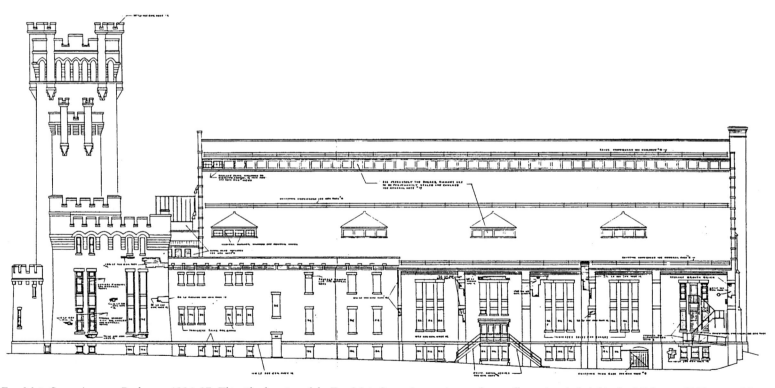

East Main Street Armory, Rochester, 1904–07. This side elevation of the East Main Street Armory is one of many illustrations included in the 2 February 1907 issue of the American Architect.

East Main Street Armory, Rochester, 1904–07. Photograph (1995) by David Lamb Photography.

1906–07   WEST JEFFERSON STREET ARMORY (FORTY-FIRST
          SEPARATE COMPANY)
          SYRACUSE, ONONDAGA COUNTY

236 West Jefferson Street
Architect: Heins

Other armories in Syracuse:
1858–59   Syracuse Arsenal, West Jefferson Street
1873   Syracuse Armory, West Jefferson Street
1941–43   East Genesee Street Armory

This was the last of three armories built on Jefferson Park for Syracuse's militia. The first was the Syracuse Arsenal, built in 1858; the second

was built in 1873 for the Fifty-first Regiment, which, in 1881, was reorganized as the Forty-first Separate Company. In his *Annual Report* for the year 1900, the adjutant general singled out Syracuse's 1873 armory as a particularly decrepit facility, remarking that it was "in need of such extensive repairs that it is believed it will be [cost-efficient] to dispose of it and erect a new building more suitable to the times and military needs of [the company]."[16] Pleas for a new armory were repeated nearly verbatim in the next four annual reports. Finally, in 1905, the Forty-first received a $175,000 appropriation for the construction of a new armory; contracts were let in 1906. The 1873 armory was razed and the new armory was built on the cleared site. Work began in early 1907 and was completed later that year. The National Guard vacated the facility in 1994; it is now privately owned and houses the Museum of Science and Technology (MOST).

West Jefferson Street Armory, Syracuse, 1906–07. Historic postcard from the collection of the author.

West Jefferson Street Armory, Syracuse, 1906–07. Detail of the side entrance to the armory. Photograph (1983) courtesy of OPRHP (SHPO, NR files).

1902 TROY ARMORY (SIXTH AND TWELFTH SEPARATE COMPANIES) TROY, RENSSELAER COUNTY

Ferry Street
Architect: Heins

Other armories in Troy:

1830s	Fulton Market Armory, River Street at Fulton Street
1884–86	Troy Armory, Ferry Street
1918–19	Troy Armory, Fifteenth Street

Originally built in 1886, the Ferry Street armory was expanded and extensively remodeled in 1902 to the design of Heins. This armory was the home of Troy's oldest militia unit, the Citizens' Corps, which, in 1898, became Company A, Second (later 105th) Infantry Regiment. (The 1886 facility also housed the Twelfth Separate Company, which appears to have disbanded during the first decade of the twentieth century.) In 1900 the adjutant general remarked in his *Annual Report* that "for the past two years the Armory Commission has recommended a special appropriation for enlarging and repairing the [1886] Troy Armory. It is understood that the board of supervisors of Rensselaer County are ready to purchase the necessary land on which to extend the drill shed, provided the State will pay the cost of construction. It is hoped that the Legislature will provide the necessary means for making this improvement at its next session."[17]

In 1901 a $100,000 appropriation was made and contracts were let for the project; work was completed in 1902. The new and improved armory, boasted the adjutant general in his annual report for that year, "compares favorably with the best buildings in the state."[18] The armory was destroyed by fire in 1917; a new armory, located on Fifteenth Street, was erected shortly thereafter.

Troy Armory, 1902. The armory was completely destroyed by fire in 1917. Photograph courtesy of the Rensselaer County Historical Society.

233

1909–10 WHITE PLAINS ARMORY (FORTY-NINTH SEPARATE COMPANY)
WHITE PLAINS, WESTCHESTER COUNTY

South Broadway at Mitchell Place
Architect: J. E. Ware

The Forty-ninth Separate Company was mustered into the National Guard in May 1907; two years later construction began on its new armory. With its massive, square central tower flanked by octagonal bastions, the White Plains Armory is essentially a scaled-down version of Heins's design for the East Main Street Armory (1904–1907) in Rochester. Decommissioned by the National Guard in 1976, the armory was subsequently converted into housing for senior citizens.

White Plains Armory, 1909–10 (above). Cannon motifs are fashioned into decorative columns around the fireplace in the southeast corner room of the second floor of the armory. Photograph (1979) courtesy of OPRHP (SHPO, NR files).

White Plains Armory, 1909–10. This artist's rendering of the proposed White Plains Armory appeared in the 31 March 1909 issue of the American Architect.

1914 NEW SCOTLAND AVENUE ARMORY (TROOP B)
ALBANY, ALBANY COUNTY

New Scotland Avenue
Architect: Pilcher

Other arsenals/armories in Albany:
1799   Albany Arsenal, Broadway at North Lawrence Street
1858   Albany Arsenal, Hudson and Eagle streets
1889–93   Washington Avenue Armory

Albany's first cavalry militia unit appears to have been the Albany Cavalry Corps, created during the early nineteenth century. Descendants of the Cavalry Corps include the Third Signal Corps, organized in 1893 and attached to the Tenth Battalion, which was housed in the Washington Avenue Armory (1889–1893). Troop B, which evolved from the Signal Corps, was created in 1902.[19] In 1913

Troop B was attached to the newly formed First Regiment of Cavalry, which had been formed by consolidating cavalry units from Utica, Rochester and Geneseo.[20] Bolstered by its association with the First Regiment, Troop B flourished and outgrew its small quarters in the Washington Avenue facility.

In 1914 Troop B acquired a large lot on what were then the suburban fringes of Albany and erected an armory to the design of Pilcher. It was sold to a private concern in the late 1990s.

New Scotland Avenue Armory, Albany, 1914. Photograph (ca. 1939) courtesy of the McKinney Library, Albany Institute of History and Art, Morris Gerber Collection (1993.010.7475).

Troop B poses behind the Washington Avenue Armory (1889–93), the cavalry unit's first home, shortly before the unit moved to its new quarters on New Scotland Avenue. Photograph (ca. 1910s) courtesy of the New York State Military Museum.

| 1917 | WEST DELAVAN AVENUE ARMORY (TROOP I) |
| | BUFFALO, ERIE COUNTY |

1015 West Delavan Avenue
Architect: Pilcher

Other arsenals/armories for the Seventy-fourth:

1858	Broadway Arsenal, Broadway
1868	Virginia Street Armory, Virginia Street at
	North William Street
1882	Virginia Street Armory, Virginia Street at Fremont Place
1884–86	Virginia Street Armory, Virginia Street at Elmwood Avenue
1896–99	Connecticut Street Armory

Other arsenals/armories for the Sixty-fifth:

1858	Broadway Arsenal, Broadway
1884	Sixty-fifth Regiment Armory, Broadway
1902–07	Masten Avenue Armory
1932–33	Masten Avenue Armory

The West Delavan Avenue Armory was built for Troop I, a cavalry unit formed in May 1912. Buffalo's first cavalry unit, Company R (formed in 1858), was attached to the Seventy-fourth Regiment. Nearly identical to the slightly earlier New Scotland Avenue Armory in Albany and the contemporaneous Culver Road Armory in Rochester, the West Delavan Avenue Armory featured a symmetrical, restrained Tudor Revival–style administration building, a drill shed surmounted by a massive, barrel-vaulted roof with a clerestory and a large, attached stable wing. The unit was later redesignated Troop E and attached to the 101st (later the 121st) Cavalry. The armory was vacated by the National Guard in the late 1970s and turned over to the city for use by its highway maintenance department. The city demolished the facility in 2000.

West Delavan Avenue Armory, Buffalo, 1917. This rendering of the recently demolished armory was drawn in 2006 by Mark L. Peckham, OPRHP.

The Armory, Cornell University, Ithaca, N. Y.

405870

1914–18 ITHACA ARMORY/BARTON HALL
ITHACA, TOMPKINS COUNTY

Cornell University
Architect: Pilcher

Ithaca's militia originated in the early 1800s. The most notable unit was the DeWitt Guards, which, by the mid-nineteenth century, was attached to the Forty-ninth Regiment in nearby Auburn. It is not clear where Ithaca's citizen soldiers were quartered during the early nineteenth century. During the third quarter of the nineteenth century, Ithaca's Cornell University began offering professional military training to future commanders of the militia. For several decades, Cornell used its old chapel for training purposes and produced many notable militiamen who later served in the upper echelons of the New York National Guard. Ithaca's citizen soldiers were allowed to drill in the old chapel.

Thus, Cornell University was a logical location for the state's centralized training armory and educational facility. Completed in 1918, the facility is essentially a giant drill shed with a nominal administration building. In the early 1980s the National Guard turned the facility over to Cornell University; the building, now known as Barton Hall, was converted into recreational space.

At some point during the mid-nineteenth century, Ithaca's militia began to drill in the old chapel on the campus of Cornell University (top, left). Historic postcard from the collection of the author.

Ithaca Armory/Barton Hall, 1914–18 (left). Now used as a recreation center by Cornell University, the Ithaca Armory originally served as a centralized indoor training and educational facility for numerous units in Upstate New York during the first half of the twentieth century. Downstate and New York City units used the Brooklyn Arsenal (1924–26). Historic postcard courtesy of Gayle N. Carpenter, DMNA.

Olean Armory, 1919. Historic postcard courtesy of Gayle N. Carpenter, DMNA.

1919 OLEAN ARMORY (FORTY-THIRD SEPARATE COMPANY)
OLEAN, CATTARAUGUS COUNTY

119 Times Square
Architect: Pilcher

Other armories in Olean:
1889–91   Olean Armory, North Barry and North streets
                     (drill shed only)

The Forty-third Separate Company was organized in March 1887; two
years later it acquired an old Second Empire–style house on Times
Square and had a drill shed (designed by Perry) added to the rear of
the house. The house served as the unit's administration building until
1919, when it was replaced by a restrained Tudor Revival–style facility
designed by Pilcher. The 1891 drill shed was retained; both portions of
the complex are still occupied by the National Guard.

1917 CULVER ROAD ARMORY (TROOP H [LATER F])
ROCHESTER, MONROE COUNTY

145 Culver Road
Architect: Pilcher

Other arsenals/armories in Rochester:
1836–37   Center Market Armory, Front and Market streets
1868–70   Rochester Arsenal, Woodbury Boulevard
1904–07   East Main Street Armory

Similar to Pilcher's designs for the New Scotland Avenue Armory in
Albany and the West Delavan Avenue Armory in Buffalo, the Culver
Road Armory features a modest, Tudor Revival–style administration
building, a massive, barrel-vaulted drill shed and a large stable wing.
Troop F, originally organized as Troop H in April 1912, was attached
to the 101st Cavalry Regiment during and following World War I.
Subsequently, Troop F joined with all other upstate cavalry units to
form the 121st Cavalry Regiment. The Culver Road Armory was
enlarged during the second quarter of the twentieth century with
the addition of a third story. The facility is still occupied by the
National Guard.

*Culver Road Armory, Rochester, 1917. Photograph (ca. 1996) by Raymond W.
Smith, OPRHP.*

239

1918–19   TROY ARMORY
TROY, RENSSELAER COUNTY

Fifteenth Street, Rensselaer Polytechnic Institute
Architect: Pilcher

Other armories in Troy:

1830s	Fulton Market Armory, River Street at Fulton Street
1884–86	Troy Armory, Ferry Street
1902	Troy Armory, Ferry Street

This facility was built to replace the 1902 Ferry Street armory that burned in 1917. Between 1919 and 1936, the 105th (formerly Second) Infantry Regiment was headquartered here. The administration building's façade, dominated by two massive, Norman-inspired entrance towers, recalls Pilcher's slightly earlier design for the Kingsbridge Armory in the Bronx, executed during the architect's tenure in private practice in New York City during the early twentieth century. The National Guard vacated the armory in 1971 and sold it to nearby Rensselaer Polytechnic Institute, which converted it for use as an athletic and recreational facility.

Troy Armory, 1918–19. Historic postcard from the collection of the author.

Troy Armory, 1918–19. Detail of towers at front entrance. Photograph (1995) by the author.

1918 YONKERS ARMORY
      YONKERS, WESTCHESTER COUNTY

North Broadway at Quincy Place
Architect: Pilcher

Other armories in Yonkers:
1890s   Yonkers Armory, Waverly Street

This was the second of two armories built for the infantry militia in Yonkers. The first, a castellated-style fortress designed by Perry, was built in the 1890s. The new one, a restrained, Tudor Revival–style edifice designed by Pilcher, was completed in 1918. The National Guard vacated the 1918 armory in 1988, when it moved to its new armory across the street. Both the 1890s and 1918 armories survive intact under private ownership.

Yonkers Armory, 1918. Historic postcard courtesy of Gayle N. Carpenter, DMNA.

This image of the Harlem Hellfighters, a late twentieth-century interpretation of the 369th Regiment in battle during World War I, is part of the U.S. Army Art Collection, managed by the Center of Military History (Washington, D.C.) and licensed to the National Guard Bureau (NGB) for reproduction as part of the National Guard Heritage Series.

Chapter 9

Armories Built in New York State between World War I and World War II

Armory construction in New York State after the end of World War I in 1918 falls into two categories, conveniently coinciding with two separate decades, the Roaring Twenties and the Depression Era of the 1930s. The 1920s saw a significant decrease in new armory building programs and a dramatic increase in the use of existing armories as civic centers. The ten-year hiatus ended abruptly in 1930 with the construction of the first of more than a dozen new armories, most of which were designed by State Architect William E. Haugaard, before the United States became embroiled in World War II in 1941. Of particular note is the 369th Regiment Armory in Harlem, built for New York State's only African American regiment.

Hiatus in Armory Building: 1920s

The virtual lack of armory building programs during the third decade of the twentieth century reflected the post–World War I, antimilitary sentiment of the American public as well as the continued uncertainty of the status of the National Guard in the wake of the Dick Act of 1903 and the National Defense Acts of 1916 and 1920. New York City had the additional constraints of economic factors: the costs of large-scale building programs in New York City, particularly Brooklyn and Manhattan, were simply too high. Of course, labor and materials had always been more costly in New York City, but by the early twentieth century, these costs were astronomical, particularly for state-funded projects that were never intended to generate future profits. Fortunately, most New York City units had acquired relatively ade-

quate, permanent quarters before World War I, and most of these "old" armories were satisfactory in fulfilling the Guard's needs.

Only three militia facilities were built in New York State during the 1920s: the Staten Island Armory, the Brooklyn Arsenal and the Hempstead Armory on Long Island. The largest of these, the Art Moderne–style Brooklyn Arsenal, is a massive, reinforced concrete edifice built to replace the old State Arsenal (1858) on North Portland Avenue in Brooklyn. The Staten Island facility is a retardetaire, castellated-style fortress, while the Hempstead Armory is a symmetrical, restrained Tudor Revival–style building.

The Armory as Civic Center

The building hiatus of the 1920s coincided with the increased popularity of the armory as civic center. Large and small armories across the state were suddenly in great demand by public and private groups in search of indoor spaces in which to hold a variety of civic events. Armories had always served in a limited capacity as centers of community activity. For example, several national musical festivals were held at the Seventh Regiment Armory during the 1880s; a charity fair was held at the Geneva Armory in the 1890s; and the International Exhibit of Modern Art (the "Armory Show") was held at Manhattan's Sixty-ninth Regiment Armory on Lexington Avenue in 1913.

By the 1920s, however, the role of armories as civic centers almost eclipsed their primary function as military facilities. Virtually every armory in New York State served the general public: more often than not, armories were the only civic buildings large enough to host communitywide events, such as traveling circuses, professional boxing matches, trade shows and Big Band dances. For example, Rochester's young veterans of World War I staged a Mardi Gras celebration that was open to the public at the city's East Main Street Armory in February 1921. The party at the armory "was one of the largest, gayest, and most animated dances Rochester had seen. [The chief of police], who had boasted two years earlier that 'all immodest and suggestive dances are prohibited,' could do little on such an occasion, and the 'lack of all modesty in dress of women' prompted him to appeal for help to dressmakers as well as dancing masters."[1]

Professional wrestling exhibitions, featuring the likes of Charlie "Midget" Fisher and Schenectady's "Pink Gardner," drew record crowds at the Thirty-sixth and Thirty-seventh separate companies' armory in the Electric City. The Schenectady Armory also hosted roller derbies, scout-o-ramas for the local chapter of the Boy Scouts of America and auto shows; and the Amsterdam Armory was home to the Hurricanes, the world's champion roller polo club. The adjutant general's annual report for 1930 estimated that 3,389,250 nonmilitary persons used the state's armories during the year; "nearly 10,000 of our citizens use our armories every day in the year."[2]

During the Depression, armories also served as temporary shelters for the homeless. A 1931 issue of the *New York National Guardsman* reported that the Middletown Armory (1892) was "believed to be the first Armory in New York State to be opened for housing homeless or stranded unemployed."[3] On 25 November 1930, thirty-one out-of-work laborers were taken care of by members of Middletown's Battery D with numerous donations supplied by the National Guardsmen and local citizens.

The militiamen themselves often used their facilities to show off their own athletic prowess and entertain local sports fans. Dozens of semiprofessional basketball and baseball leagues composed solely of unit-specific militiamen hosted regular public competitions against rival National Guard units or nonmilitary teams. Units in Gloversville and Whitehall were particularly known for their athletic accomplishments and lively sporting events.

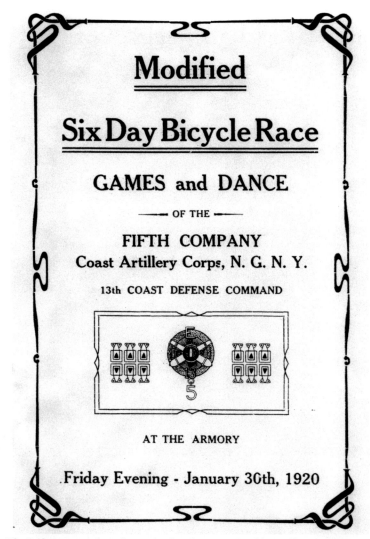

The Fifth Company hosted a six-day bicycle race at Brooklyn's Thirteenth Regiment Armory on 30 January 1920. Program courtesy of the New York State Military Museum.

An indoor bicycle race was held at the Masten Avenue Armory (1902–07) in Buffalo. Photograph (ca. 1920s) courtesy of the Buffalo and Erie County Historical Society.

A boat and auto show was presented at the Whitehall Armory during the early 1960s. Photograph courtesy of the New York State Military Museum.

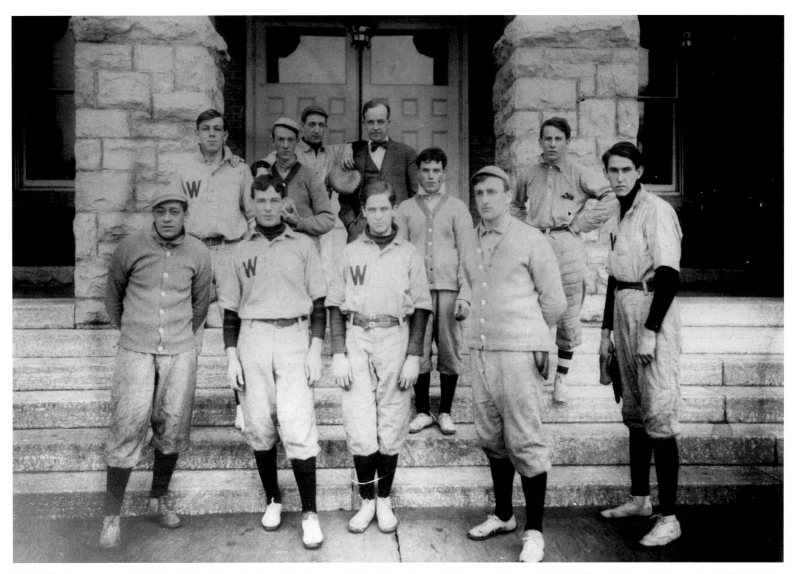

Whitehall militiamen pose in their baseball uniforms in front of their armory during the early twentieth century. Many of New York's units formed their own baseball, football or basketball teams, both for inter-unit competitions or friendly tournaments with rival civic entities, such as local police or firefighter teams. Photograph (early to mid-twentieth century) courtesy of the New York State Military Museum.

The armory as a civic center has been eclipsed by the proliferation of huge arenas and various types of sports complexes; nonetheless, armories continue to be in demand for a broad range of midsize community events. Pictured here is Allie Dermont, enjoying a hands-on exhibit at a traveling children's museum hosted by the Poughkeepsie Armory in 1995. Photograph by the author.

Even more important than providing entertainment, the armory as a civic center engendered local pride and patriotism and renewed citizens' commitment to the welfare of their communities. More than ever, the public began to view the local armory with a sense of personal ownership and renew its respect for the National Guard. This widespread, grassroots support of the militia was crucial to the welfare of the institution of citizen soldiery, particularly after the Dick Act of 1903 and the National Defense Acts of 1916 and 1920 redefined the role of America's militia. Once again, the National Guard was elevated to an exalted position; its renewed popularity would have a profound impact on armory construction during the 1930s.

William E. Haugaard: 1930s

The completion of the Oneida and Utica armories in 1930 marked the beginning of a new wave of armory construction upstate that occurred during William E. Haugaard's tenure as state architect. While in office between 1928 and 1944, Haugaard designed a dozen armories; all manifested the hallmarks of the building type set forth in the Seventh Regiment Armory in 1879. Like their predecessors, armories built during the 1930s consisted of administration buildings with attached drill sheds at ground level. Brick and stone continued to be the primary building materials, although methods of construction continued to evolve with technological improvements. The massive roofs of the drill sheds continued to be supported by exposed steel truss work, although the components became lighter and stronger as well as cheaper and easier to construct. Finally, armories built during the 1930s continued to serve as quarters for local units of the National Guard and as imposing reminders of governmental presence, but they were now explicitly intended for use as civic centers as well.

However, there were notable differences between Haugaard's armories and their late nineteenth- and early twentieth-century counterparts, particularly in terms of setting and architectural design and decoration. Whereas most armories built before World War I had been built on urban lots (or blocks) in densely built-up areas, almost all of Haugaard's armories were built on large lots in sparsely populated suburbs. Now in possession of new fleets of mechanized vehicles, the National Guard needed large plots of cheap land for parking lots as well as ample space for parade practice and the grazing of cavalry and artillery units' horses. The suburbs offered sprawling tracts of affordable land suited for the militia's new programmatic requirements.

In terms of design and decoration, Haugaard's armories cover a wide spectrum of architectural styles. Castellated and noncastellated styles are equally well represented. Traditional examples of Gothic-inspired fortresses coexist with Neoclassical-, Tudor Revival– and Art Deco–style buildings. For example, the Oneida and Syracuse armories are relatively simplified, classically flavored interpretations of the Tudor Revival style, while the Binghamton, Ticonderoga, Corning and Jamestown armories refer more directly to the Tudor Revival idiom. With its towered entrance pavilion, flanking end turrets and long, narrow plan, the design of the Utica Armory was clearly influenced by Pilcher's designs for the Kingsbridge and Troy armories. The Masten Avenue Armory in Buffalo is an exuberant, polychromatic, Tudor-inspired edifice, and the Schenectady Armory reflects the influence of Art Deco.

Still others, including the Kingston, Peekskill and Newburgh armories, all completed around 1932 for subunits of the 156th Field Artillery Regiment, are extremely utilitarian and unremarkable in terms of their overall decorative character. Nonetheless, all three embody the distinctive characteristics of the building type, and each is regarded as an important local landmark.

New York City Armories: 1930s

Two regimental armories were built in New York City in the 1930s, the 369th Regiment Armory in Harlem (Manhattan) and the Fourth Regiment Armory in Jamaica (Queens). Both are fine examples of the Art Deco style. The 369th Regiment Armory is particularly distinguished for its association with New York State's only African American regiment.

The 369th Regiment Armory, built in two stages during the early 1920s and the early 1930s, is a monument to the role of African Americans not only in the New York National Guard in particular but in American military history in general. Founded in 1913 as the Negro Regiment of Infantry and redesignated the Fifteenth Regiment upon mustering into the U.S. Army in 1917, it was the only African American unit in the New York National Guard. The unit was later redesignated the 369th Regiment.

Prior to 1913 a number of separate companies and full regiments had been organized according to ethnicity, but the creation of the Fifteenth Regiment was the first instance of organizing a unit in New York State according to race. Since their arrival in the New World, African Americans had always been a part of the country's military force: first as chattel deemed worthy of only menial chores and hard labor and later as full-fledged soldiers fighting side by side with whites. Clearly, individual blacks and groups of African Americans had distinguished themselves in military service since the colonial era, but it was not until the creation of all-black regiments that African American servicemen finally received widespread recognition and sanction.

Funding for Armories: The PWA and WPA Programs

Ironically, New York State's ambitious armory building program of the early to mid-1930s was beginning to wind down just as the federal government agreed to fund the construction of National Guard facilities with Public Works Administration (PWA) and/or Works Progress Administration (WPA) money. Part of President Franklin D. Roosevelt's New Deal, the PWA (established in 1933) and the WPA (created in 1935) were federal work relief programs designed to stimulate the economy and create jobs for the unemployed during the Great

Depression. Initially, PWA and WPA officials were reluctant to fund projects for the armed forces primarily because the nation was still deeply in debt over World War I. Furthermore, the general public continued to express an overall sense of war-weariness that made it difficult for government officials to justify spending public money on military causes. Noncontroversial, nonmilitary projects such as bridges, roads, schools and post offices were more appealing to the general public.

However, unrest in Europe during the mid-1930s motivated Americans to reassess their attitude toward the military. Formerly neutral and even antimilitary citizens and government officials began to argue for, or at least reluctantly agree with, the need for increased military readiness. The first PWA/WPA money for armories was released in 1936, and major funding was made available in 1937 and 1938. This financial assistance enabled many states, particularly those in the Midwest, South and Southwest, to embark on aggressive armory building campaigns. More than four hundred new armories were built and approximately five hundred armories were repaired or remodeled in the United States under the auspices of the PWA or WPA. Many of the new buildings were erected in states that had never before had armories.

New York, however, did not benefit greatly from this windfall of federal money. Not a single new armory was built with PWA or WPA funding in the Empire State, and only a few older armories received grants for remodeling. For example, Albany's Tenth Battalion received $30,000 from the federal program (augmented by a $6,000 state match) to refurbish the drill shed in its Washington Avenue Armory. A number of small projects, including the renovation of the officers' club rooms at the 106th Infantry (formerly Twenty-third) Regiment Armory on Bedford Avenue in Brooklyn, were also completed in New York City with WPA funding.[4]

Embracing the spirit of the New Deal, the New York National Guard supported a broad range of relief programs during the Great Depression. Many of the state's armories, especially those in New York City, played crucial roles in aiding the poor and unemployed throughout the period. Armories served as homeless shelters and soup kitchens, while unemployed laborers were given short-term repair and maintenance jobs.[5] In addition, a number of WPA-funded circus performances, designed to employ destitute circus workers as well as provide free entertainment for impoverished Americans, were held at several New York City armories.[6]

The following catalog entries are arranged as follows:

Armories built in the 1920s, organized chronologically
Armories designed by Haugaard in the 1930s in Upstate New York, organized alphabetically
Armories built in New York City in the 1930s, organized chronologically

1922   STATEN ISLAND ARMORY (101ST CAVALRY SQUADRON)
        STATEN ISLAND, RICHMOND COUNTY

321 Manor Road
Architect: Werner and Windolph

Built for Staten Island's cavalrymen, this is the only National Guard facility constructed in Richmond County. With its crenelated, Norman-inspired towers, the armory harkens back to the castellated style popular during the 1880s and 1890s. Still owned and occupied by the National Guard, the armory houses an important collection of military memorabilia.

Staten Island Armory, 1922. Mid-twentieth-century photograph courtesy of Gayle N. Carpenter, DMNA.

1924–26 Brooklyn Arsenal (Second Division)
Brooklyn, Kings County

Second Avenue between 63rd and 64th streets
Architect: Jones

Other arsenals for the division:
1858 State Arsenal, North Portland Avenue

This facility was designed to serve as a centralized storage space for Brooklyn's various militia units. Between 1858 and the late 1870s, the State Arsenal on North Portland Avenue had served in this capacity. Between 1878, when Brooklyn's Fourteenth Regiment took over the North Portland Avenue building for its sole use, and 1926, when the Second Avenue arsenal was completed, the city (later borough) of Brooklyn had no centralized storage facility.

The arsenal on Second Avenue is conveniently located adjacent to the former U.S. Army Military Ocean Terminal (the earliest components of which were built in 1918) in South Brooklyn. Like the main buildings of the army base, the arsenal features modern construction technology, that is, reinforced concrete, and epitomized early modern industrial design. The construction cost was funded by the $1,350,000 profit derived from the sale of the North Portland Avenue arsenal/armory in 1924. Sullivan W. Jones, state architect at the time under Governor Alfred E. Smith, designed the facility and oversaw its construction. "New York State," reported a current account, "is surely going to have 'the last word' in Arsenals."[7] The National Guard vacated the facility in the late 1950s when it built its new warehouse at Camp Smith in Peekskill. The arsenal is currently owned by the city of New York.

Brooklyn Arsenal, 1924–26. During the second and third quarters of the twentieth century, the arsenal was a centralized storage, training and educational center for all downstate and New York City units. Upstate units used the Ithaca Armory (1914–18) at Cornell University. Historic postcard courtesy of Colonel Michael J. Stenzel, DMNA.

1927–29   HEMPSTEAD ARMORY
           HEMPSTEAD, NASSAU COUNTY

216 Washington Street
Architect: Jones

The Hempstead Armory, formally opened on 21 November 1929, was designed by State Architect Sullivan W. Jones for companies K and L of Brooklyn's Fourteenth Regiment. (Jones also designed the 1924–1926 State Arsenal on Second Avenue in Brooklyn.) The restrained, classically inspired facility was vacated by the National Guard in 1993 and converted for use as local government offices.

Hempstead Armory, 1927–29. This photograph of the Hempstead Armory appeared in the Guardsman, *December 1929.*

1932–34 BINGHAMTON ARMORY
         BINGHAMTON, BROOME COUNTY

85 West End Avenue
Architect: Haugaard

Other armories in Binghamton:
1880s   Binghamton Armory, State Street
1904–06   Binghamton Armory, Washington Street

The West End Avenue facility was built for subunits of the Tenth Regiment Infantry (headquartered in Albany) and the 104th Field Artillery. The official opening of the armory was held on 10 October 1934. In his keynote speech at the dedication, Major General Franklin W. Ward, adjutant general of the state of New York, voiced a variety of sentiments held by proponents of the volunteer militia since the colonial era. He praised Binghamton's new armory as "a schoolhouse for the teaching of true Americanism and respect for law and order. . . . Binghamton has been built . . . by its citizenry, and it will be defended, if necessary, by its citizen-soldiers who will be trained in this building."[8] The facility, which looks more like a large suburban estate house than a military facility, was the last of three historic armories built in Binghamton. It is still occupied by the National Guard.

Binghamton Armory, 1932–34. Drawing of proposed armory, courtesy of the New York State Military Museum.

1932–33	MASTEN AVENUE ARMORY (SIXTY-FIFTH REGIMENT) BUFFALO, ERIE COUNTY

27 Masten Avenue (between Best and North streets)
Architect: Haugaard

Other armories for the unit:

1858	Broadway Arsenal
1884	Sixty-fifth Regiment Armory, Broadway
1902–07	Masten Avenue Armory

The Masten Avenue Armory, still occupied by the National Guard, was built to replace an earlier armory on the site, a massive, castellated edifice designed by State Architect George L. Heins and completed in 1907. Heins's armory burned to the ground in 1931 and a new facility, costing nearly one million dollars, was promptly built on the rubble. The cornerstone for the new armory was laid on 11 December 1932; the building, covering nearly four acres of land, was completed the following year and officially dedicated on 5 December 1933. It was the fourth home of the Sixty-fifth Regiment, Buffalo's oldest militia unit, which, by the time Haugaard's armory was erected, was known as the 106th Field Artillery.

Masten Avenue Armory, Buffalo, 1932–33. Photograph (mid-1930s) courtesy of the Buffalo and Erie County Historical Society.

1935–36 CORNING ARMORY
CORNING, STEUBEN COUNTY

Centerway
Architect: Haugaard

Other arsenals/armories in Corning:
1858   Corning Arsenal, First Street

The Corning Armory, a fanciful, Tudor Revival–style building, was the second of two historic facilities built for Corning's militia; the first, completed around 1858, was the Corning Arsenal. The area's militia languished after the Civil War and, by the 1870s, the arsenal was vacated due to lack of troops. National Guard activity was revived in Corning during the early to mid-1920s.[9] On 15 April 1926, Corning's unit was designated the 105th Hospital Company, 102nd Medical Regiment.[10] By the early 1930s, enrollment in the company was sufficient to petition the legislature for a permanent armory. The cornerstone for the new building was laid on 30 April 1935. The armory was completed in March 1936 and dedicated in September of the same year "with appropriate and inspiring ceremonies. The participation of the citizens of Corning in these ceremonies was most gratifying and they feel that additional educational and social advantages have now been provided for this community."[11] Vacated by the National Guard in 1978, the building now houses the local branch of the YMCA.

Corning Armory, 1935–36. Details of stone and terra-cotta trim. Photograph (1998) by the author.

1932   JAMESTOWN ARMORY
        JAMESTOWN, CHAUTAUQUA COUNTY

Porter Avenue and Front Street
Architect: Haugaard

Other armories in Jamestown:
1890–92   Jamestown Armory, South Main Street

This restrained, Chateauesque/Tudor Revival–style building was the second of two armories built for Jamestown's militia. The first was built on South Main Street in 1892 for the Thirteenth Separate Company, which was formed in 1875 and known as Fenton's Guard. For a while during the early twentieth century, the Thirteenth (under the designation Company E) was attached to the Sixty-fifth Regiment in nearby Buffalo; at the close of World War I, it became Company E, 174th (formerly Seventy-fourth) Infantry, also headquartered in Buffalo. The facility, reminiscent of an early twentieth-century suburban estate house, is still occupied by the National Guard.

Jamestown Armory, 1932. Photograph (1999) by Kathleen Howe, Bero Associates.

1932   KINGSTON ARMORY
       KINGSTON, ULSTER COUNTY

North Manor Road
Architect: Haugaard

Other armories in Kingston:
1879   Kingston Armory, Broadway

The North Manor Road facility was designed for Kingston's field artillery unit (Battery A), which was attached to the region's 156th Field Artillery Regiment. The 156th, although not officially designated as such until 1924, had its roots in a field artillery unit that had formed during the Spanish American War. After 1905, but prior to its association with the 156th, Kingston's artillery unit was known as Company M of the Tenth Infantry Regiment.[12] Similar to the

Haugaard-designed armories in nearby Newburgh and Peekskill, the four-part facility in Kingston is an unadorned, utilitarian building featuring a 65' x 112' administration building, a 60' x 120' drill hall, a 112' x 200' riding hall and an 80' x 94' stable wing. Built to replace Kingston's aging armory on Broadway (1879), the North Manor Road building still functions as an active National Guard armory.

1931–32   NEWBURGH ARMORY
          NEWBURGH, ORANGE COUNTY

South William Street
Architect: Haugaard

Other armories in Newburgh:
1879   Newburgh Armory, Broadway

This is the second of two armories built for Newburgh's militia; the first, built in 1879, is located on Broadway. The cornerstone of the new armory was laid on 23 October 1931, and the building was completed the following year. This is one of three armories built in the mid-Hudson Valley between 1930 and 1932, all of which were erected to house subunits of the 156th Field Artillery Regiment (formed in 1924). Like those in Kingston and Peekskill, the Newburgh Armory is a plain, four-part facility comprising an unornamented administration building, a gymnasium, a drill shed and a stable wing. It was designed for Newburgh's field artillery unit (formerly the Fifth Separate Company). The facility on South William Street still functions as an active National Guard armory.

Kingston Armory, 1932. Historic postcard from the collection of the author.

Newburgh Armory, 1931–32. Photograph (1996) by the author.

Oneida Armory, 1929–30. Photograph (1995) by the author.

1929–30   ONEIDA ARMORY
               ONEIDA, MADISON COUNTY

217 Cedar Street
Architect: Haugaard

The Oneida Armory was the only armory built in Madison County. It housed Company K, Tenth Infantry, composed of militiamen from the city of Oneida and nearby communities. The cornerstone was laid in October 1929; the restrained, Tudor Revival–style armory with classical overtones was completed the following year. Vacated by the National Guard in 2002, the building is now owned by the city of Oneida.

Oneida Armory, 1929–30. Cast concrete trim, including a bas-relief medallion depicting the official emblem of the state of New York. Photograph (1995) by the author.

1932–33   PEEKSKILL ARMORY
          PEEKSKILL, WESTCHESTER COUNTY

955 Washington Street
Architect: Haugaard

This was the only permanent armory built in Peekskill for the area's militia, a field artillery unit that was organized in 1922. During the 1920s, the artillerymen appear to have been quartered in a temporary armory at the corner of James and Park streets.[13] In 1931 the legislature appropriated $315,000 for the construction of a new facility for Peekskill's militiamen, which, by then, were attached to the region's 156th Field Artillery Regiment. The cornerstone was laid on 14 August 1932 by Governor Franklin D. Roosevelt, who deftly worked the event into his busy presidential campaign schedule. Ground had been broken earlier that year, and the building, which cost about $400,000, was completed and dedicated on 22 April 1933. The armory still houses the National Guard.

Peekskill Armory, 1932–33. This artist's rendering of the newly opened armory appeared in the May 1933 issue of the Guardsman.

1936 SCHENECTADY ARMORY
SCHENECTADY, SCHENECTADY COUNTY

125 Washington Avenue
Architect: Haugaard

Other arsenals/armories in Schenectady:
1868   Schenectady Arsenal, State Street at Crescent Park
1898–99   Schenectady Armory, State Street at Crescent Park

The Schenectady Armory was built to house companies E and F (formerly the Thirty-sixth and Thirty-seventh separate companies) and as headquarters for the region's 105th Infantry Regiment. (The 105th

Schenectady Armory, 1936. Historic postcard courtesy of Gayle N. Carpenter, DMNA.

Schenectady Armory, 1936. Detail of front entrance of the armory. Note the stylized, Gothic letters above the archway that spell out "N Y State Armory." Photograph (1995) by the author.

was formerly headquartered at the Troy Armory [1919].) During the nineteenth and early twentieth centuries, the Thirty-sixth and Thirty-seventh had been quartered in the Schenectady Arsenal and the first Schenectady Armory. Both were located on Crescent (later Veterans') Park; neither survives. The 1936 facility, an outstanding example of an Art Deco–style armory, is still occupied by the National Guard.

Schenectady Armory, 1936. This historic postcard, highlighting the Western Gateway Bridge (built in 1925), shows the prominent downtown location of the armory. Also shown is the Van Curler Hotel, built in 1925, which now houses Schenectady County Community College. From the collection of the author.

Schenectady Armory, 1936. Detail of cast concrete trim around and above windows. Photograph (1995) by the author.

1941–43   East Genesee Street Armory
             Syracuse, Onondaga County

1055 East Genesee Street
Architect: Haugaard

Other arsenals/armories in Syracuse:
1858–59   Syracuse Arsenal, West Jefferson Street
1873   Syracuse Armory, West Jefferson Street
1906–07   West Jefferson Street Armory

The East Genesee Street Armory, completed in 1943, was built for Syracuse's battery of field artillery (organized in 1911). Prior to the construction of the battery's permanent armory, the artillerymen had been housed in rented quarters known as the Arena Building. With the exception of the segmentally arched sally port, the East Genesee Street Armory is virtually devoid of medieval-inspired, military-like features; it is more like a modest civic or educational building of the early 1940s. Erected while America was embroiled in World War II, the armory is a reflection of the economies of scale and design preferred for public buildings during the period. It was surplussed by the National Guard in late 2002.

East Genesee Street Armory, Syracuse, 1941–43. Photograph (1995) by the author.

1935   TICONDEROGA ARMORY
        TICONDEROGA, ESSEX COUNTY

315 Champlain Avenue
Architect: Haugaard

The Ticonderoga Armory, dedicated on 7 June 1935, was the only permanent facility built to house Essex County's militia. A 1937 issue of the *Guardsman* described the armory as follows:

> The drill hall measures 60 x 100 feet, with a 34-foot high ceiling. Also on the ground floor are the locker and shower rooms and a splendid suite of offices for the officer personnel. On the second floor there are recreation rooms for both officers and enlisted men, a ladies' rest room, and in the basement are to be found a large mess hall, a well-equipped kitchen, a spacious garage, supply room and a fine rifle range. The structure is of brick and presents a very comfortable, attractive appearance from the outside.[14]

It was built for the 106th Ambulance Company, which, although not officially designated as such until 1922, had its roots in the First Ambulance (later First Field Hospital) Company, formed in 1910. The 106th was attached to the 102nd Medical Regiment, which was headquartered at the old First Battery Armory (1903) on West 66th Street in Manhattan.[15] The armory was vacated by the National Guard in 2003.

Ticonderoga Armory, 1935. Historic postcard courtesy of Gayle N. Carpenter, DMNA.

1929–30   UTICA ARMORY
             UTICA, ONEIDA COUNTY

1700 Parkway East
Architect: Haugaard

Other arsenals/armories in Utica:
1862   Utica Arsenal, Bleecker Street
1893–94   Utica Armory, Rutger and Steuben streets at
                 Steuben Park

Built for Utica's cavalrymen (Troop A, 121st Cavalry), this was the
last of several armories built for the city's militia, the roots of which

date back to the Utica Citizens' Corps, established in 1835. Other
early facilities occupied by Utica's militia included Chubbuck Hall on
Hotel Street, the Utica Arsenal on Bleecker Street and the Utica
Armory on Steuben Park, all of which were built for infantry units
and none of which survives. The Parkway East facility was Troop A's
first permanent armory. Organized around 1918, the cavalry unit had
rented various temporary quarters until the construction of its state-of-
the-art armory on the suburban fringes of the city. The cornerstone
was laid on 3 August 1929, and the building was completed and
officially opened in November 1930.[16] The facility is still owned by
the National Guard.

Utica Armory, 1929–30.
Historic postcard from the
collection of the author.

2366 Fifth Avenue (between West 142nd and West 143rd streets)
Architect: Tachau and Vought (1920s drill shed)
             Van Wart and Wein (1930–33 administration building)

The 369th Regiment Armory, built in two stages during the early 1920s and early 1930s, was the home of New York's only African American regiment. The roots of the regiment date to 1913, when members of Harlem's Lenox Community Center banded together to form what was first known as the Negro or Colored Regiment of Infantry. The unit was housed initially in a rowhouse at 58 West 130th Street.

Upon mustering in for service during World War I, the Negro Regiment became the Fifteenth Regiment, although it quickly acquired the moniker Harlem Hellfighters for its military prowess. While attached to the French Army, the regiment achieved international acclaim for its heroics during the war, particularly on the Reims-Argonne front and during the Battle of Le Mesnil. Several individual members of the regiment as well as the unit itself were awarded the coveted Croix de Guerre by the French. Several members also received the Medal of Honor, the Distinguished Service Cross and/or the Legion of Honor Award from their own countrymen.

After World War I, the Fifteenth was redesignated the 369th. Around 1921 the regiment acquired a site in Harlem between West 142nd and West 143rd streets just west of Fifth Avenue. The firm of

369th Regiment Armory, 1930–33.
Photograph (1995) by Merrill E. Hesch,
OPRHP.

Members of the 369th Regiment return home from serving with the French Army during World War I. Courtesy of the National Archives and Records Administration, Records of the War Department (Record Group 165, ARC Identifier 533548).

Features of the Art Deco–style detailing in the lobby of the 369th Regiment Armory appear in this 2005 photograph taken at a homecoming ceremony hosted for troops returning from service in Iraq. Courtesy of DMNA.

Tachau and Vought (the successor firm of Pilcher and Tachau, which had designed the Troop C Armory in Brooklyn and the Kingsbridge Armory in the Bronx) was commissioned to design a drill shed for the unit. The drill shed was completed in 1924. Additional land fronting Fifth Avenue and overlooking the Harlem River was acquired by the regiment in 1929, and a massive, Art Deco–style administration building, designed by the New York City firm of Van Wart and Wein, was added to the front of the drill shed in 1930–1933. The visual prominence and architectural sophistication of this monumental administration building attests to the high status then accorded New York's only all-black regiment. The building remains an important reminder of the role of African Americans in American military history.

1936 JAMAICA ARMORY (FOURTH REGIMENT)
JAMAICA, QUEENS COUNTY

93–05 168th Street
Architect: Meyers

The Art Deco–style Jamaica Armory was designed by Charles B. Meyers and completed in 1936. It was built for the 104th Field Artillery, formerly and still commonly known as the Fourth Regiment. The drill shed and the iron grilles that ornament the first-story windows reveal the building's service as a military facility; otherwise, it could easily be mistaken for an early to mid-twentieth-century civic or educational building. The armory is still occupied by the National Guard.

Jamaica Armory, 1936. Artist's rendering (1930s) courtesy of the New York State Military Museum.

Armories constructed in New York State after World War II no longer employed design or decorative features associated with any recognized architectural style. Instead, they were designed with an eye to utilitarianism, convenience and functionality. Pictured here is an artist's rendering of the proposed Rome Armory, built in 1959. Courtesy of Gayle N. Carpenter, DMNA.

Conclusion

The Army National Guard played a vital role during World War II and the cold war era as a critical reserve to the U.S. Army, although by the 1950s, the federal reserves superceded the state-based citizen troops as the country's primary reserve force. National Guardsmen and women have served overseas in virtually every military engagement between the mid-twentieth and early twenty-first centuries and in numerous international relief and peacekeeping missions. Most recently, the Guard has achieved distinction for its role in the Global War on Terror, especially for its service in Operation Iraqi Freedom. Closer to home, the National Guard continues to serve as domestic peacekeepers and disaster relief aides, from suppressing rioters to assisting authorities in homeland security efforts; from aiding hundreds of thousands of victims of hurricanes, floods, ice storms and wildfires to assisting local communities in public service projects.

Today, military readiness remains the National Guard's top mandate, and armories remain the home bases of all National Guard activity. As early as the 1950s, government and military officials became acutely aware that many of the state's armories, particularly those built before World War I, were woefully inadequate for the needs of the National Guard during the cold war era. Of particular concern was the lack of land associated with the pre–World War I armories, most of which were built on small city lots in the congested cores of their respective communities. Expansive parking lots and room for large storage buildings and repair shops were needed for the militia's ever expanding fleets of vehicles. Consequently, a major armory building program occurred in New York in the 1950s, 1960s and early 1970s, occasionally on the suburban fringes of communities whose armories were more than fifty years old, but primarily in regions where it was convenient to merge several units in a more centralized location. Most of these mid-twentieth-century armories are utilitarian facilities that are easily mistaken for standardized educational or civic buildings of the period. Like their pre–World War II counterparts, these new armories were designed to function as quarters for local units of the New York National Guard, and most feature administration buildings with attached drill sheds. In all cases, the administration buildings are virtually devoid of aesthetic embellishment, and none feature the luxurious interior appointments—such as elegant lounges, libraries or company meeting rooms—that had characterized all nineteenth-century armories and many early twentieth-century armories. The drill sheds of these late twentieth-century armories are scaled-down versions of their nineteenth-century counterparts, designed to serve athletic or recreational purposes rather than full-scale training or drilling spaces. (After World War II, most official training occurred out-of-doors, particularly at the several expansive state training grounds in Youngstown, Newark, Guilderland and Peekskill.) Further precluding the need for large drill sheds was the fact that in most cases, the armories were no longer needed as civic centers—by the 1970s and 1980s, most communities had their own modern arenas or convention centers.

For nearly every armory built during the third quarter of the twentieth century, a pre–World War II armory was released from state ownership. This process of assessing the condition and usefulness of the state's various armories was simply a continuum of a centuries-old tradition: as early as the second quarter of the nineteenth century, the militia began disposing of obsolete buildings that were barely several decades old. By the 1850s, it was a common practice. Sometimes the state razed an old armory and built anew upon the same site; in other cases, the militia simply vacated the facility and built a new armory elsewhere, oftentimes giving or selling the armory to the community or a private developer. For example, when the state built the 1858 arsenal for the First Division in Manhattan, the old Central Park Arsenal (1848) was turned over to the city and eventually became the first home of the Museum of Natural History and later the headquarters for the city's Department of Parks and Recreation. Albany's 1799 arsenal became a public school when the Tenth Regiment moved from its North Broadway home to a new armory on Hudson Street in 1858. Similarly, the ca. 1809 arsenal in Russell was converted for use as a public school during the mid-nineteenth century; the 1858 arsenal in Corning became a convent; and the Ballston Spa Arsenal, also built in 1858, was converted during the early 1870s for use as a parish hall by a nearby church. The Walton Armory (1886) became a grange hall and a school; when the school became obsolete, a grocery store took over (with the grange still intact). Equally frequently, however, the state simply demolished an older armory and built a new one on the same site. For example, the 1858 arsenal in Syracuse was razed to make way for a new armory in 1873, which, in turn, was razed to make way for yet another armory in 1906; the 1868 arsenal in Schenectady was demolished in 1898, and a new armory was promptly erected; and the 1885 armory in Oneonta was replaced twenty years later with a new one.

The National Guard continued to abandon obsolete facilities during the early twentieth century. For example, the Binghamton Armory (1906), vacated by the National Guard in 1934, became the Broome County Technical College; the Kingston Armory (1879) became a community center and neighborhood recreational facility in the 1930s/40s; and the Sixty-fifth Regiment Armory (1884) in Buffalo was converted for use by the city as a public auditorium around 1907. The motivation behind these adaptations was purely economical: it was not a matter of preserving a significant historic resource; it was simply financially prudent to reuse an existing building.

As the state began to surplus its armories in the nationwide boom years of the 1950s and 1960s, few developers had the need or desire to reuse old buildings. The post–World War II ideology of "new is better" prevailed in all construction programs, with only a few lone voices calling out for the appreciation and protection of American history as embodied in the built environment. In 1969 proponents of the nascent preservation movement focused their attention on New York State's armories. Manhattan's Squadron A Armory (1895) on Madison Avenue (attached to the old Eighth Regiment Armory [1889] on Park Avenue) had been turned over to New York City authorities and was being demolished in order to construct a new school. At the eleventh hour, when everything but the Madison Avenue façade of the 1895 administration building had been razed, the final phase of demolition was stopped by a court order. The façade was saved, and local preservationists worked with state and federal agencies to list it in the National Register of Historic Places; the surviving fragment became the rear wall of the school's playground.

During the 1970s and 1980s, more than a dozen pre–World War II armories were listed in the National Register; about half were still owned by the state, and half were owned by various types of public or private entities. Not surprisingly, the state-owned Seventh Regiment Armory (1879) was the second armory in the state to achieve National Register listing; several other massive, nationally known armories (such as the Kingsbridge Armory [1917] in the Bronx and the Twenty-third Regiment Armory [1895] in Brooklyn) were listed shortly thereafter. Slightly more surprising was how quickly local communities joined the preservation movement and recognized the significance of their respective National Guard facilities, regardless of size or relative architectural sophistication. Armories (and former arsenals) all across the state, including those in Binghamton (1880s), Elmira (1888), Ogdensburg (1858), Newburgh (1879), Poughkeepsie (1892) and Glens Falls (1895), were soon added to the National Register. In 1986 the Seventh Regiment Armory was declared a National Historic Landmark, the first armory in America to receive such an honor. During the 1990s, a partnership between DMNA and OPRHP, utilizing funding from the U.S. Department of Defense's Legacy Resource

Management Program, resulted in the National Register listing of more than a dozen state-owned armories. Concurrently, nearly one-half dozen non-DMNA-owned armories were also listed.

A review of the fate of New York's historic armories that left state ownership during the last quarter of the twentieth century yields a few remarkable success stories, an equal number of dismal failures or complete losses and a respectable number of accomplishments in between. Bearing in mind that success is not always measured in terms of financial profits, some of the "best" examples of well-preserved armories are owned or occupied by not-for-profit entities such as local governments, YMCA branches or social service organizations. For example, the Mohawk Armory (1892) and the Corning Armory (1936) both became local branches of the YMCA; the Troy and Ithaca armories, both dating from the second decade of the twentieth century, were turned over to local universities for use as athletic/recreational facilities; the Ogdensburg Arsenal (1858) serves as a public works storage facility; and the Mount Vernon Armory (1889) became a senior citizens' center. The armories in Hempstead and Flushing were both converted into local government offices during the 1990s. More recently, the armories in Ticonderoga (1935), Oneonta (1905) and Malone (1892) were acquired by their respective local governments. Many large regimental armories in New York City are used as homeless shelters, a trend that peaked during the 1980s and 1990s: their drill sheds and gymnasiums were often filled with thousands of cots. In more recent years, the homeless are placed in smaller, more private spaces in the armories' administration buildings.

In terms of "financial" successes, the Rochester Arsenal (1870) has been a profitable convention center (and later a performing arts venue) for decades; the Syracuse Armory (1907) houses a popular science and technology museum in the city's central business district. The White Plains Armory (1910) was converted into private apartment units and the Hudson Armory (1898) provides dealers of high-end antiques with showroom space.

A depressing number of "failures" also abound: many armories, including those in Utica (1894), Schenectady (1899), Auburn (1873) and Watertown (1879), were demolished in the name of urban renewal. Others were lost to fire, such as the Russell Arsenal (ca. 1809) and the Binghamton Armory (1906). In other cases, private commercial ventures undertaken at certain armories, such as the ones in Cohoes (1893) and Walton (1896), were not particularly successful. Both buildings went through a series of owners and both are, as of early 2006, vacant. The West Delavan Avenue Armory (1917) in Buffalo succumbed to the wrecking ball in the early twenty-first century after several decades of underutilization and neglect by the city. The fate of other vacant or neglected armories no longer in state ownership appears equally bleak; for example, the city of Rochester has yet to find a buyer or an economically feasible use for the massive East Main Street Armory (1907).

The fate of the roughly two dozen armories still owned by the state remains to be seen. Since the partnership between DMNA and OPRHP began in 1992, nearly a dozen pre–World War II armories were vacated by the state, mostly because the facilities were obsolete and far too expensive to maintain. Not unsympathetic to the value of its old armories, DMNA made valiant attempts during the 1980s and early 1990s to preserve, protect and make better use of its aging facilities. The public was invited to expand its use of armories as civic centers, and efforts were made to retrofit obsolete facilities with modern conveniences. However, several factors worked to undermine the success of armories as income-generating civic centers. First, the proliferation of modern arenas and recreation facilities superceded old drill sheds as viable sites for massive public gatherings. Second, in many cases, DMNA was required by law to provide its drill sheds free of charge to public groups, thereby greatly increasing its operation costs while adding nothing to its coffers. And even when DMNA could charge private groups for their use of its facilities, it was statutorily required—and still is—to turn all proceeds over to the state's general fund. Consequently, the harder DMNA worked to make its facilities available to the public, the less it profited.

This inability to generate revenue, compounded by decreased state and federal funding during the post–cold war era of military downsizing, has forced DMNA to neglect many of its oldest and neediest armories. Federal cutbacks are matched with declining state funding, preventing DMNA from carrying out even the most basic maintenance of its properties; what little money there is goes not to preservation efforts, but to meeting building code mandates such as fire protection, handicapped accessibility and lead and asbestos abatement. Understandably, but regrettably, one of the most viable solutions for both DMNA and the state's Office of General Services (OGS) during the last decade of the twentieth century and the first

decade of the twenty-first century has been to simply sell the old buildings.

In closing, a case study of the Newburgh Armory (1879) is offered to illustrate the fact that in no instance is an armory beyond salvation, given the proper political, economic and social climate of the community in particular and the state in general. Newburgh's armory, built on Broadway in 1879 to the design of John Wood, was

Newburgh Armory, 1879. Historic postcard courtesy of the author.

first vacated by the National Guard in 1932 when a new armory was built on South William Street. The old armory, located in the core of Newburgh's central business district, was used by a succession of private concerns for several decades. Many of these concerns prospered, as did Newburgh in general, at least until the third quarter of the

twentieth century, when the city began to experience a severe economic downturn. By the early 1980s, the building had been completely abandoned; by the early 1990s, the roof had collapsed; by the mid-1990s, nearly everything but the exterior shell of the building had become rubble.

Underutilized since the mid-twentieth century and virtually abandoned since the 1970s, the partially deteriorated Newburgh Armory was listed in the National Register in 1981. Photograph (1981) courtesy of OPRHP (SHPO, NR files).

In 1996 Orange County officials entered into a partnership with a New York City development firm to rehabilitate the building for use by the county's district attorney and social services department. Utilizing a combination of private investment funds and public development monies, the restored building is now a major example of a successful historic preservation project in this still-struggling community. Hopefully, it will serve as a focal point of the city's economic revitalization and as a testimony to public-private partnerships in salvaging the state's historic armories.

Rehabilitated in 1996–1997 to house several departments of the Orange County government, the ribbon-cutting ceremony at the reopening of the Newburgh Armory drew a large crowd of local dignitaries and interested citizens. Photograph (1997) by the author.

Notes

Introduction

1. Federal arsenals, built for the regular army (a small but not insignificant component of the American military system during the eighteenth and nineteenth centuries), are not included in this study.

2. Although construction of the Seventh Regiment Armory spanned a five-year period between 1877 and 1881, the date 1879 consistently appears in many secondary sources about the National Guard and its armories as the official date of construction.

3. The following entities are beyond the scope of this book: the New York Air National Guard, the New York Naval Militia and the New York Guard.

4. Many of the illustrations reproduced in this book are historic. They were derived from archival collections of various local, regional or state historical societies or governmental repositories; nineteenth- and early twentieth-century magazines, journals and newspapers; and, particularly regarding old postcards, private individuals' personal collections. Contemporary photographs of several arsenals and armories were taken by the author, Merrill E. Hesch, David J. Lamb, Kathleen Howe and Raymond W. Smith.

5. General DeWitt Clinton Falls, "Regimental Historical Sketches," *New York National Guardsman* 3 (August 1929): 9.

6. Within each chapter, the various arsenals/armories are organized in slightly different manners, depending upon the nature of the group. Most are organized chronologically, although some (such as those in New York City) are organized by location according to the borough in which they were built, and some (such as those designed by a single architect) are organized alphabetically.

7. See Appendix I for a list organized alphabetically by location.

Chapter 1. History of the Army National Guard

1. Provincial Convention of Maryland. 1774. Quoted by Edward E. Britton, "In What Way Can the National Guard Be Modified so as to Make It an Effective Reserve to the Regular Army in Both War and Peace," *Journal of the Military Service Institution of the United States* 26 (1900): 156.

2. *Annual Report of the Adjutant General of the State of New York*, 1867, 13–14.

3. Thomas M. Anderson, "Nationalization of the State Guards," *Forum* 30 (1901): 653–57. The *Forum* was a popular, conservative, men's monthly magazine.

4. During the Civil War, New York State officially adopted the name National Guard, formerly claimed by the Seventh Regiment, as the rubric for its coalition of militia units. By the early twentieth century, the federal government began to use the term National Guard to encompass all state-controlled militia units.

5. Alan Aimone and Barbara Aimone, "New Netherland Defends Itself," *Military Collector and Historian* (Summer 1980): 53.

6. Moses King, *King's Handbook of New York City* (Boston, 1893). Reprint, 2 volumes (New York: Benjamin Blom, 1972), 2: 531.

7. Prior to 1898, the term New York City referred only to the island of Manhattan. Brooklyn was a separate city, and the future boroughs of the Bronx, Queens and Staten Island were merely neighborhoods within larger geopolitical units.

8. Alexander C. Flick, *History of the State of New York* (Port Washington: Friedman, 1962), 5: 227.

9. Many of these units were joined with other units or evolved into full regiments by the mid-nineteenth century. For example, the National Guards became the Seventh Regiment, the Washington Greys became the Eighth Regiment, the Brooklyn Light Guard became the Thirteenth Regiment, the Brooklyn Chasseurs became the Fourteenth Regiment, the Washington Continentals became the Tenth Regiment, the Twenty-eighth Artillery became the Sixty-fifth Regiment, the Willard Guards became the Forty-ninth Regiment, the Oswego Guards became the Forty-eighth Regiment and the Penfield Pioneers became the Fifty-fourth Regiment.

10. Numerous sources, particularly labor histories and histories of New York City, contain information about these mid-nineteenth-century riots. For a specific analysis of the militia's role in subduing rioters, see William R. Wright, "Service in Aid of Civil Authorities," a multipart series published in monthly installments in the *Guardsman* 3 and 4 (November 1926–October 1927).

11. William Swinton, *History of the Seventh Regiment, National Guard, State of New York* (New York: Dillingham, 1869), 15–16.

12. Ibid., 16.

13. Wright, *Guardsman* 3 (February–March 1927): 18–19.

14. "The Eighth Regiment at Staten Island," *Frank Leslie's Illustrated Newspaper*, 25 September 1858, 255–63; "Colonel Vosburgh's Tent at Camp Washington, Staten Island," *Leslie's*, 6 November 1858.

15. John C. Churchill, *Landmarks of Oswego County, New York* (Syracuse: Mason, 1895), 411.

16. Wright, *Guardsman* 3 (February–March 1927): 18.

17. "The Inauguration of Clark Mills's Statue of Washington, on February 22, 1860," *Harper's Weekly*, 3 March 1860, 136.

18. "The Prince of Wales in New York," *Leslie's*, 20 October 1860, 335.

19. *History of the DeWitt Guard, Company A, 50th Regiment, NGNY* (Ithaca: Andrus, McChain, 1866), 154.

20. Ibid., 155.

21. J. H. French, *Gazetteer of the State of New York* (Syracuse: Smith, 1860), 43.

22. Wright, *Guardsman* 4 (April 1927): 9, 17.

23. The short-lived NLU died out in 1872–73. The Knights of Labor flourished throughout the late 1870s and 1880s, particularly under the leadership of Terence Powderley.

24. The Haymarket Affair was sparked when a bomb exploded and killed a police officer at a rally of labor unionists at Haymarket Square. An anarchist of Eastern European origin was accused of and eventually hung for setting the bomb. The Carnegie Steel Strike erupted when angry steelworkers revolted against low wages, poor working conditions and the mill manager's refusal to recognize the Amalgamated Association of Iron and Steelworkers. The Pullman Strike broke out when George Pullman, maker of luxurious Pullman Palace sleeping cars, cut his workers' wages and increased the rents he charged in his company town. In sympathy with their comrades in Chicago, 260,000 railroad workers in twenty-six states across the country shut down virtually all lines carrying Pullman Palace cars.

25. George Wood Wingate, *History of the Twenty-second Regiment of the National Guard of the State of New York from Its Organization to 1895* (New York: Dayton, 1896), 574.

26. Wright, *Guardsman* 4 (May 1927): 9; 4 (June 1927): 8; 4 (July 1927): 8–9.

27. E. L. Godkin, "The Late Riots," *Nation* 25 (2 August 1877): 68.

28. "The Great Strike," *Harper's Weekly*, 11 August 1877, 626.

29. "New York in the Late Troubles," *Harper's Weekly*, 18 August 1877, 639.

30. Daniel S. Mercein, "The National Guard of New York State in Active Service in Brooklyn," *Outing* 25 (March 1895): 518.

31. Ibid., 524.

32. Alexander G. Marshall, "The Necessity for Armories," *Bostonian* 1 (March 1895): 611–12; 2 (April 1895): 49–50.

33. B. O. Flower, "Plutocracy's Bastiles: Or Why the Republic Is Becoming an Armed Camp," *Arena* 10 (October 1894): 604, 614, 616.

34. These brigades, along with their respective separate companies, were again reorganized at the outbreak of the Spanish American War in 1898; subsequent major restructuring occurred when New York's National Guard was mustered into federal service during World War I.

35. The Dick Act was named after Congressman Charles Dick of Ohio. On the surface, the Dick Act and the two subsequent National Defense Acts appeared to ring the death knell for the National Guard; in reality, however, all three laws reinforced the importance of perpetuating the state-controlled militia, in spite of opponents' efforts to abolish the National Guard altogether.

36. The defeat of the Populist and Democratic parties in the 1896 election signaled a major political coup for the predominantly pro-industrialist Republican Party and a devastating setback for America's struggling rural farmers and urban workers. Furthermore, President McKinley's willingness and ability to address international issues (as evidenced by his decision to send military aid to Cuba in 1898) signaled the beginning of the end of American isolationism.

Chapter 2. Arsenals and Armories Built in New York State during the Republican, Antebellum and Civil War Eras

1. French, 44, n. 5.

2. Flick, 5: 224.

3. J. W. Lewis, *History of Clinton and Franklin Counties* (1880). Reprinted by Duane Hamilton Hurd (1978), 404.

4. Tetra Tech, Inc. "Survey of Cold War–Era Buildings and Structures at Plattsburgh Air Force Base," November 1995, 1–4. See also French, 44, n. 5.

5. William L. Stone, *History of New York City from the Discovery to the Present Day* (New York: Virtue and Yorston, 1872), 457.

6. Other sources indicate that the arsenal was not completed until 1853 or 1854. See, for example, Robert Koch, "The Medieval Castle Revival: New York Armories," *Journal of the Society of Architectural Historians* 14 (1955): 23.

7. French, 436, n. 3.

8. Albany, Ballston Spa, Buffalo, Corning, Dunkirk, Ogdensburg and Syracuse.

9. Later armories designed by White include the Fifty-first Regiment's second armory in Syracuse and the Forty-eighth's East Side Armory in Oswego; both date from 1873.

10. Clarence S. Martin, *Seventy-five Years with the Tenth Regiment Infantry* (Albany: Lyon, 1935), 13–14.

11. Herbert J. Ellis, "The Story of Arsenal Hill," *Daily Messenger*, 6 September 1968, 2.

12. Franklin B. Hough, *History of St. Lawrence and Franklin Counties, New York, from the Earliest Period to the Present Time* (Albany: Little, 1853), 407; Marie Rocca, Russell Town Historian, Research Files.

13. Henry O'Reilly, *Sketches of Rochester with Incidental Notices of Western New York* (1838), as quoted by William F. Peck, *History of Rochester and Monroe County* (New York and Chicago: Pioneer, 1908), 70. The "market-house" referred to in Boston is Faneuil Hall, which was also partially occupied by the local militia.

14. Wright, *Guardsman* 3 (February–March 1927): 18.

15. Churchill, 411.

16. Henry W. B. Howard, *The Eagle and Brooklyn: History of the City of Brooklyn from Its Settlement to the Present Time*, part 2 (Brooklyn: Brooklyn Daily Eagle, 1893), 837.

17. Howard, 819; companies D and E were both known as the Williamsburgh Light Artillery.

18. Henry R. Stiles, *History of the County of Kings and the City of Brooklyn, NY*, Volume 2 (New York: Munsell, 1884), 1195.

19. Howard, 829.

20. New York City Landmarks Preservation Commission, *Fourteenth Regiment Armory Designation Report* (LP–1965) (New York: City of New York, 1998), prepared by Donald G. Presa; 3. In 1849 the city's offices were moved to the newly built Brooklyn City (later Borough) Hall. The old city hall was demolished to make way for the Henry Street Armory in 1858.

21. French, 436, n. 3.

22. *New York Times*, 2 August 1871 and 26 July 1888.

23. French, 44, n. 5.

24. "The New State Arsenal," *Gleason's Pictorial Drawing-Room Companion*, 2 September 1854, 133.

25. *Leslie's*, quoted in "The Old Seventh Regiment's Armory 70 Years Ago," *Guardsman* 7 (March 1931): 11.

26. One source reports that by the end of the Civil War, the Fourteenth was housed with the city's fire department in an 1864 building known as the Armory and Fireman's Hall. See Robert M. Fogelson, *America's Armories: Architecture, Society and Public Order* (Cambridge: Harvard University Press, 1989), 11.

27. Falls, *Guardsman* 2 (May 1925): 5.

28. In strictly chronological terms, this catalog entry could be placed near the end of the chapter, perhaps after the discussion of the arsenals built (or at least designed) in Upstate New York during the state's 1858 arsenal building program. Instead, it is somewhat arbitrarily grouped here with facilities built in New York City during the very last years of the antebellum era and the early years of the Civil War. Despite its slightly later date of construction, it seems more appropriate to group it with its nearly contemporaneous, geographic neighbors, including the unit-specific Tompkins Market and Henry Street armories and the First Division and Second Division arsenals.

29. Wingate, 140–41.

30. "Destruction of the New York State Arsenal," *Leslie's*, 4 December 1858, 9.

31. *New York Times*, 29 April 1858 and 26 October 1858; *Brooklyn Eagle*, 19 November 1858.

32. Hans A. Pohlsander, interview, 6 March 2001; *Albany Evening Journal*, 28 February 1877; *Albany Morning Express*, 30 May 1898; *Albany Times Union*, 30 May 1898.

33. The southern units of the Eighth Division were served by an arsenal built in Dunkirk in 1858.

34. *Souvenir, 74th Regiment, N.G., S.N.Y.* (Buffalo: Valentin and Munchausen, 1889), 1.

35. This "new" park was actually an improved and expanded version of the old Regimental Park on which Syracuse's militia had drilled since 1851. A particularly good rendering of the arsenal in its setting is found on a panoramic map of Syracuse published in 1868 by E. Sachse and Company. Scores of historic panoramic maps of villages and cities all across the country are kept in the Geography and Maps Division of the Library of Congress. Many contain renderings of New York's historic arsenals and armories in their respective settings.

36. *Syracuse Standard*, 16 September 1859.

37. *St. Lawrence Republican*, 27 April 1858, as quoted in the *Watertown Daily Times*, 7 January 1961.

38. *St. Lawrence Republican*, 19 April 1859, as quoted by Lawrence Bovard, "History of the Arsenal Building," 23 September 1963, 4.

39. *Ballston Journal*, 3 August 1858.

40. The Rochester Arsenal, which served as headquarters for the northern components of the Seventh Division, was not built until after the Civil War.

41. "Utica Citizens' Corps Centennial," *Guardsman* 14 (July 1937): 13, 24–26.

42. The money appears to have been derived from funds set aside in 1858 for the construction of twelve new arsenals in Upstate New York. By 1868 only eight of those twelve had been built or were under construction. For some reason, Oswego, Troy and Auburn were dropped from the original list and Schenectady was added.

43. The Seventh's southern units were headquartered in Corning.

44. Blake McKelvey, *Rochester: The Flower City, 1855–1890* (Cambridge: Harvard University Press, 1949), 133.

45. Wright, *Guardsman* 4 (June 1927): 8.

Chapter 3. Armories Built in New York City during the 1870s and in Upstate New York during the 1870s and 1880s

1. Falls, *Guardsman* 2 (June 1925): 5; "Diamond Jubilee Planned," *Guardsman* 13 (January 1937): 7.

2. Stiles, 1196.

3. Ibid., 1197.

4. Fogelson, 11.

5. Crisfield Johnson, *History of Oswego County* (Philadelphia: Everts, 1877), 131.

6. Henry Hale, *History of Auburn* (Auburn: Dennis, 1869), 108–09.

7. Ibid., 479.

8. The 1873 armory may have been built on the site of the 1830s gunhouse.

9. Wright, *Guardsman* 4 (June 1927): 8.

10. Russel Headley, *History of Orange County, New York,* Volume 2 (Middletown: Van Deusen and Elms, 1908), 369.

11. *Daily Journal*, quoted in *The Newburgh Centennial 1783–1883* (Newburgh: Ritchie and Hull, 1883), 19.

12. Ibid., 17.

13. Ibid., 34.

14. The Fourth Battery was disbanded on 25 February 1887 (*Annual Report*, 1887, 7).

15. "New State Armory at Troy, N.Y., Brown and Dawson, Architects, Troy, N.Y.," *American Architect and Building News* 15 (21 June 1884): 294–95.

Chapter 4. The Seventh Regiment Armory

1. Swinton, 16.

2. The "s" in Guards was dropped over the course of the next few decades. In 1862 the state usurped the name National Guard as the official term for all of its militia units; during the early twentieth century, federal officials adopted the term for all militia units across the country.

3. "The Seventh Regiment Armory," *Harper's Weekly*, 13 October 1877, 801.

4. Colonel Clark commanded the unit until 1889. In 1890 Clark wrote a definitive history of the Seventh Regiment, the two-volume *History of the Seventh Regiment of New York, 1806–1889.*

5. Clinton, born in 1838, was a New York City architect who had trained with Richard Upjohn. Although appreciated for his work on the Seventh Regiment Armory, Clinton did not achieve widespread renown until the 1890s, when he joined in practice with William H. Russell. Between 1894 and 1920, Clinton and Russell were noted for their civic and commercial buildings in New York City. The only other armory designed by Clinton and Russell was the Seventy-first Regiment's second armory on Park Avenue (1904–06).

6. Highly detailed descriptions of the interior of the armory can be found in numerous articles, reports and booklets, for example, "Seventh Regiment Armory, Illustrated," *Decorator and Furnisher Magazine* (New York: May 1885); New York City Landmarks Preservation Commission, *Seventh Regiment Armory Designation Report* (LP–1884) (New York: City of New York, 1994), prepared by Jay Shockley; and Mary Anne Hunting, "The Seventh Regiment Armory in New York City," *Magazine Antiques* (January 1999).

Chapter 5. Armories Built in Brooklyn and Manhattan during the 1880s and 1890s

1. J. Hollis Wells, "Armories for the Organized Militia," *Brickbuilder* 17 (1908): 120, 139.

2. "Our Armories," *Seventh Regiment Gazette, A Military Review,* 1 April 1888, 94.

3. King, 535.

4. Ibid., 536.

5. "The Seventy-first's Armory," *Harper's Weekly,* 27 February 1892, 199.

6. "Brooklyn's Great Armory," *Harper's Weekly,* 28 April 1894, 404.

7. "Brooklyn's New Armories," *Harper's Weekly,* 16 July 1892, 679.

8. E. E. Hardin, "The National Guard of New York State," *Outing* 25 (January 1895): 344.

9. When the New York City Armory Board was first created, its purview was restricted to New York City, that is, the island of Manhattan. When the present-day New York City was created in 1898 by joining Manhattan, Brooklyn, the Bronx, Queens and Staten Island, the purview of the New York City Armory Board was expanded to encompass all five boroughs.

10. Stiles, 1201.

11. Ibid., 1202.

12. "New Buildings in Brooklyn," *Harper's Weekly,* 9 August 1890, 619.

13. "Brooklyn's New Armories," 679.

14. "Brooklyn's Great Armory," 404.

15. Unlike most other armories built in Manhattan and Brooklyn during the 1880s, which were city-owned and funded, the Twenty-third Regiment Armory was a state facility overseen by the State Armory Board.

16. "New Buildings in Brooklyn," 619.

17. "Brooklyn's New Armories," 679.

18. *The Armory Board, 1884–1911* (New York: New York City Armory Board, 1912), 6.

19. King, 535.

20. The regiment comprised the following units: the Light Guard, City Musketeers (later named the Washington Light Guard), Tompkins Blues, City Blues, Guard Lafayette (later named the Webster Guard), Lafayette Fusiliers, Independence Guard, Baxter Blues, Baxter Guards (later named the National Greys) and New York Riflemen (later named the Black Rifles); see Falls, *Guardsman* 2 (July 1925): 7 and Monroe Mayhoff, "Ninety Years of the 12th Regiment," *Guardsman* 13 (March 1937): 14, 22.

21. *Souvenir of the Grand Opening of the New Armory of the Eighth Regiment, N.G.S.N.Y.* (30 January 1890): 6.

22. King, 534.

23. Wright, *Guardsman* 3 (December 1926): 6; see also, "Look at Your Mother's Arm," an article in an unnamed newspaper of the late 1800s found in the *Scrapbook of the Eighth Regiment* on file at the New York State Military Museum in Saratoga Springs. The *Scrapbook* and many other regiment-related materials were salvaged from the Kingsbridge Armory during the mid-1990s when DMNA turned the facility over to city officials. Unfortunately, many literary and pictorial items in the collection record neither the date nor the original source of specific documents.

24. *New York Herald*, undated clipping in *Scrapbook*.

25. Various clippings, *Scrapbook*.

26. *Eighth Coast Artillery District Athletic Association: Inaugural Games, November 27th, Nineteen Hundred and Nine* (Souvenir Pamphlet): 23; see also *New York Times*, 2 August 1871 and *Scientific Review, Special Armory Edition* 6, 3 (February 1916): 3, 11.

27. Thomas later designed the Seventy-first Regiment's first armory in 1892–1894 and the Squadron A Armory in 1894–1895.

28. Wingate, 491.

29. Ibid., 492, 495.

30. King, 536.

31. *Harper's Weekly*, 27 February 1892, 199.

32. Falls, *Guardsman* 6 (June 1929): 9.

33. *The Armory Board*, 12.

34. One of the rejected plans, that of Smyth and McIlvaine, was reproduced in the 19 May 1894 issue of *American Architect and Building News*; oddly enough, Cable and Sargent's design was not featured.

35. *Annual Report*, 1894, viii.

36. Hardin, 524.

37. Subsequent National Guard cavalry units included Troop C in Brooklyn, Troop B in Albany, Troop H in Rochester and Troop I in Buffalo.

38. *The Armory Board*, 13.

39. The squadron was organized in February 1895; in 1911 it was merged with the First Regiment of Cavalry. Two years later it became known as the First Squadron of Cavalry; in 1914 it readopted the official name Squadron A.

Chapter 6. Upstate Armories Designed by Isaac G. Perry between 1888 and 1899

1. The Office of the State Architect was established in 1899 by Governor Theodore Roosevelt; see chapter 8. For a full account of Perry, see Wesley Haynes, "Isaac G. Perry: Architect, Builder and Craftsman," master's thesis, Columbia University, 1983.

2. Perry's Twenty-third Regiment Armory (1891–95) in Brooklyn is discussed in the preceding chapter.

3. This is true for twenty-four of Perry's twenty-seven armories. The anomalies are as follows: the Washington Avenue Armory was built for a battalion; the Connecticut Street Armory in Buffalo was built for a regiment; and the Olean "armory" was merely a drill shed attached to an older building that served as the local unit's headquarters.

4. *Annual Report*, 1887, 11.

5. In Albany, Hoosick Falls, Saratoga Springs, Mount Vernon, Catskill, Poughkeepsie, Olean, Cohoes, Mohawk, Jamestown and Middletown.

6. "In Due and Ancient Form: The Corner Stone of the New State Armory Laid Today," *Daily Saratogian*, 22 November 1889.

7. Ibid.

8. *Souvenir*, unpaginated.

9. *Buffalo Express*, 5 July 1898, quoted in Warren R. Baltes, *The Story of the 74th Regimental Armory, Buffalo, New York* (Buffalo: Research Foundation of the State University of New York, Buffalo State College, 1989), 40–41.

10. "Tonawanda's Armory," *Niagara Falls Daily Cataract*, 16 February 1897, 6.

11. Baltes, 14. Much of the information in the following narrative is derived from Baltes's book, republished in honor of the armory's centennial.

12. The *Buffalo News*, 2 January 1898, as quoted by Baltes, 10.

13. Wright, *Guardsman* 4 (August 1927): 9.

14. According to the adjutant general's *Annual Report* for the year of 1930 (page 8), "reconstruction of the Hudson armory, made necessary by fire which practically destroyed the building, was completed in November and [it] is now occupied by troops."

15. "New Armory at Jamestown Inspected," *Guardsman* 10 (August 1933): 14.

16. Jamestown, New York. Fenton Historical Center. Research files, newspaper clipping from an unknown date in 1938.

17. Lewis, 404–05.

18. *Malone Palladium*, 1879, quoted by Lewis, 417.

19. Franklin B. Williams, *Middletown, A Biography* (Middletown: Toepp, 1928) 78.

20. "Using Armories for the Unemployed," *Guardsman* 7 (January 1931): 6. The use of armories as homeless shelters discontinued after the Depression ended. However, when New York City was faced with increasing numbers of homeless men, women and families during the last quarter of the twentieth century, armories were once again converted for use as temporary housing.

21. "History of the 156th Field Artillery," *Guardsman* 13 (June 1936): 14.

22. "The Tonawanda Ball—A Successful Affair," *Niagara Falls Daily Cataract*, 23 February 1897, 5.

23. T. Wood Clarke, *Utica for a Century and a Half* (Utica: Widtman, 1952), 70–71.

24. *Utica Weekly Herald*, 26 February 1895, as quoted by John J. Walsh, "From Frontier Outpost to Modern City: A History of Utica, 1784–1920," 409. (Copy on file at the Oneida County Historical Society in Utica.)

25. In 1898 the unit became Company I, Second (later 105th Infantry) Regiment; still later, it became the Howitzer Company, 105th Infantry Regiment.

26. The Fourth later became Company C, 105th Infantry Regiment.

Chapter 7. Armories Built in New York City between 1900 and World War I

1. An eighth armory, designed by State Architect George L. Heins for the Seventeenth Separate Company in Flushing in 1904–05, will be discussed in chapter 8 in the context of Heins's other early twentieth-century armories.

2. Further discussion about the office of the state architect is included in the next chapter.

3. *Annual Report*, 1907, 103.

4. Montgomery Schuyler, "Two New Armories," *Architectural Record* 29 (April 1906): 262.

5. Ibid., 264.

6. Wells, 161.

7. "Architectural Criticism, Armory, 2nd Battery, Field Artillery, N.G.N.Y., N.Y.," *Architecture* 22 (15 July 1910): 97–99.

8. Montgomery Schuyler, "An Oasis in the Bronx," *Architectural Record* 41 (February 1917): 181–82.

9. New York City Landmarks Preservation Commission, *First Battery Armory Designation Report* (LP–1670) (New York: City of New York, 1989), prepared by Michael Corbett; 9.

10. Schuyler, 1906, 261.

11. "The Bronx's Great New Armory Will Be a Mighty Fortress," *New York Herald*, 26 November 1911, 3.

12. William Francis Stanton Root, *The 69th Regiment in Peace and War* (New York: Blanchard, 1905), 35–36.

13. Schuyler, 1917, 181–82.

14. New York City Landmarks Preservation Commission, *First Battery Armory Designation Report* (LP–1670) (New York: City of New York, 1989), prepared by Michael Corbett; 2–6.

15. Ibid., 3.

16. Ibid., 9.

17. "Captain Wendel Accused of Taking Much Graft," *New York Times*, 23 December 1906.

18. *Armory Board*, 22.

19. Schuyler, 1906, 261.

20. Wells, 120–29.

21. *Armory Board*, 39.

Chapter 8. Armories Built in Upstate New York between 1900 and World War I

1. Flick, 7: 193.

2. Ibid., 194.

3. The New York State Department of Architecture was created in 1914 via a legislative amendment to the 1899 act that created the Office of the State Architect.

4. A. D. F. Hamlin, "The State Architect and His Works," *Architectural Record* 53 (January 1923): 27.

5. James H. Rowe, "History, Company L [Saratoga Springs], 105th Infantry, NYNG," n.d. (ca. 1930), 4–5. Typescript on file with the City Historian of Saratoga Springs; see also Wright, *Guardsman* 4 (August 1927): 9.

6. *Annual Report*, 1905, 51–67.

7. Included in this group is the Flushing Armory in Queens. Although built in New York City, it belongs with the group of separate company armories designed by Heins.

8. "The Rochester State Armory," *American Architect and Building News* 91 (2 February 1907) and *Brickbuilder* 17 (1908).

9. "The Finest Armory for Militia in the World," *Harper's Weekly*, 22 May 1909, 25.

10. Hamlin, 43.

11. Ibid., 42–43.

12. Ibid., 35–36.

13. Ibid., 43.

14. Frank M. Foley, "Flushing's Military History," *Guardsman* 15 (September 1939): 18–19.

15. Edsel Grinnell, "State Armory," 16 October 1994, on file at the Medina Historical Society; Russell J. Waldo, "25th Anniversary of the National Guard's Mobilization for WW II," 1964, on file at OPRHP.

16. *Annual Report*, 1900, 287–88.

17. Ibid., 288.

18. *Annual Report*, 1902, 304.

19. Falls, *Guardsman* 6 (April 1929): 9.

20. During World War I, these units were joined by troops from Buffalo and Syracuse to form the 101st Cavalry Regiment, which later became the 121st Cavalry.

Chapter 9. Armories Built in New York State between World War I and World War II

1. Blake McKelvey, *Rochester: The Quest for Quality, 1890–1925* (Cambridge: Harvard University Press, 1956), 358.

2. *Annual Report*, 1930, 32; see also "National Guard Armories Serve Many Purposes," *Guardsman* 8 (April 1931): 21.

3. "Using Armories for the Unemployed," *Guardsman* 7 (January 1931): 6.

4. *Annual Report*, 1937, 28–29; "New Club-Rooms," *Guardsman* 13 (May 1936): 14.

5. See *Annual Reports* from the 1930s, especially 1930, page 34, and 1935, pages 43–44.

6. "W.P.A. Circuses in Armories," *Guardsman* 12 (December 1935): 9.

7. *Guardsman* 1 (April 1924): 24. A conflicting, but unsubstantiated secondary source records Ely Jacques Kahn as the architect of the arsenal; see Marcus Whiffen, *American Architecture Since 1780, A Guide to the Styles* (Cambridge: MIT Press, 1969), 235.

8. Portions of Ward's address, as quoted by Philip J. Wurtelle, "New Armory for Binghamton Units Opened," *Guardsman* 11 (December 1934): 16.

9. *Annual Report*, 1927, 7.

10. "Cornerstone Laid at Corning," *Guardsman* 12 (June 1935): 15. Administrative headquarters of the 102nd were located at the former First Battery Armory on West 66th Street in Manhattan.

11. *Annual Report*, 1936, 16.

12. "History of the 156th Field Artillery," *Guardsman* 13 (June 1936): 14.

13. "The Governor Lays Cornerstone for the Peekskill Armory," *Guardsman* 9 (September 1932): 6.

14. "Comfort in Ticonderoga," *Guardsman* 14 (May 1937): 29.

15. *Annual Report*, 1933, 11; *Annual Report*, 1927, 6; Falls, *Guardsman* 5 (June 1928): 9.

16. "The New Cavalry Armory at Utica," *Guardsman* 7 (February 1931): 10.

Bibliography

Adams, Annon. "J. A. Wood." Unpublished typescript. Poughkeepsie: Annon Adams, 1997.

Aimone, Alan and Barbara Aimone. "New Netherland Defends Itself." *Military Collector and Historian* (Summer 1980): 52–57.

Albany Evening Journal, 28 February 1877.

Albany Morning Express, 30 May 1898.

Albany Times Union, 30 May 1898.

Anderson, Thomas M. "Nationalization of the State Guards." *Forum* 30 (1901): 653–57.

Annual Reports of the Adjutant General of the State of New York for the Years of 1856–1942.

"Architectural Criticism, Armory, 2nd Battery, Field Artillery, N.G.N.Y., N.Y." *Architecture* 22 (15 July 1910): 97–99.

The Armory Board, 1884–1911. New York: New York City Armory Board, 1912.

"Armory for the Eighth." *American Architect and Building News* 32 (11 April 1891): 29–30.

"Armory for Squadron C." *American Architect* 89 (20 January 1906): drawings and construction photographs, eight unnumbered plates.

"Armory of the Seventy-first Regiment." *American Architect and Building News* 46 (15 December 1894): 118–19.

"Armory of the Seventy-first Regiment." *American Architect* 89 (10 March 1906): drawings and photographs, three unnumbered plates.

Auburn: 200 Years of History. Souvenir Celebration Booklet, Auburn Bicentennial Committee. Lakeside, 1992.

Ballston Journal, 3 August 1858.

Baltes, Warren R. *The Story of the 74th Regimental Armory, Buffalo, New York.* Buffalo: Research Foundation of the State University of New York, Buffalo State College, 1989.

Beha, Anne. "Armories of New York City." January 1987. Copies of typescript on file at the New York City Landmarks Preservation Commission.

Bovard, Lawrence. "History of the [Ogdensburg] Arsenal Building." 23 September 1963. Typescript on file at the New York State Office of Parks, Recreation and Historic Preservation.

Brayer, Betsy. *The [Andrew J.] Warner Legacy in Western New York.* Rochester: Landmark Society of Western New York, 1984.

Britton, Edward E. "In What Way Can the National Guard Be Modified so as to Make It an Effective Reserve to the Regular Army in Both War and Peace." *Journal of the Military Service Institution of the United States* 26 (1900): 155–88.

"The Bronx's Great New Armory Will Be a Might Fortress." *New York Herald*, 26 November 1911: 3.

"Brooklyn's Great [Thirteenth Regiment] Armory." *Harper's Weekly*, 28 April 1894: 404.

"Brooklyn's New Armories." *Harper's Weekly*, 16 July 1892: 679.

Buffalo Express, 2 May 1909.

Buffalo, New York. Buffalo and Erie County Historical Society. Archives.

"Captain Wendell Accused of Taking Much Graft." *New York Times*, 23 December 1906.

Churchill, John C. *Landmarks of Oswego County, New York*. Syracuse: Mason, 1895.

"The Citizen Soldier; The Address Delivered at the Laying of the Corner Stone of the New York State Armory, at Ballston Spa, August 26th, 1858." *Ballston Journal*, 7 September 1858: 2.

Clark, Colonel Emmons. *History of the Seventh Regiment of New York 1806–1889*. New York: Seventh Regiment, 1890.

Clarke, T. Wood. *Utica for a Century and a Half*. Utica: Widtman, 1952.

"Company E Returns to Its Armory." *Utica Saturday Globe*, 31 December 1898.

"Competitive Design for Ninth Regiment Armory." *American Architect and Building News* 44 (19 May 1894): unnumbered plate.

"Corner Stone Ceremonies." *Daily Saratogian*, 19 November 1889.

Dunson, Fred W. *A History of Co. L, 105th Infantry, 27th Division, NYNG*. n.d. (mid-1950s). Booklet on file with the Saratoga Springs City Historian.

Eighth Coast Artillery District Athletic Association: Inaugural Games, November 27th, Nineteen Hundred and Nine. Souvenir Pamphlet.

Ellis, Herbert J. "The Story of Arsenal Hill [Canandaigua]." *Daily Messenger*, 6 September 1968: 2.

Falls, Colonel (later General, later Brigadier General) DeWitt Clinton. "Regimental Historical Sketches." *New York National Guardsman* 2–8 (April 1925–February 1932).

"Festival of Mars, Dedication of the New [Seventy-fourth Regiment] Armory Last Evening." *Buffalo Express*, 25 February 1868: 4.

"Finest Armory for Militia in the World." *Harper's Weekly*, 22 May 1909: 25.

Flick, Alexander C. *History of the State of New York*. Vols. 4–7. Port Washington: Friedman, 1962.

Flower, B. O. "Plutocracy's Bastiles: Or Why the Republic Is Becoming an Armed Camp." *Arena* 10 (October 1894): 601–21.

Fogelson, Robert M. *America's Armories: Architecture, Society and Public Order*. Cambridge: Harvard University Press, 1989.

Foley, Frank M. "Flushing's Military History." *New York National Guardsman* 15 (September 1939).

Frank Leslie's Illustrated Newspaper, 3 June 1882, 132; and various volumes from the late 1850s to the early 1880s on file at the New York State Historical Association in Cooperstown, New York.

French, J. H. *Gazetteer of the State of New York*. Syracuse: Smith, 1860.

Garand, Reverend P. S. *The History of the City of Ogdensburg*. Ogdensburg: 1927.

Godkin, E. L. "The Late Riots." *Nation* 25 (2 August 1877): 65; 68–69.

"The Great Strike." *Harper's Weekly*, 11 August 1877: 626.

Grinnell, Edsel. "[Medina] State Armory." 16 October 1994.

Hale, Henry. *History of Auburn*. Auburn: Dennis, 1869.

Hamilton, W. R. "Merits and Defects of the National Guard." *Outing* 15 (1889; 1890): 173–82; 252–59.

Hamlin, A. D. F. "The State Architect and His Works." *Architectural Record* 53 (January 1923): 27–43.

Hardin, E. E. "The National Guard of New York State." *Outing* 25 (1894): 251–56; 25 (1895): 340–44; 427–32.

Harris, Cyril M. *Dictionary of Architecture and Construction*. New York City: McGraw-Hill, 1975.

Haynes, Wesley. "Isaac G. Perry: Architect, Builder and Craftsman." Master's thesis, Columbia University, 1983.

Headley, Russel. *History of Orange County, New York.* Volume 2. Middletown: Van Deusen and Elms, 1908.

History of the DeWitt Guard, Company A, 50th Regiment, NGNY. Ithaca: Andrus, McChain, 1866.

Hough, Franklin B. *History of St. Lawrence and Franklin Counties, New York, from the Earliest Period to the Present Time.* Albany: Little, 1853.

Howard, Henry W. B. *The Eagle and Brooklyn: History of the City of Brooklyn from Its Settlement to the Present Time.* Part 2. Brooklyn: Brooklyn Daily Eagle, 1893.

Hunting, Mary Anne. "The Seventh Regiment Armory in New York City." *Magazine Antiques* (January 1999).

Hylton, Renee K., and Robert K. Wright. *A Brief History of the Militia and the National Guard: 357 Years, 1636–1993.* Washington, D.C.: Historical Services Division, Office of Public Affairs, National Guard Bureau, 1993.

"In Due and Ancient Form: The Corner Stone of the New State Armory Laid Today." *Daily Saratogian,* 22 November 1889.

"The Inauguration of Clark Mills's Statue of Washington." *Harper's Weekly,* 3 March 1860: 136.

Israel, Fred L. "New York's Citizen Soldiers: The Militia and Their Armories." *New York History, the Quarterly Journal of the New York State Historical Association* 42 (1961): 145–56.

Johnson, Crisfield. *History of Oswego County.* Philadelphia: Everts, 1877.

Kelton, J. C. "Requirements for National Defense." *Forum* 8 (1889): 317–25.

King, Moses. *King's Handbook of New York City.* Boston: 1893. Reprint, 2 volumes. New York: Benjamin Blom, 1972.

Koch, Robert. "The Medieval Castle Revival: New York Armories." *Journal of the Society of Architectural Historians* 14 (1955): 23–29.

"The Labor Troubles, II, Class Organization." *American Architect and Building News* 3 (2 February 1878): 38–39.

"The Labor Troubles, III, Communism." *American Architect and Building News* 3 (23 February 1878): 62–63.

Latham, New York. New York State Division of Military and Naval Affairs (DMNA). Research files.

"Lawn Tennis in the Seventh Regiment Armory." *Harper's Weekly,* 10 December 1881: 823–24.

"Laying the Stone." *Daily Saratogian,* 20 November 1889.

Lewis, J. W. *History of Clinton and Franklin Counties.* 1880. Reprint. Duane Hamilton Hurd, 1978.

Marshall, Alexander G. "The Necessity for Armories." *Bostonian* 1 (1895): 611–14; 2 (1895): 49–53; 617–25.

Martin, Clarence S. *Seventy-five Years with the Tenth Regiment Infantry.* Albany: Lyon, 1935.

Mayhoff, Monroe. "Ninety Years of the 12th Regiment." *New York National Guardsman* 13 (March 1937).

McKee, Harley J. "Horatio Nelson White, 1814–1892." *Empire State Architect* (March/April 1961): 28–29.

McKelvey, Blake. *Rochester: The Flower City, 1855–1890.* Cambridge: Harvard University Press, 1949.

———. *Rochester: The Quest for Quality, 1890–1925.* Cambridge: Harvard University Press, 1956.

Mercein, Daniel S. "The National Guard of New York State in Active Service in Brooklyn." *Outing* 25 (1895): 517–24.

"The Military Ball." *Tonawanda Herald,* 28 February 1897.

"The Monroe Obsequies." *Frank Leslie's Illustrated Newspaper*, 7 August 1858: 150–51.

"The Musical Festival." *Harper's Weekly*, 6 May 1882: 279–81.

"New Buildings in Brooklyn: The New Armory for the Thirteenth Regiment, The New Armory for the Twenty-third Regiment." *Harper's Weekly*, 9 August 1890: 616, 619.

"New State Armory at Troy, N.Y., Brown and Dawson, Architects, Troy, N.Y." *American Architect and Building News* 15 (21 June 1884): 294–95.

"The New State Arsenal." *Gleason's Pictorial Drawing-Room Companion*, 2 September 1854.

New York City Landmarks Preservation Commission. Research files and Designation Reports.

New York City, NY. New-York Historical Society. Research and photo files.

"New York in the Late Troubles." *Harper's Weekly*, 18 August 1877: 639.

"The New York Musical Festival." *Harper's Weekly*, 21 May 1881: 332–33, 335.

New York Times, 2 August 1871.

The Newburgh Centennial 1783–1883. Newburgh: Ritchie and Hull, 1883.

"Ogdensburg's Arsenal, 102 Years Old, Has Proud Past." *Watertown Daily Times*, 7 January 1961.

"Old Armory Knew Many Joys, Thrills, Heartbreaks." *Utica Observer-Dispatch*, 22 July 1956.

O'Reilly, Henry. *Sketches of Rochester with Incidental Notices of Western New York*. Rochester: William Alling, 1838.

"Our Armories." *Seventh Regiment Gazette, A Military Review*, 1 April 1888.

Pacelli, Tony. *Past and Present: Amsterdam and Surrounding Communities*. Amsterdam: Anthony Pacelli, 1987.

Parker, John H. "The 'National Guard' Problem." *Forum* 28 (1899): 190–96.

Peck, William F. *History of Rochester and Monroe County*. New York and Chicago: Pioneer, 1908.

Platt, Edmund. *History of Poughkeepsie, from the Earliest Settlements, 1683 to 1905*. Poughkeepsie: Platt and Platt, 1905.

Porter, Horace. "Militia Service." *Cosmopolitan* 12 (1891): 102–04.

"The Pullman Strike." *Harper's Weekly*, 21 July 1894: 686–89.

Ray, Gerda W. "'We Can Stay Until Hell Freezes Over': Strike Control and the State Police in New York, 1919–1923." *Labor History* 36 (1995): 403–25.

"The Rochester State Armory." *American Architect* 91 (2 February 1907): completion photograph, one unnumbered plate.

Root, William Francis Stanton. *The 69th Regiment in Peace and War*. New York: Blanchard, 1905.

Rowe, James H. "History, Company L [Saratoga Springs], 105th Infantry, NYNG." n.d. (ca. 1930). Typescript on file with the City Historian of Saratoga Springs.

St. Lawrence Republican, 27 April 1858; 18 May 1858; 29 November 1858.

"Saratoga's Beautiful New Building." *Saratoga Union*, 25 December 1889.

Schenectady, NY. Schenectady City History Museum, City Hall. Research files.

———. Schenectady County Historical Society. Research files.

Scientific Review, Special Armory Edition, February 1916.

Schuyler, Montgomery. "Two New Armories [Sixty-ninth and Seventy-first regiment armories]." *Architectural Record* 29 (April 1906): 259–64.

———. "An Oasis in the Bronx [Second Battery Armory]." *Architectural Record* 41 (February 1917): 177–82.

Scrapbook of the Eighth Regiment. Newspaper clippings and regimental memorabilia from the late nineteenth to mid-twentieth century; bound and on file at the New York State Military Museum, Saratoga Springs, New York.

Seaver, Frederick J. *Historical Sketches of Franklin County, Several Towns.* Albany: Lyon, 1918.

"The Seventh Regiment Armory." *Harper's Weekly*, 13 October 1877: 801.

"Seventh Regiment Armory, Illustrated." *Decorator and Furnisher Magazine* (May 1885).

"The Seventh's Athletic Club." *Harper's Weekly*, 8 April 1882: 220.

"The Seventh's Great Fair." *Harper's Weekly*, 13 December 1879: 965, 971.

"The Seventy-first Regiment Armory." *Harper's Weekly*, 7 April 1894: 333.

[The Seventy-first Regiment] *Souvenir.* 1884. Booklet on file at the New York State Military Museum.

"The Seventy-first's Armory." *Harper's Weekly*, 27 February 1892: 197, 199.

Souvenir, 74th Regiment, N.G., S.N.Y. Buffalo: Valentin and Munchausen, 1889.

Souvenir of the Grand Opening of the New Armory of the Eighth Regiment, N.G.S.N.Y. 30 January 1890.

"Squadron A's New Home." *Harper's Weekly*, 4 January 1896: 4, 7.

"Squadron C Armory." *American Architect* 89 (13 January 1906): 15–16 and four unnumbered plates.

"State Armory, White Plains." *American Architect* 95 (31 March 1909): artist's rendering and architect's drawings, four unnumbered plates.

Stiles, Henry R. *The History of the County of Kings and the City of Brooklyn, NY.* Vol. 2. New York: Munsell, 1884.

Stone, William L. *History of New York City from the Discovery to the Present Day.* New York: Virtue and Yorston, 1872.

Swinton, William. *History of the Seventh Regiment, National Guard, State of New York.* New York: Dillingham, 1869.

Syracuse, NY. Onondaga Historical Association. Research files.

Syracuse Standard. 16 September 1859.

Taylor, Daniel Morgan. "The Militia." *Cosmopolitan* 8 (1890): 566–71.

Tetra Tech, Inc. "Survey of Cold War–Era Buildings and Structures at Plattsburgh Air Force Base." November 1995.

"The Thirteenth Regiment New York State Militia Leaving Their Armory in Brooklyn for the War." *Harper's Weekly.* 11 May 1861: 295, 298.

"The Tonawanda Ball—A Successful Affair." *Niagara Falls Daily Cataract*, 23 February 1897: 5.

"Tonawanda's Armory." *Niagara Falls Daily Cataract*, 16 February 1897: 6.

"Two New Armories [Eighth and Twenty-second regiment armories]." *Harper's Weekly*, 16 February 1889: 124, 127.

"The [Seventh Regiment] Veterans' Room." *Harper's Weekly*, 25 June 1881: 413–14.

Waldo, Russell J. "25th Anniversary of the [Medina] National Guard's Mobilization for WWII." 1964.

Walsh, John J. "From Frontier Outpost to Modern City: A History of Utica, 1784–1920." Undated.

Watertown Daily Times. 7 January 1961.

Weise, A. J. *The City of Troy and Its Vicinity.* 1886.

Wells, J. Hollis. "Armories for the Organized Militia." *Brickbuilder* 17 (Nos. 6, 7 and 8, 1908): 120–62.

Whiffen, Marcus. *American Architecture Since 1780, A Guide to the Styles.* Cambridge: MIT Press, 1969.

Withey, Henry F. and Elsie Rathburn Withey. *Biographical Dictionary of American Architects (Deceased).* Los Angeles: Hennessey and Ingalls, 1970.

Williams, Franklin B. *Middletown, A Biography.* Middletown: Toepp, 1928.

Wingate, George Wood. *History of the Twenty-second Regiment of the National Guard of the State of New York from Its Organization to 1895.* New York: Dayton, 1896.

Wright, William R. "Service in Aid of Civil Authorities," a multipart series published in installments in 1926 and 1927 in the *New York National Guardsman* 3 and 4 (November 1926–October 1927).

Appendix I
Arsenals and Armories by Location

This table is organized alphabetically by location and generally chronologically within each location. Shaded entries denote arsenals/armories that no longer survive.

Many entries include the unit(s) for which the facility was built or that had clear and lengthy affiliations with a specific arsenal or armory. Some entries, especially those for post–World War I armories, contain no specific unit, primarily because the names changed so frequently during the twentieth century that it is virtually impossible

(and somewhat meaningless) to assign discreet units to any given armory.

In addition to the forty-three (43) arsenals/armories listed in the National Register of Historic Places, there are two facilities that have been designated as National Historic Landmarks. They are the Seventh Regiment Armory (1879) on Park Avenue and the Sixty-ninth Regiment Armory (1906) on Lexington Avenue. Both are located in Manhattan.

Location	Armory	Unit	Address	Date, Architect	Date of National Register Listing
Albany Albany County	Albany Arsenal		Broadway at North Lawrence Street	1799 Hooker	
Albany Albany County	Albany Arsenal	Tenth Regiment, Third Division (South)	Hudson Street (later Avenue) and Eagle Street	1858 von Steinwehr	
Albany Albany County	Washington Avenue Armory	Tenth Batallion	195 Washington Avenue	1889–93 Perry	1995
Albany Albany County	New Scotland Avenue Armory	Troop B	New Scotland Avenue	1914 Pilcher	1994
Amsterdam Montgomery County	Amsterdam Armory	Forty-sixth Separate Company	Florida Avenue at DeWitt Street	1895 Perry	1994
Auburn Cayuga County	Auburn Armory	Forty-ninth Regiment	57 Water Street	1873 Hamblin	
Ballston Spa Saratoga County	Ballston Spa Arsenal	Third Division (North)	Ballston Avenue	1858 White	
Binghamton Broome County	Binghamton Armory	Sixth Battery and Twentieth Separate Company	202–208 State Street	1880s	1986

Entries that are shaded denote facilities that no longer survive.

Location	Armory	Unit	Address	Date, Architect	Date of National Register Listing
Binghamton Broome County	Binghamton Armory	Sixth Battery and Twentieth Separate Company	Washington Street	1904–06 Heins	
Binghamton Broome County	Binghamton Armory		85 West End Avenue	1932–34 Haugaard	
Bronx Bronx County	Franklin Avenue Armory	Second Battery	1122 Franklin Avenue (at East 166th Street)	1908–11 Haight	
Bronx Bronx County	Kingsbridge Armory	Eighth Coastal Artillery District	29 West Kingsbridge Road (between Jerome and Reservoir avenues)	1912–17 Pilcher and Tachau	1982
Brooklyn Kings County	Gothic Hall	Thirteenth and Fourteenth regiments	Adams Street	1830s	
Brooklyn Kings County	Henry Street Armory	Thirteenth and Fourteenth regiments	Henry Street at Cranberry Street	1858	
Brooklyn Kings County	State Arsenal	Second Division	North Portland Avenue at Auburn Place	1858	
Brooklyn Kings County	Flatbush Avenue Armory	Thirteenth Regiment	Flatbush Avenue at Hanson Place	1874–75	
Brooklyn Kings County	North Portland Avenue Armory	Fourteenth Regiment	North Portland Avenue at Auburn Place	1877–78	
Brooklyn Kings County	Clermont Avenue Armory	Twenty-third Regiment	Clermont Avenue between Myrtle and Willoughby avenues	1872–73 (extensively remodeled in 1911) Mundell	
Brooklyn Kings County	Clermont Avenue Armory	First Battalion of Field Artillery	Clermont Avenue between Myrtle and Willoughby avenues	1911	
Brooklyn Kings County	Forty-seventh Regiment Armory	Forty-seventh Regiment	355 Marcy Avenue (between Heyward and Lynch streets)	1883–84 Mundell (1899 drill shed: Perry)	
Brooklyn Kings County	Dean Street Armory	Second Signal Corps	793–801 Dean Street	1909–11 (originally designed by Dixon ca. 1884 for the Third [Gatling] Battery) Robinson and Kunst	

Entries that are shaded denote facilities that no longer survive.

Location	Armory	Unit	Address	Date, Architect	Date of National Register Listing
Brooklyn Kings County	Thirteenth Regiment Armory	Thirteenth Regiment	357 Sumner Avenue (now Marcus Garvey Boulevard; between Atlantic Avenue and Pacific Street)	1892–94 Daus	
Brooklyn Kings County	Twenty-third Regiment Armory	Twenty-third Regiment	1322 Bedford Avenue (between Atlantic Avenue and Pacific Street)	1891–95 Fowler and Hough (with Perry)	1980
Brooklyn Kings County	Fourteenth Regiment Armory	Fourteenth Regiment	1402 Eighth Avenue (between 14th and 15th streets)	1891–95 Mundell	1994
Brooklyn Kings County	Troop C Armory	Troop C	1579 Bedford Avenue (between President and Union streets)	1903–07 Pilcher and Tachau	
Brooklyn Kings County	Brooklyn Arsenal		Second Avenue (between 63rd and 64th streets)	1924–26 Jones	
Buffalo Erie County	Broadway Arsenal	Sixty-fifth and Seventy-fourth regiments	Broadway (formerly Batavia Road)	1858 Otis	
Buffalo Erie County	Virginia Street Armory	Seventy-fourth Regiment	Virginia Street at North William Street (later Fremont Place, later Elmwood Avenue)	1868	
Buffalo Erie County	Virginia Street Armory	Seventy-fourth Regiment	Virginia Street at Fremont Place (formerly North William Street, later Elmwood Avenue)	1882 Beebe	
Buffalo Erie County	Virginia Street Armory	Seventy-fourth Regiment	Virginia Street at Elmwood Avenue (originally Fremont Place, subsequently North William Street)	1884–86 Bethune and Bethune	
Buffalo Erie County	Connecticut Street Armory	Seventy-fourth Regiment	184 Connecticut Street (between Niagara Street and Prospect Avenue)	1896–99 Perry (with Lansing)	1995
Buffalo Erie County	Sixty-fifth Regiment Armory	Sixty-fifth Regiment	Broadway between Potter and Milner streets	1884	
Buffalo Erie County	Masten Avenue Armory	Sixty-fifth Regiment	27 Masten Avenue	1902–07 Heins	
Buffalo Erie County	Masten Avenue Armory	Sixty-fifth Regiment	27 Masten Avenue	1932–33 Haugaard	

Entries that are shaded denote facilities that no longer survive.

Location	Armory	Unit	Address	Date, Architect	Date of National Register Listing
Buffalo Erie County	West Delavan Avenue Armory	Troop I, 121st Calvary	1015 West Delavan Avenue	1917 Pilcher	
Canandaigua Ontario County	Canandaigua Arsenal		Arsenal Hill	1808	
Catskill Greene County	Catskill Armory	Sixteenth Separate Company	78 Water Street	1888–89 Perry	
Cohoes Albany County	Cohoes Armory	Seventh Separate Company	Hart Street (current legal address: 41 Columbia Street)	1892–93 Perry	
Corning Steuben County	Corning Arsenal	Seventh Division (South)	First Street between Washington and Hamilton streets	1858	
Corning Steuben County	Corning Armory		Centerway	1935–36 Haugaard	2003
Dunkirk Chautauqua County	Dunkirk Arsenal	Eighth Division (South)	Central Avenue and East Fourth Street	1858 White	
Elmira Chemung County	Elmira Armory	Thirteenth Separate Company	307 East Church Street	1886–88 Pierce	1980
Flushing Queens County	Flushing Armory	Seventeenth Separate Company	137–58 Northern Avenue	1904–05 Heins	1995
Geneva Ontario County	Geneva Armory	Thirty-fourth Separate Company	300 Main Street	1892 (with 1906 expansion by Heins) Perry	1995
Geneva Ontario County	Geneva Armory	Thirty-fourth Separate Company	300 Main Street	1906 Heins	1995
Glens Falls Warren County	Glens Falls Armory	Eighteenth Separate Company	147 Warren Street	1895 Perry	1984
Gloversville Fulton County	Gloversville Armory	Nineteenth Separate Company	87 Washington Street	1904–05 Heins	1995
Hempstead Nassau County	Hempstead Armory		216 Washington Street	1927–29 Jones	
Hoosick Falls Rensselaer County	Hoosick Falls Armory	Thirty-second Separate Company	Church Street at Elm Street	1888–89 Perry	1995

Entries that are shaded denote facilities that no longer survive.

Location	Armory	Unit	Address	Date, Architect	Date of National Register Listing
Hornell Steuben County	Hornell Armory	Forty-seventh Separate Company	100 Seneca Street	1894–96 Perry	1980
Hudson Columbia County	Hudson Armory	Twenty-third Separate Company	Fifth and State streets	1898 Perry	
Ithaca Tompkins County	Ithaca Armory/ Barton Hall		Cornell University	1914–18 Pilcher	
Jamaica Queens County	Jamaica Armory	Fourth Regiment (104th Field Artillery)	168th Street	1936 Meyers	
Jamestown Chautauqua County	Jamestown Armory	Thirteenth Separate Company	South Main Street	1890–92 Perry	
Jamestown Chautauqua County	Jamestown Armory		Porter Avenue and Front Street	1932 Haugaard	1995
Kingston Ulster County	Kingston Armory	Fourteenth Separate Company	467 Broadway (at Hoffman Street)	1879 Wood	
Kingston Ulster County	Kingston Armory		North Manor Road	1932 Haugaard	
Malone Franklin County	Malone Armory	Twenty-seventh Separate Company	116 West Main Street	1891–92 Perry	1995
Medina Orleans County	Medina Armory	Twenty-ninth Separate Company	302 Pearl Street (at Prospect Street)	1901 Heins	1995
Middletown Orange County	Middletown Armory	Twenty-fourth Separate Company	Highland Avenue at Wickham Avenue	1891–92 Perry	
Mohawk Herkimer County	Mohawk Armory	Thirty-first Separate Company	83 East Main Street	1891–92 Perry	
Mount Vernon Westchester County	Mount Vernon Armory	Eleventh Separate Company	North Fifth Avenue at North Street	1888–89 Perry	
New York City (Manhattan) New York County	Centre Market Armory	Seventh Regiment (et alia)	Grand and Centre streets	1830s	
New York City (Manhattan) New York County	Downtown Arsenal	First Division	White, Elm, Center and Franklin streets	1844	

Entries that are shaded denote facilities that no longer survive.

Location	Armory	Unit	Address	Date, Architect	Date of National Register Listing
New York City (Manhattan) New York County	Central Park Arsenal	First Division and Seventh Regiment	Fifth Avenue at East 64th Street	1848 Thompson	1963
New York City (Manhattan) New York County	Tompkins Market Armory	Seventh Regiment	Third Avenue at the Bowery between East 6th and East 7th streets	1857–60 Bogardus (and Lefferts)	
New York City (Manhattan) New York County	State Arsenal	First Division	Seventh Avenue at West 35th Street	1858 Cleveland and Backue	
New York City (Manhattan) New York County	Twenty-second Regiment Armory	Twenty-second Regiment	West 14th Street near Sixth Avenue	1863	
New York City (Manhattan) New York County	Seventh Regiment Armory	Seventh Regiment	643 Park Avenue (between East 66th and East 67th streets)	1877–81 Clinton	1975
New York City (Manhattan) New York County	Twelfth Regiment Armory	Twelfth Regiment	Columbus Avenue between West 61st and West 62nd streets	1886–87 J. E. Ware	
New York City (Manhattan) New York County	Eighth Regiment Armory	Eighth Regiment	Park Avenue between East 94th and East 95th streets	1888–89 Thomas	
New York City (Manhattan) New York County	Twenty-second Regiment Armory	Twenty-second Regiment	Western Boulevard (later Broadway) at Columbus Avenue (between West 67th and West 68th streets)	1889–92 Leo	
New York City (Manhattan) New York County	Seventy-first Regiment Armory	Seventy-first Regiment	Park Avenue between East 33rd and East 34th streets	1892–94 Thomas	
New York City (Manhattan) New York County	Squadron A Armory	Squadron A	Madison Avenue between East 94th and East 95th streets	1894–95 Thomas	1972
New York City (Manhattan) New York County	Ninth Regiment Armory	Ninth Regiment	West 14th Street between Sixth and Seventh avenues	1894–96 Cable and Sargent	

Entries that are shaded denote facilities that no longer survive.

Location	Armory	Unit	Address	Date, Architect	Date of National Register Listing
New York City (Manhattan) New York County	First Battery Armory	First Battery	56 West 66th Street	1901–03 Horgan and Slattery	
New York City (Manhattan) New York County	Sixty-ninth Regiment Armory	Sixty-ninth Regiment	68 Lexington Avenue (between East 25th and East 26th streets)	1904–06 Hunt and Hunt	1994
New York City (Manhattan) New York County	Seventy-first Regiment Armory	Seventy-first Regiment	Park Avenue between East 33rd and East 34th streets	1904–06 Clinton and Russell	
New York City (Manhattan) New York County	Fort Washington Avenue Armory	Twenty-second Regiment Corps of Engineers	216 Fort Washington Avenue	1911 Walker and Morris	1995
New York City (Manhattan) New York County	369th Regiment Armory	369th Regiment	2366 Fifth Avenue (between West 142nd and West 143rd streets)	Early 1920s; 1930–33 Tachau and Vought (early 1920s: drill shed) Van Wart and Wein (1930–33: administration building)	1994
Newburgh Orange County	Newburgh Armory	Fifth and Tenth separate companies	145 Broadway	1879 Wood	1981
Newburgh Orange County	Newburgh Armory		South William Street	1931–32 Haugaard	
Niagara Falls Niagara County	Niagara Falls Armory	Forth-second Separate Company	901 Main Street	1895 Perry	1995
Ogdensburg St. Lawrence County	Ogdensburg Arsenal	Fourth Division	100 Lafayette Street	1858 White	1976
Ogdensburg St. Lawrence County	Ogdensburg Armory	Thirty-fifth Separate Company	225 Elizabeth Street (at Ford Street)	1898 Perry	1995
Olean Cattaraugus County	Olean Armory (new drill shed attached to an 1870s house)	Forty-third Separate Company	North Barry and North streets (later Times Square)	1889–91 Perry	1995

Entries that are shaded denote facilities that no longer survive.

Location	Armory	Unit	Address	Date, Architect	Date of National Register Listing
Olean Cattaraugus County	Olean Armory (new administration building attached to Perry's drill shed)	Forty-third Separate Company	119 Times Square	1919 Pilcher	1995
Oneida Madison County	Oneida Armory		217 Cedar Street	1929–30 Haugaard	1995
Oneonta Otsego County	Oneonta Armory	Third Separate Company	4 Academy Street (at Fairview Avenue)	1885	
Oneonta Otsego County	Oneonta Armory	Third Separate Company	4 Academy Street (at Fairview Avenue)	1904–05 Heins	1995
Oswego Oswego County	Old Market House	Oswego Guards	Water Street	1835	1974
Oswego Oswego County	East Side Armory	Forty-eighth Regiment	East First Street	1873 Attributed to White	
Oswego Oswego County	Oswego Armory	Forty-eighth Separate Company	265 West First Street	1906–08 Heins	1988
Peekskill Westchester County	Peekskill Armory		955 Washington Street	1932–33 Haugaard	
Poughkeepsie Dutchess County	Poughkeepsie Armory	Fifteenth Separate Company	61 Market Street (at Church Street)	1891–92 Perry	1982
Rochester Monroe County	Center Market Armory	Pioneer Rifleman et alia	Front and Market streets	1836–37	
Rochester Monroe County	Rochester Arsenal	Seventh Division (North) and Fifty-fourth Regiment	Woodbury Boulevard at Washington Park	1868–70 Warner	1985
Rochester Monroe County	East Main Street Armory	Third Regiment	900 East Main Street	1904–07 Heins	
Rochester Monroe County	Culver Road Armory	Troop H (later F), 121st Cavalry Headquarters	145 Culver Road	1917 Pilcher	
Russell St. Lawrence County	Russell Armory		Russell-Pyrites Road	ca. 1809	

Entries that are shaded denote facilities that no longer survive.

Location	Armory	Unit	Address	Date, Architect	Date of National Register Listing
Saratoga Springs Saratoga County	Saratoga Armory	Twenty-second Separate Company	61 Lake Avenue	1889–91 Perry	1982
Schenectady Schenectady County	Schenectady Arsenal	Fifth Division	State Street at Crescent (later Veterans') Park	1868	
Schenectady Schenectady County	Schenectady Armory	Thirty-sixth and Thirty-seventh separate companies	State Street at Crescent (later Veterans') Park	1898–99 Perry	
Schenectady Schenectady County	Schenectady Armory	105th Infantry Regiment Headquarters	125 Washington Avenue	1936 Haugaard	1995
Staten Island Richmond County	Staten Island Armory	101st Cavalry Squadron	321 Manor Road	1922 Werner and Windolph	
Syracuse Onondaga County	Syracuse Arsenal	Sixth Division and Fifty-first Regiment	West Jefferson Street	1858–59 White	
Syracuse Onondaga County	Syracuse Armory	Fifty-first Regiment	West Jefferson Street	1873 White	
Syracuse Onondaga County	West Jefferson Street Armory	Forty-first Separate Company and Troop D, 121st Cavalry	236 West Jefferson Street	1906–07 Heins	1984
Syracuse Onondaga County	East Genesee Street Armory		1055 East Genesee Street	1941–43 Haugaard	
Ticonderoga Essex County	Ticonderoga Armory		315 Champlain Avenue	1935 Haugaard	1988
Tonawanda Erie County	Tonawanda Armory	Twenty-fifth Separate Company	79 Delaware Street	1896–97 Perry	1994
Troy Rensselaer County	Fulton Market Armory	Troy Citizens' Corps	River Street at Fulton Street	1830s	
Troy Rensselaer County	Troy Armory	Sixth, Twelfth and Twenty-first separate companies	Ferry Street	1884–86 Brown and Dawson	
Troy Rensselaer County	Troy Armory	Sixth and Twelfth separate companies	Ferry Street	1902 Heins	

Entries that are shaded denote facilities that no longer survive.

Location	Armory	Unit	Address	Date, Architect	Date of National Register Listing
Troy Rensselaer County	Troy Armory	105th Infantry Regiment Headquarters	Fifteenth Street, Rensselaer Polytechnic Institute	1918–19 Pilcher	
Utica Oneida County	Utica Arsenal	Twenty-eighth Separate Company	Bleecker Street	1862 White	
Utica Oneida County	Utica Armory	Twenty-eighth and Forty-fourth separate companies	Rutger and Steuben streets at Steuben Park	1893–94 Perry	
Utica Oneida County	Utica Armory	Troop A, 121st Cavalry	1700 Parkway East	1929–30 Haugaard	1995
Walton Delaware County	Walton Armory	Thirty-third Separate Company	Stockton Avenue	1886 Randall and Gilbert	1998
Walton Delaware County	Walton Armory	Thirty-third Separate Company	Stockton Avenue	1895–96 Perry	
Watertown Jefferson County	Watertown Armory	Thirty-ninth Separate Company	190 Arsenal Street	1879 Wood	
White Plains Westchester County	White Plains Armory	Forty-ninth Separate Company	South Broadway at Mitchell Place	1909–10 F. B. Ware	1980
Whitehall Washington County	Whitehall Armory	Ninth Separate Company	62 Poultney Street (at Williams Street)	1899 Perry	1995
Yonkers Westchester County	Yonkers Armory	Fourth Separate Company	Waverly Street	1890s Perry	
Yonkers Westchester County	Yonkers Armory		127 North Broadway (at Quincy Place)	1918 Pilcher	

Entries that are shaded denote facilities that no longer survive.

Appendix II
Notes on Architects and Architectural Firms

This appendix provides an annotated list of many of the various architects and architectural firms who were responsible for armory construction in New York State. Most entries include brief biographies, all of which are based on readily available secondary sources. For the purposes of this book, extensive research on relatively unknown architects and/or firms was not conducted; thus, the information is provided as a brief overview rather than a comprehensive research tool. The following are included in the appendix:

Brown and Dawson
Cable and Sargent
Clinton, Charles W.
Daus, Rudolf L.
Fowler and Hough
Haight, Charles C.
Hamblin, G.
Haugaard, William E.
Heins, George L.
Hooker, Philip
Horgan and Slattery
Hunt, Joseph R.
Jones, Sullivan W.
Leo, Captain John P.
Mundell, William A.
Perry, Isaac G.
Pierce and Bickford
Pilcher, Lewis F.
Robinson and Kunst
Thomas, John R.
Van Wart and Wein
Walker and Morris

Ware, Franklin B.
Ware, James E.
Warner, Andrew J.
Wells, Colonel James H.
Werner and Windolph
White, Horatio N.
Wood, John A.

Brown and Dawson

1884–86   Troy Armory, River and Ferry streets

Virtually nothing is currently known about this firm, other than the fact that they designed a new armory in Troy in 1884 to replace the old quarters occupied by the local militia unit over the Fulton Market Armory.

Cable and Sargent (W. E. Cable and E. A. Sargent)

1894–96   Ninth Regiment Armory, West 14th Street, Manhattan

W. E. Cable was a former member of both the Seventh Regiment and Squadron A. No information about E. A. Sargent is available.

Clinton, Charles W. (Clinton and Russell)

1877–81   Seventh Regiment Armory, Park Avenue, Manhattan
1904–06   Seventy-first Regiment Armory, Park Avenue, Manhattan

Charles W. Clinton was born in 1838. After apprenticing with Richard Upjohn, Clinton entered into independent practice. His design for the new armory for the Seventh Regiment was one of his first professional endeavors. Later, Clinton collaborated briefly with the renowned church architect Edward T. Potter and, by 1894, had entered into partnership with William Hamilton Russell, with whom he remained associated until the latter's death in 1907. (Even after Russell's death, Clinton continued to practice under the firm's established name.) The firm of Clinton and Russell (both before and after Russell's death) gained widespread acclaim for numerous public and professional/commercial buildings primarily in New York City; notable examples include the Astor Hotel, the New York Athletic Club and the Bank of America building.

Several decades after Clinton designed the Seventh Regiment Armory, the firm of Clinton and Russell oversaw the design and construction of a new facility for the Seventy-first Regiment (1904–06). Colonel James Hollis Wells, an employee of the firm as well as a member of the Seventh-first Regiment, was the architect in charge of the project. Clinton died in 1910, but the firm lived on under the leadership of Wells.

Daus, Rudolph Laurent

1892–94   Thirteenth Regiment Armory, Sumner Avenue, Brooklyn

Born in Mexico and educated in New York, Germany and the Ecole des Beaux Arts in Paris, Rudolph L. Daus was a locally renowned architect in Brooklyn and Manhattan for more than thirty years. Notable public buildings designed by Daus include the German Hospital and the Brooklyn Hall of Records (1905) in Brooklyn and the Church of Our Lady of Lourdes and the New York County National Bank in Manhattan. Considering his classical training and his extensive affiliations with both the American Institute of Architects (AIA), a predominantly conservative, classically oriented organization, and the similarly inclined Beaux Arts Society of Architects, the highly picturesque, medieval-inspired Thirteenth Regiment Armory is surprisingly atypical of Daus's general aesthetic predilections.

Fowler and Hough (Halstead Parker Fowler and William Hough)

1891–95   Twenty-third Regiment Armory, Bedford Avenue, Brooklyn

The firm of Fowler and Hough was locally renowned in the New York City area during the late nineteenth and early twentieth centuries. The firm maintained offices at 280 Broadway in Manhattan. Prominent public buildings in Brooklyn designed by Fowler and Hough include the Throop Avenue Presbyterian Church, the Cumberland Street Hospital and the Dudley Memorial Building at 110 Amity Street in the Cobble Hill neighborhood.

Halstead Parker Fowler was born in 1859 and died on 11 March 1911. He was a member of the Twenty-third Regiment, as was William Hough, about whom little else is known. Although the execution of the building was carried out by Fowler and his partner, the form and design of the edifice was created—or perhaps influenced or even dictated—by Isaac G. Perry who, at the time, was the state architect. Unlike most armories built in New York City, which were locally owned buildings designed by private firms and overseen by the New York City Armory Board, the new armory for the Twenty-third Regiment was a state-owned facility that was funded, overseen and completely controlled by the state. The Romanesque Revival armory, with its bold, heavy massing, polychrome masonry and asymmetrical form dominated by a six-and-one-half-story corner tower, is a quintessential embodiment of Perry's aesthetic.

Haight, Charles Coolidge

1908–11	Franklin Avenue Armory, Bronx

Born in New York City in 1841, Charles C. Haight apprenticed with the architectural offices of Emlyn T. Littel after recuperating from severe injuries incurred during the Civil War. After several years with Littel, Haight opened his own offices and was promptly appointed architect of the Trinity Church Corporation in New York City. (His father was, for many years, assistant rector at the church.) Haight's earliest, most important commissions included the School of Mines at Columbia University (1874) and Hamilton Hall at Columbia University (1880). The latter was an important example of the nascent Collegiate Gothic mode, which Haight later used in the Second Battery Armory on Franklin Avenue in the Bronx. Other notable public buildings in Manhattan designed by Haight during the late nineteenth century included the first Cancer Hospital on Central Park West; the Down Town Club at Pine and Cedar streets; Trinity Parish Offices on Church Street; the Eye and Ear Hospital; the General Theological Seminary; the Lawyers' Title Insurance Building on Maiden Lane; Christ Church on Broadway at West 71st Street; the Church of the Holy Nativity; and St. Ignatius at West 87th Street and Amsterdam Avenue.

During the first decade of the twentieth century, Haight collaborated with Alfred W. Githens on a number of Collegiate Gothic buildings at Yale University. The Franklin Avenue Armory in the Bronx was one of the last major commissions undertaken by Haight during his thirty-year professional career; he died in 1917.

Hamblin, G.

1873	Auburn Armory, Water Street

Virtually nothing is currently known about G. Hamblin, who designed the Auburn Armory for the Forty-ninth Regiment in 1873.

Haugaard, William E.

1932–34	Binghamton Armory, West End Avenue
1932–33	Masten Avenue Armory, Buffalo
1935–36	Corning Armory, Centerway
1932	Jamestown Armory, Porter Avenue
1932	Kingston Armory, North Manor Road
1931–32	Newburgh Armory, South William Street
1929–30	Oneida Armory, Cedar Street
1932–33	Peekskill Armory, Washington Street
1936	Schenectady Armory, Washington Street
1941–43	East Genesee Street Armory, Syracuse
1935	Ticonderoga Armory, Champlain Avenue
1929–30	Utica Armory, Parkway East

William E. Haugaard, state architect between 1928 and 1944, was born in 1889 in Brooklyn and educated at Pratt Institute, the Massachusetts Institute of Technology and the Ecole des Beaux Arts. Between 1912 and 1917, he was employed by the drafting department of the Isthmusian Canal Commission in New York City and oversaw several major building projects in the Panama Canal Zone. During World War I, he was appointed assistant construction quartermaster at Fort McHenry in Baltimore, Maryland. After the Great War, he worked in a number of different New York City firms, including Mowbray and Uffinger, William T. Stoddard and Warren and Wetmore.

Haugaard was appointed state architect on 11 February 1928 by Governor Alfred E. Smith. During his sixteen-year tenure in state office, Haugaard was responsible for the design of dozens of public buildings, including prisons, schools, asylums and armories. After retiring from state service in 1944, Haugaard moved to Manhasset, Long Island, where he designed buildings for the Long Island Park Commission and the Brooklyn Board of Transportation. In 1947 he was appointed Chief of Planning for the New York Housing Authority; he died the following year.

Heins, George Lewis

1904–06	Binghamton Armory, Washington Street
1902–07	Masten Avenue Armory, Buffalo
1904–05	Flushing Armory, Northern Avenue
1906	Geneva Armory, Main Street
1904–05	Gloversville Armory, Washington Street
1901	Medina Armory, Pearl Street
1904–05	Oneonta Armory, Academy Street
1906–08	Oswego Armory, West First Street
1904–07	East Main Street Armory, Rochester
1906–07	West Jefferson Street Armory, Syracuse
1902	Troy Armory, Ferry Street

George L. Heins, who was born in Philadelphia on 4 May 1860 and died on 25 September 1907, served as state architect between 1899 and 1907. He attended the University of Pennsylvania and graduated from the Massachusetts Institute of Technology in 1882. Shortly after graduating, Heins worked for several different architectural firms in Minnesota; subsequently, he moved to New York City and in 1886 established himself with Christopher G. LaFarge, renowned church architect and son of artist John LaFarge. During their twenty-year partnership (which overlapped Heins's tenure as state architect), LaFarge and Heins achieved widespread acclaim for a series of monumental religious buildings across the Northeast and mid-Atlantic states, including the Church of the Blessed Sacrament in Providence, Rhode Island, St. Paul's in Rochester, New York, the Cathedral of St. John the Divine in New York City, the Church of the Good Shepherd in Shelton, Connecticut, the Roman Catholic churches at both Tuxedo Park and West Point, New York, St. Matthew's Roman Catholic Cathedral in Washington, D.C., and the Fourth Presbyterian Church in New York City. The firm also designed the original subway stations for the Rapid Transit Commission in New York City, as well as private residences for a number of distinguished families in New York City and Washington, D.C.

In 1899 Heins was appointed by Governor Theodore Roosevelt to succeed Isaac G. Perry as state architect. During his tenure in state service Heins oversaw numerous renovations conducted during the ongoing building program at the State Capitol in Albany. In the context of Heins's oeuvre, his early twentieth-century armories pale in comparison to his late nineteenth-century churches. In the context of armory construction in New York State, Heins's armories carry on the traditions established by his predecessor, Isaac G. Perry: most are quintessential castellated-style fortresses, despite their cleaner, flatter, more modern character.

Hooker, Philip

1799	Albany Arsenal, Broadway

Born in 1776, Hooker was widely renowned for numerous Federal-style buildings erected in Albany, New York, between 1790 and 1830. In 1797 Hooker achieved widespread acclaim for his design for one of the first buildings at the newly established Union College (1795) in Schenectady, New York. Shortly thereafter, he began designing civic and religious buildings in nearby Albany. In 1799 Hooker was commissioned to design a state arsenal on North Broadway in Albany.

Hooker's most famous Federal-style buildings in Albany date from the first three decades of the nineteenth century. Notable examples in Albany include St. Peter's Church (1802), the New York State Bank (1803), South (Middle) Dutch Church (1805), the first State Capitol (1804–1806), Albany Academy (1815), the Lancaster School (1815), the First Lutheran Church (1816), the Pearl Street Theater (1824), the Fourth Presbyterian Church (1828) and the first City Hall (1829); only the Albany Academy survives.

Hooker also designed numerous renowned civic and/or religious buildings in nearby Utica, Cooperstown, Cazenovia and Clinton in the Mohawk Valley, Cherry Valley and central regions of Upstate New York. He died in 1836.

Horgan and Slattery (Arthur J. Horgan and Vincent Slattery)

1901–03   First Battery Armory, West 66th Street, Manhattan

The New York City firm of Horgan and Slattery operated between 1889 and 1910, during which time they achieved widespread notoriety as Tammany Hall's unofficial "City Architects." Through their questionable association with the infamous Mayor Robert Van Wyck (following their refurbishing of the Democratic Club in 1897), Horgan and Slattery landed virtually every commission for city-sponsored buildings erected by the Department of Corrections, the Charities Department and the Tax Department during Van Wyck's tenure. Notable projects executed by the team included numerous recreation piers, interior work at the Tombs, many fire stations, the completion of the New York City Hall of Records, Harlem Hospital and the Sanitarium at Sailors' Snug Harbor.

Horgan, who was born in 1868 and died on 2 September 1912, came from a family active in the building business. He trained as an apprentice with his godfather, Colonel Arthur Crooks. (Crooks, locally renowned for his Victorian-era religious buildings in the New York City area, had trained with Richard Upjohn, the famous mid-nineteenth-century church architect.)

Slattery was born in 1867 and died in 1939. Before joining Horgan in architectural practice, Slattery was in the coal business. While teamed professionally, Horgan handled the technical and architectural aspects of the firm's commissions and Slattery dealt with the administrative aspects of the business.

Horgan, an honorary member the First Regiment, was commissioned in 1900 to design a new armory for his unit. Several years later, Horgan and Slattery almost acquired the commission to design a new armory for the Sixty-ninth Regiment on Lexington Avenue in Manhattan, but lost the project amid continuing scandals at Tammany Hall. (The Sixty-ninth Regiment Armory was subsequently designed by the New York City firm of Hunt and Hunt.) After Horgan's death in 1912, Slattery worked in the insurance and real estate fields.

Hunt, Joseph Howland (Hunt and Hunt)

1904–06   Sixty-ninth Regiment Armory, Lexington Avenue, Manhattan

Joseph Howland Hunt, born in 1870, was the younger son of the famous Richard Morris Hunt. In 1901 Hunt joined his older brother, Richard Howland Hunt, to form the firm of Hunt and Hunt. (Richard Howland had practiced with his father until the latter's death in 1896.) Like their father before them, the sons carried on the tradition of Beaux Arts classicism; both—like their father—had trained in the Ecole des Beaux Arts in Paris. The design for the Sixty-ninth Regiment Armory, one of their earliest commissions, is primarily the work of Joseph; the pair went on to achieve widespread acclaim for a number of public and private commissions in the New York City region, including the East Wing of the Metropolitan Museum, the Fiske Office Building on Broadway at West 57th Street, the Old Slip Police Station and the Alumni Building and Williams Hall at Vassar College in Poughkeepsie. They were also renowned for their palatial urban and country residences designed for many members of New York City's elite during the early twentieth century.

Jones, Sullivan W.

1924–26   Brooklyn Arsenal, Second Avenue
1927–29   Hempstead Armory, Washington Street

Jones was born in West Brighton (Rockland County) in 1878 and served as state architect beginning in 1923. He was educated in public schools in New York City and Hoboken before enrolling in the Massachusetts Institute of Technology (Class of 1900). Other well-known buildings designed by Jones include the Alfred E. Smith State Office Building in Albany and City Hall in Buffalo.

Leo, Captain John P.

1889–92   Twenty-second Regiment Armory, Western Boulevard
(later Broadway), Manhattan

The initial commission for the Twenty-second Regiment Armory was awarded to George B. Post, a renowned New York City architect as well as a retired colonel, a Civil War veteran and a former commander of the Twenty-second Regiment. Post's proposal proved far too elaborate and costly for the $300,000 allocated to the project by the New York City Armory Board; unwilling or unable to scale down his original design, Post gave up the commission. Captain Leo, a member of the Twenty-second Regiment at the time, was subsequently hired to design a new armory for his comrades. Nothing is known about Leo's background in building, architecture or engineering—or whether he even had training in any of these areas at all.

Mundell, William A.

1872–73   Clermont Avenue Armory, Clermont Avenue,
Brooklyn
1883–84   Forty-seventh Regiment Armory, Marcy Avenue,
Brooklyn
1891–95   Fourteenth Regiment Armory, Eighth Avenue,
Brooklyn

Born in 1844, Mundell is best remembered for several public buildings erected in Brooklyn during the late nineteenth century, including the first Brooklyn Hall of Records (Adams Street), the Kings County Almshouse (Flatbush Avenue) and the Clermont Avenue, Forty-seventh Regiment and Fourteenth Regiment armories. According to a letter to the editor published in the 20 July 1890 issue of the *Brooklyn Eagle*, Mundell also designed an armory in 1888–1889 for the Thirty-second Regiment on Stagg Street and Bushwick Avenue. Little else currently is known of his professional life. He died in 1903.

Perry, Isaac G.

1889–93   Washington Avenue Armory, Albany
1895   Amsterdam Armory, Florida Avenue
1896–99   Connecticut Street Armory, Buffalo
1888–89   Catskill Armory, Water Street
1892–93   Cohoes Armory, Hart Street
1892   Geneva Armory, Main Street
1895   Glens Falls Armory, Warren Street
1888–89   Hoosick Falls Armory, Church Street
1894–96   Hornell Armory, Seneca Street
1898   Hudson Armory, Fifth Street
1890–92   Jamestown Armory, South Main Street
1891–92   Malone Armory, West Main Street
1891–92   Middletown Armory, Highland Avenue
1891–92   Mohawk Armory, East Main Street
1888–89   Mount Vernon Armory, North Fifth Avenue
1895   Niagara Falls Armory, Main Street
1898   Ogdensburg Armory, Elizabeth Street
1889–91   Olean Armory, North Barry and North streets
1891–92   Poughkeepsie Armory, Market Street
1889–91   Saratoga Springs Armory, Lake Avenue
1898–99   Schenectady Armory, State Street
1896–97   Tonawanda Armory, Delaware Street
1893–94   Utica Armory, Rutger and Steuben streets
1895–96   Walton Armory, Stockton Avenue
1899   Whitehall Armory, Poultney Street
1890s   Yonkers Armory, Waverly Street

See chapter 6 for a discussion of State Architect Isaac G. Perry.

Pierce and Bickford (Joseph Hart Pierce and Henry H. Bickford)

1886–88   Elmira Armory, East Church Street

Pierce was born in Dundee (Yates County) and apprenticed in the office of Warren H. Hayes in Elmira (Chemung County). In 1884 Pierce joined with Otis A. Dockstader, also of Elmira; the partnership lasted only a few years. Shortly thereafter, Pierce joined with Henry H. Bickford to form a solid and prolific partnership that lasted until the latter's death in 1928. Bickford was born in 1863 in Vermont, where he received his formal education.

Upon the demise of Bickford, his son, Robert T. Bickford, became Pierce's partner after serving nine years as a draftsman for the original partners. Notable buildings in Elmira designed by Pierce and Bickford include the Elmira City Hall (1894), the Hedding Methodist Episcopal Church (1900), the Elmira Free Academy (1913), the Southside High School (1924), the Central YMCA Building (1926) and several buildings at Elmira College. Outside of Elmira, the firm achieved acclaim for its designs for the Baptist Church in Corning (Steuben County) and the Sanitarium and Nurses' Home in Clifton Springs (Ontario County).

Pilcher, Lewis F.

1914	New Scotland Avenue Armory, Albany
1914–18	Ithaca Armory/Barton Hall, Cornell University
1917	West Delavan Avenue Armory, Buffalo
1919	Olean Armory, Times Square
1917	Culver Road Armory, Rochester
1918–19	Troy Armory, Fifteenth Street
1918	Yonkers Armory, North Broadway

Lewis F. Pilcher was born in 1871 in Brooklyn and attended Columbia University's School of Architecture from which he graduated in 1895.

He gained practical experience after graduation in the office of Mercein Thomas in Brooklyn and, for a short time, in independent practice. In 1900 he joined with former classmate W. G. Tachau, and they maintained a joint practice in New York City until 1921. Pilcher and Tachau received widespread acclaim for their design for the Troop C Armory on Bedford Avenue in Brooklyn in 1903; subsequent, well-received projects in New York State included several buildings at Vassar College in Poughkeepsie (Dutchess County), the Haviland Building in New York City and the First Church of Christ Scientist in Glens Falls (Warren County). Pilcher and Tachau were also widely recognized for their design for the famous Kingsbridge Armory (1912–1917) in the Bronx for the Eighth Coastal Artillery District.

Pilcher, appointed state architect in 1913 by reform-minded Governor William Sulzer, was responsible for the design (or oversight) of seven state armories, including three facilities for cavalry troops (the New Scotland Avenue Armory in Albany, the Culver Road Armory in Rochester and the West Delavan Avenue Armory in Buffalo) and three facilities for infantry troops (the Yonkers, Troy and Olean armories). He also designed a huge state drill hall on the campus of Cornell University in Ithaca that served as a centralized facility for independent units all across the state to join together for drills and exhibitions.

During his ten-year tenure as state architect, Pilcher was also responsible for a wide variety of other types of public buildings, such as prisons, hospitals and military hospitals. After leaving his position with the state in 1923, Pilcher served for three years as a consulting architect to the U.S. Veterans' Bureau in Washington, D.C. In 1926 he removed to Philadelphia, where he served for many years at both Pennsylvania State College and the University of Pennsylvania. During the Depression, he administered the city's Public Works Administration (PWA) School Program in Philadelphia. He retired from professional life in 1939 and died in 1941.

Robinson and Kunst

1909–11   Dean Street Armory, Brooklyn

Robinson and Kunst, a New York City firm about whom little is known, is believed to have been responsible for the major remodeling of the Dean Street Armory in 1909–1911. Robert Dixon, also about whom little is known, is believed to have designed the original building around 1884.

According to currently available information, Robinson and Kunst also carried out the expansion and remodeling program at the Seventh Regiment Armory (1879, Manhattan) between 1909 and 1914.

Thomas, John Rochester

1888–89   Eighth Regiment Armory, Park Avenue, Manhattan
1892–94   Seventy-first Regiment Armory, Park Avenue, Manhattan
1894–95   Squadron A Armory, Madison Avenue, Manhattan

According to Witheys' *Biographical Dictionary of American Architects (Deceased)*, Thomas is reputed to have designed more buildings in New York City than any other architect of his time. Thomas was born in Rochester in 1886. He studied architecture in the office of a Dr. Anderson at Rochester University and, later, in several European schools. After practicing in Elmira and Rochester for a few years, he came to New York City, where, in 1884, he established a private architectural practice that lasted until his death in 1901. New York City buildings for which he is noted include the Calvary Baptist Church on West 57th Street; the Hayes Building on Maiden Lane; a remodeling of the Stock Exchange building; and the Second Reformed Church on Lenox Avenue. Outside of New York City, Thomas is remembered for his designs for the Rahway State Prison (New Jersey) and the Willard Asylum for the Insane on Seneca Lake in Seneca County. He is also reputed to have designed several armories in "other cities," although that has not been substantiated. As for armories in New York State, the only ones attributed to him are the three cited herein.

Van Wart and Wein (John S. Van Wart and Sidney Wein)

1930–33   369th Regiment Armory, Fifth Avenue, Manhattan

Information about the firm of Van Wart and Wein is found in the New York City Landmarks Preservation Commission's designation report (1985) for the 369th Regiment Armory. John S. Van Wart, who died in 1950, and Sidney Wein, who died in 1960, are believed to have specialized in the design of apartment houses, particularly in New York City. Among their known works are neo-Georgian apartment houses at 40 Fifth Avenue and 7–13 Greenwich Avenue in Greenwich Village and the Beekman Mansion apartment building at 435–443 East 51st Street; the Classical/Art Deco apartment building at 21 East 79th Street; and the Tudor-inspired Blind Brook Lodge garden apartment complex in Rye (Westchester County). In 1930–1933, Van Wart and Wein were commissioned to design an administration building for the 369th Regiment Armory to tower over Fifth Avenue in Harlem. Ten years earlier, a large, utilitarian drill shed had been built to the design of Tachau and Vought, the successor firm to the more renowned Pilcher and Tachau. The monumental Art Deco administration building was attached to the east end of the 1920s drill shed.

Walker and Morris (Richard Walker and Charles Morris)

1911   Fort Washington Avenue Armory, Manhattan

Walker and Morris designed several large public buildings and structures in New York City, including the South Ferry Building and the bridge and pavilions at West 95th Street and Riverside Drive in Manhattan, and several libraries in Brooklyn. To date, no other information is readily available about Walker and/or Morris.

Ware, Franklin B.

1909–10   White Plains Armory, South Broadway

Franklin B. Ware, who served as state architect between 1907 and 1912, was born in New York City in 1874 and graduated from Columbia University in 1894. He was the son of James E. Ware (see the following entry) who, in 1886–1887, had designed the Twelfth Regiment Armory on Columbus Avenue in Manhattan. Franklin and his younger brother Arthur joined their father in 1900 to form the firm of James E. Ware and Sons. Little is known of the fruits of this eighteen-year association, which ended with Ware Sr.'s death in 1918. (Ware Sr. is most frequently remembered for his pre-1900, independent architectural endeavors.) Franklin and Arthur formed their own partnership after their father's death, and gained renown for a variety of religious and collegiate buildings, as well as private mansions for wealthy clients on Long Island and in Westchester County (New York) and New Jersey.

When State Architect George L. Heins died in 1907, Ware was appointed by the governor to fill the vacancy. During his five-year tenure in state service, Ware was responsible for the construction of the State Education Building in Albany as well as numerous alterations at the state capitol. In 1909 he designed the White Plains Armory. His service in state office ended abruptly in April 1912 under scandalous political circumstances.

Ware, James E.

1886–87   Twelfth Regiment Armory, Columbus Avenue, Manhattan

James E. Ware, born in 1846 and educated in New York City, practiced alone between 1875 and 1900; after 1900 he was joined by his two sons, Franklin B. and Arthur. The trio practiced under the name of James E. Ware and Sons. He died in 1918.

Major works completed under his sole proprietorship, in addition to the Twelfth Regiment Armory, include Halcyon Hall in Millbrook (Dutchess County) and the Madison Avenue Presbyterian Church at East 73rd Street in Manhattan. During the late 1870s, Ware was a member of the Seventh Regiment. Little is known about his later undertakings in partnership with his sons.

Warner, Andrew Jackson

1868–70   Rochester Arsenal, Woodbury Boulevard

Warner came to Rochester in 1847 at age fourteen and apprenticed in the office of his uncle, Merwin Austin, who was the younger brother of Henry Austin, a well-known architect active in New Haven, Connecticut, during the mid-nineteenth and early twentieth centuries. From 1853 to 1857, Warner worked in partnership with his uncle. Between 1857 and when he retired in 1894, Warner alternated between assorted short-term partnerships and practicing alone. At one point, Warner partnered with his nephew, Frederick A. Brockett. Warner's most important work was executed in Rochester, including, for example, the Powers Block, the Powers Hotel, City Hall, the Wilder Building, the Ellwanger and Barry Building, the First Presbyterian Church, the Asbury Methodist Church, St. Bernard's Seminary, the Mount Hope Cemetery Gatehouse and the Rochester Free Academy. Noteworthy Warner-designed buildings in other parts of the central and western regions of New York include the Willard Memorial Chapel-Welch Memorial Building in Auburn, Cayuga County; the New York State Hospital (with H. H. Richardson) and the Erie County Municipal Building in Buffalo, Erie County; City Hall in Corning, Steuben County; the Soldiers' and Sailors' Home in Bath, Steuben County; and the Richardson-Bates House in Oswego, Oswego County. Most of his designs incorporate elements associated with the Richardsonian Romanesque, High Victorian Gothic or Romanesque Revival styles. Warner died in 1910.

Wells, Colonel James Hollis

| 1904–06 | Seventy-first Regiment Armory, Park Avenue, Manhattan |

James H. Wells was born in England in 1864 and raised in New York City. He studied civil engineering and architecture at Lehigh University during the 1880s and subsequently joined the New York City firm of Clinton and Russell. (Charles W. Clinton [see earlier entry] designed the Seventh Regiment Armory before joining with William Hamilton Russell in 1894.) During his tenure as commander of the Seventy-first Regiment, Wells (representing the firm of Clinton and Russell) undertook the design of a new armory for his unit when its first armory was destroyed by fire in 1902. After the demise of Russell in 1907 and Clinton in 1910, Wells continued to practice architecture under the well-established name of Clinton and Russell. Wells died in 1926.

Werner and Windolph

| 1922 | Staten Island Armory, Manor Road |

To date, no information about the individuals or the firm seems to be available.

White, Horatio Nelson

1858–59	Syracuse Arsenal, West Jefferson Street
1858	Ogdensburg Arsenal, Lafayette Street
1858	Ballston Spa Arsenal, Ballston Avenue
1858	Dunkirk Arsenal, Central Avenue
1873	East Side Armory, East First Street, Oswego
1873	Syracuse Armory, West Jefferson Street

White was born in Middletown, New Hampshire, in 1814. Prior to moving to Syracuse in 1843, White trained as a carpenter and builder in Andover, Massachusetts. Between 1847 and 1851, White spent time in Brooklyn and San Francisco, earning money to cover financial obligations incurred in Syracuse in the mid-1840s. After returning to Syracuse in 1851 and redeeming himself with his debtors, White secured a commission to design the Church of the Messiah in 1853. His success with that edifice allowed him the opportunity to design the new Onondaga County Courthouse (1857) in Syracuse's Clinton Square, for which he drew immediate acclaim. Firmly established as a talented architect, White went on to design numerous civic, religious and commercial buildings in the region. Well-known works of White include the Chemung County Courthouse in Elmira (1860) and the Jefferson County Courthouse in Watertown (1861).

In terms of public service, White represented the Seventh Ward as alderman in 1855–1856 and 1860–1862. He was a major in the National Guard, but was too old when the Civil War broke out to serve at the front. As an established architect and respected militiaman, White was selected to design arsenals in Syracuse, Ballston Spa and Ogdensburg during the state's late 1850s arsenal building program. White's association with the New York National Guard lasted throughout his lifetime. In early 1873, he was called upon to design an armory in Syracuse for the Fifty-first Regiment to replace the old arsenal he had designed in 1858; shortly thereafter, he designed an armory in Oswego (also 1873) for the Forty-eighth Regiment. White died in 1892.

Wood, John A.

1879	Kingston Armory, Broadway
1879	Newburgh Armory, Broadway
1879	Watertown Armory, Arsenal Street

John A. Wood was born in 1835 in Bethel (Sullivan County) and practiced architecture in Poughkeepsie from ca. 1864 to ca. 1871; around 1872 he opened an office on Broadway in Manhattan but retained his residency in Poughkeepsie. He designed numerous religious, civic, commercial and residential buildings in the mid-Hudson Valley region between the late 1860s and early 1880s. Between the late 1870s and 1910, Wood achieved acclaim for not only three state armories, but for several large hotel projects in the Hudson Valley as well as in Georgia and Florida. His professional career appears to have ended around 1911, although the bulk of his work seems to have been done before about 1892; the date of his death is unknown.

Index

This book was designed and typeset in Goudy Oldstyle
by Partners Composition and printed and bound
by Brodock Press—both of Utica, New York.